Women and Men in
World Cultures

Women and Men in World Cultures

Laura F. Klein
Pacific Lutheran University

Boston   Burr Ridge, IL   Dubuque, IA   Madison, WI   New York
San Francisco   St. Louis   Bangkok   Bogotá   Caracas   Kuala Lumpur
Lisbon   London   Madrid   Mexico City   Milan   Montreal   New Delhi
Santiago   Seoul   Singapore   Sydney   Taipei   Toronto

The McGraw·Hill Companies

Higher Education

WOMEN AND MEN IN WORLD CULTURES

1 2 3 4 5 6 7 8 9 0 DOC/DOC 0 9 8 7 6 5 4 3

ISBN 0-7674-1769-0

Publisher: *Phillip A. Butcher*
Sponsoring editor: *Kevin Witt*
Developmental editor: *Kathleen Cowen*
Senior marketing manager: *Daniel M. Loch*
Media producer: *Shannon Gattens*
Project manager: *Jill Moline*
Production supervisor: *Janean A. Utley*
Design manager: *Laurie Entringer*
Supplement associate: *Kathleen Boylan*
Photo research coordinator: *Alexandra Ambrose*
Associate art editor: *Carin C. Yancey*
Photo researcher: *Robin Sand*
Cover design: *Laurie Entringer*
Cover image: *©Private Collection/Diana Ong/SuperStock*
Interior design: *Laurie Entringer*
Typeface: *10/12 New Aster*
Compositor: *Lachina Publishing Services*
Printer: *R.R. Donnelley and Sons, Inc.*

Library of Congress Cataloging-in-Publication Data

Klein, Laura F. (Laura Frances), 1946–
    Women and men in world cultures / Laura F. Klein.
        p.   cm.
    Includes bibliographical references and index.
    ISBN 0-7674-1769-0 (softcover : alk. paper)
    1. Culture. 2. Gender identity. 3. Sex discrimination. I. Title.

HM621K582 2004   2003046359
305.3—dc21

www.mhhe.com

Brief Contents

Contents

Preface and Acknowledgments

All books are very personal books, at least in the way that the author writes herself and her interests into the work. I first came to be interested in topics of gender and anthropology as a graduate student in the early 1970s. Not much had been written, but there was a keen excitement that there was a universe of knowledge out there to learn. Women in similar situations in the San Francisco Bay area, in Madison, Wisconsin, and in New York City sent their works back and forth in mimeographs and photocopies. It fun, exciting, and naïve. As dissertations were written, papers given, and articles published, we all settled down to the hard work of academic anthropology. Over the years, these women and their colleagues and students have created a subfield of anthropology that remains exciting but is far less naïve.

In my career, I have focused on a set of interests and developed a frame of mind that is reflected in this book, as in all my work. It might be worthwhile to make these biases transparent from the start. First, I am interested in power: Who has it? How do you get it? What do you do with it? Who controls the lives of men and women in societies? This theme runs throughout the chapters that follow. Second, I am very distressed by the glorification of victimization that all too often appears in the popular literature and media. It is important to realize that a person or category of people is being victimized. This is identifying a social problem. The reaction, however, must be to solve the problem rather than to accept victimization as a noble situation. In this book I tend to value the solution of problems and the strength of women and men in different cultures.

Third, I am interested in gender. Women and men, and other genders, only make sense in reference to one another. No culture is male and no culture is female. I try to emphasize this here. Unfortunately, many more books and articles have been written on women than men in the pursuit of information on gender. Many might disagree and argue that the first century of anthropological writings was on men, and this is substantially correct. However, that body of literature rarely consciously looked as men as gendered beings. Consequently, a fuller view of gender that equally includes men and women is still in the future.

CONTENT AND ORGANIZATION

Women and Men in World Cultures is an overview of anthropological understandings of the nature of sex and gender as they appear throughout the world. The book begins with a review of the theories about the role gender may have played in past societies. Using data and ideas from both biological anthropology and archaeology, we question the methods of recreating a gendered past as well as the theories that are reached. The second section focuses on the place of women and men in a wide variety of ways of life from foragers to members of the global community. Questions including the relationship of social stratification to gender stratification, the nature of sexual divisions of labor, and definitions of power in diverse contexts run throughout this section. It introduces students to a number of cases of societies that they can use throughout the class. A third section refocuses toward topics that are most often of key interest to students. The roles that women and men play in the family and what this means to the lives of individuals are discussed and analyzed. Similarly the definition of power is challenged with issues of autonomy, authority, prestige discussed along with those of formal elites. Similarly the roles that supernatural beliefs and religious leaders play in the defining of gender are also considered. Students are further challenged to look at the history of colonialism and the role that it has played in creating new gender concepts throughout the world. The realities of globalization and transnationalism are considered as they differentially influence the lives of men and women. Finally, as a conclusion, students are challenged to confront the complexities of the concepts of sex and gender themselves.

PEDAGOGY

Writing Style: Although concepts of gender, power, and society are anything but simple, this book is written with clear, concise, student-friendly language. I hope to engage the readers and help them to think critically about gender constructs with this enjoyable yet scholarly tone.

Chapter Opening Questions: By providing challenging, thought-provoking questions at the start of each section rather than at the end, *Women and Men in World Cultures* gives readers the opportunity to reflect on key concepts before chapter reading begins. This is designed not only to encourage more productive reading, but to help readers explore critical concepts in anthropology and gender beyond their immediate world.

Chapter Summaries: This book contains end-of-chapter summaries, intended to more completely explore gender studies in both an evolutionary and global context.

Readings: A comprehensive, end-of-chapter readings section references all works cited.

SUPPLEMENTS

Website: This free, web-based student supplement features quizzes as well as helpful links to anthropology of gender sites.

Instructor's Manual/Test Bank: This indispensable instructor supplement features chapter outlines, key terms, and a complete test bank.

ACKNOWLEDGMENTS

I do not know where to start to acknowledge those who have helped me so generously with this work. I have to start with my mother, my aunts, senior women anthropologists, especially Ruth Freed, Happy Leacock, and Connie Sutton, and nearly every Tlingit woman I have ever met. They have all presented roles of women who are strong, socially concerned, and contentedly female. Friends like Ann Sullivan, Faye Anderson, and Alina Urbanec fill these roles as well, while others like my father and Stephen Sullivan, thought these roles were normal. Thanks also to my students throughout the years, who teach even more than they learn. Colleagues at Pacific Lutheran University have been very supportive and special thanks go to Elizabeth Brusco, Ann Kelleher, Greg Guldin, Veeda Gargano-Ray, and Judith Pine, who always help by challenging. Other friends and anthropologists, including, notably, Helen Fisher and Lillian A. Ackerman, have also been there to prod me on. Librarians, including the ever-knowledgeable Gail Egbers, are the unsung heroes of any academic work. Critiques from reviewers are not always welcomed at first blush, but the then anonymous reviewers who gave their time and efforts to this book made it a much better work than it would have been without them. The editors and staff from Mayfield and McGraw-Hill, especially Jan Beatty, Kevin Witt, Kathleen Cowan, Jill Moline, and Simone Rico have been supportive and generous with their time. Too many people to thank and too many remain unnamed. Thank you all.

I'm also very grateful to the prepublication reviewers of the manuscript, who include:

Noel Anne Brennan—University of Rhode Island
Joyce Hammond—Western Washington University

Barbara Hoffman—Cleveland State University
Kathleen Young—Western Washington University
Abigail Adams—Central Connecticut State University
Anita Schwartz—Nassau Community College

Laura F. Klein
Pacific Lutheran University

Women and Men in World Cultures

SECTION I

Looking at the Past for Clues to the Future

The two chapters that begin this book review the findings of the anthropological fields of biological anthropology and archaeology. Using these fields we can look at the past in order to discover what they can tell us about sex and gender in the human present. That these questions and answers are flavored by the very contemporary concerns of those who ask and respond to them is true, and this recognition must be a part of the analysis of all work. The study of the development of humans, biologically and culturally, may offer clues to the lives of people living in technologically simpler times when the complexities of modern urban life did not intervene.

Chapter 1 is a discussion of the possible lessons of these anthropologists concerning sex and gender. Biological, or physical, anthropology is the study of the biological variations in people over space and time. Human evolution is the core theoretical model for the study of biological change. In this pursuit, anthropologists study the remains of earlier forms of humans and the nature and lives of monkeys and apes, our closest living cousins, in order to get a broader view of the nature of human biology. The works of primatologists and evolutionary scientists, in particular, have been used in recent years to construct hotly debated models of innate male and female qualities. Paleoarchaeologists, who study the cultures of early humans through their material remains, expand biological studies by adding the cultural dimension. Together, these scientists have created images of the lives of early women and men.

Chapter 2 reviews more recent societies, where cultural differences are becoming apparent. Many archaeological sites of these later times yield artifacts and settlements that have been used to explain the cultural beginnings of human gender differences. However, it is a common scholarly lesson that you only find what you look for. This is not an absolute, of course, because scholars often discover unexpected results in their research. However, scientists develop their research plans in the light of existing knowledge. As a hypothetical example, if a paleontologist were looking for remains of an early farming community and it is known that this region was arid during the period being investigated, that scientist would be foolish to establish a field site in this area when more temperate sites were available. To do otherwise would be a waste of time and resources. But what if the initial assumption were incorrect? What if early farmers did live in deserts but only in the rainiest season? The point is that scholarly assumptions are critical in the progress of science. What is known, or is thought to be known, limits the extent of further research.

This directly relates to the study of gender in archaeology. Basic assumptions about what men and women do and about which industries are connected to women and which to men are used in the development of study problems and the analysis of collected data. Because gender has not been an object of study in archaeology until very recently, there is no body of archaeological data upon which to build these assumptions. Archaeologists, then, must search with analytical tools built from what they know from living cultures as reported by cultural anthropologists. There are two distinct problems with doing this: (1) Cultural anthropologists have only begun to seriously study gender as an important part of culture in the last two decades. Most of the earlier ethnographies, or descriptions of cultures, shed little light on gender or, worse, reflect the biases of their day. (2) Working from analogies with the present makes finding differences in the past most unlikely. What if past cultures lived gendered lives different than their contemporary descendants, just like they lived technological lives that were very different? Assuming that gender patterns in the past were the same as those in contemporary times may mean that this different understanding of gender may never be found. This is a very difficult problem for working archaeologists, and a review of archaeological method and analysis may clarify the nature of discovery and the reliability of results in archaeology. Moreover, it should form a series of questions that every student of gender should ask when running into a new theory of gender in the past. For example, where do the data for this theory come from, and what form of analysis allows the authors to come to their conclusions?

These first chapters look for the origins of human gender diversity.

CHAPTER ONE

Origins: Searching for the Essence of a Gendered Humanity?

> *Is there something in the basic makeup of human beings that dictates the behavior of people along gender lines?*
> *If such a mandate does exist, would it be evident in humans from the beginning of time?*

These questions and assumptions have engaged many people who believe that the key to understanding contemporary humans lies in knowing their distant past. Others discount such deterministic reasoning for studying the past but still hope to find clues to the development of modern gender traits through seeing people in a wide variety of environments and levels of technology. Even others applaud these attempts but warn that views of the past are almost always based on views of the present. Origin tales in many societies can be shown to change over time to protect the integrity of the modern experience. The past is used to justify the present. No doubt even scientific searches for beginnings are strongly influenced by the values of the present.

ORIGINS: THE NATURE OF THE ARGUMENT

Stories of origins, both folk and scientific, tend to set a baseline for understanding who a group of people are and should be. For example, the story of Adam and Eve in the Bible sets the beginnings of humanity in a religious context. For believers, it explains why people look like they do and act like they do. These are innate and right. God determined them. This narrative also explains what people should be like and, thus, establishes the tenets of morality. This particular origin story also sets a clear picture of two sexes and the appropriate relationship between them. Origin stories are important. Thousands of years after this was written, this story enriches the lives of countless believers. Other religions similarly offer their believers maps of creation. The Hijras, discussed in Chapter 11, for example, can trace their place in the universe to the Hindu story of creation. Understanding the cultures of believers often demands a close study of these stories.

Western science also offers an important story of human creation: human evolution. This tells of the slow development of contemporary humans through a long series of stages from the first life on earth to the present. This construct sets humans firmly in the same realm as other life forms because it defines humans as members of the primate order. Animal groups diverged over time, based on the mechanism of natural selection—which meant that as animals moved into new environments, they adapted physical traits that allowed them to live and breed successfully in those environments. The most recent division of significance for people was the split between human ancestors and other primates more than five million years ago. While the paradigm or theoretical orientation of human evolution is not a moral blueprint, in that it does not claim a religious creator with a moral agenda for humanity, it does establish a picture of baseline humanity. As anthropologist Linda Fedigan pointed out in a 1986 review of gender and evolution, "What more significant guide to comprehending the structure of our own underlying nature could we discover than the original blueprint for human society? That is why the practice of modeling the life of early humans, although shunned by many anthropologists, is nevertheless a scientific game played with great determination; its reward is the right to propound a view of human nature." (Fedigan 1986: 26) People biologically adapted to particular circumstances, and, logic suggests, those circumstances are the best for human life. In other words, the scientific origin myth establishes how people are structured to function today.

The essential question for this chapter is whether men and women are physically programmed by the nature of evolution of humans to act differently beyond the traits necessary for biological reproduction. Many popular American cultural questions must be raised: Are males programmed to be dominant, form political groups, provide food for females and offspring? Have females developed to be submissive, nurturing, and domestic? Is there a natural way to be female or male?

ORIGINS: METHODS FOR LEARNING ABOUT THE PAST

Anthropologists searching for the origins of human form and behavior face a major challenge. The first ancestors, who are clearly on the line of humans and not also on the lines of other primates, date back several million years. They lived at the most basic technological level and left few cultural remains. Their fossilized remains and the context in which they were found provide the most important evidence of their lives. Because these early ancestors were physically similar, though not identical, to the other primates with whom they coexisted, another source of evidence defines the nature of those animals. What it means to be a human and what it means to be a primate are related questions. The evidence for human evolution, then, is drawn from many sources, but the primary areas of study explore the fossil and archaeological record or contemporary primates. Analogies based on contemporary understandings, which are discussed in Chapter 2, are used to fill in the gaps.

Exploring the Fossil Record

Fossils are the physical remains and traces left behind by long-dead animals. Most apparent are the mineralized bones and teeth that serendipitously survive in the earth over the years. Other remains of people are even more unusual. The rare discoveries of remains of meals, tools, and even footprints add valuable information. Despite the scarcity of such information, there are enough data to demonstrate a clear path of human evolution over more than five million years. The additional data found in connection with fossils allow an understanding of environments and economic systems at different parts of history. Remains of plants and other animals, found associated with human fossils, reveal the nature of the environment in which these people lived. They further suggest the availability of different foods and raw materials for their use.

Much more is missing than is present in this record. The remains of bones can tell little about the soft tissues of the body nor about when children reached sexual maturity or how they mated. They do not tell what their skin, hair, and smiles looked like. While stone tools remain, most tools were likely made of decomposable materials such as wood, netting, and skins. The bunting of animal skin that may have wrapped an infant and the containers of plant or skin materials in which food was gathered are not going to be found. They rotted away soon after being discarded. Most importantly, the abstract systems and thoughts that characterize humanity are not made of permanent materials. Scientists cannot dig up love, hate, or contemplation. It must be acknowledged that most of what makes up human life is missing from the fossil record. Even given this, it is truly amazing how much these ancestors left behind.

Physical anthropologists depend on luck and complex research to find fossils. Contemporary evidence suggests that the earliest hominid ancestors of contemporary people were Africans, and it is here that most research is located. Specific geological regions, where areas of the appropriate time are assessable, become the focus. In the study of these regions, the knowledge of the evolution of other animals and the environments has grown exponentially. It is the human remains that make the headlines, however. These are rare, and each find is examined and fit into the context of other discoveries. In this framework, the analysis of gender becomes difficult.

FOSSIL EVIDENCE

Early Hominids: Sexual Dimorphism in the Human Family

All people today belong to the biological category *Homo sapiens sapiens*. This means that everyone is assigned to the genus *Homo*, species *Homo sapiens*, and race, or subspecies, *Homo sapiens sapiens*. Given the geographical breadth and population of humans, we are remarkably homogeneous physically. This makes it particularly difficult to understand a time when there were multiple species and genuses of hominids existing co-terminously. In the period called the Plio-Pleistocene, however, this was the reality. During the period following the split between human and ape ancestors, a number of different types of hominids lived in Africa. From the fossil data, anthropologists hypothesize that species of the genuses including *Ardipithecus* and *Australopithecus*[1] lived in East Africa more than four million years ago. The australopithecines continued in a variety of forms in much of Africa until about one million years ago. These beings all shared a basic structural similarity. All were upright beings who walked bipedally. Unlike other primates, humans move through their environment on the ground using only their hind legs. The brains of these hominids were slightly larger than those of contemporary apes (controlling for body size), and their teeth approached a more human pattern. As might be expected, the earlier forms were more apelike in form and the later ones more like modern humans.

Due to the fragmentary and variable remains over time and place, it is difficult to establish secondary physical differences between males and females in these groups. The order Primates is highly variable in degrees of physical differences between males and females, called sexual dimorphism. Male savanna baboons and gorillas, for example, are generally twice as large as females of the same species. Gibbons and New World monkeys, on the contrary, exhibit little size differential. Contemporary humans demonstrate a moderate size difference, with females in some areas of the world often taller than males in others. The fossil evidence is difficult to interpret because most human bones show no sex difference. The best diagnostic bones to find would be the pelvises, but too few of these are found. A few skulls are found with pronounced sagittal crests that are characteristic of males in gorillas. However, few full skeletons have been found, and there are too few cases of male and female skeletons of the same species from the same sites.

On the other hand, there appear to be significant differences in the sizes of different fossil finds. Some anthropologists argue that these differ-

[1]Ardipithecus, Orroin, Sahelanthropus and the like are new categories, and the fossils are not yet fully analyzed. Australopithecines, on the other hand, are represented by hundreds of well-analyzed individuals. The nature of the complexity of these australopithecines is still under debate.

ences are, in part at least, evidence of extreme sexual dimorphism. It has been hypothesized that the A. afarensis "may have been as dimorphic as *any* living primate." (Jurmain et al. 2000: 268, 281) A trail of footprints of two or three individuals walking together millions of years ago indicates that one individual was about 4 feet 9 inches and another about 4 feet 1 inch. Many picture this scene as a man and woman walking together, perhaps hand in hand. Of course, other pictures, including perhaps mother or father and child, could be drawn from the same evidence. The question of sexual dimorphism in australopithecines remains an active debate.

Genus Homo: Sex and Gender?

Fossils classified as part of the contemporary human genus, Homo, first appear more than two million years ago, and these individuals coexisted with australopithecines for more than one million years. The earliest individuals lived in Africa and showed only slight differences from the australopithecines. Their brains were larger and their teeth more modern.

The trends of physical evolution from early genus *Homo* species from Africa to *Homo erectus* to *Homo sapiens* seem relatively clear. Over time brains were larger, teeth were smaller, and modern skull shape and stature emerged. While physical anthropologists debate the physical makeup of every new find and work to discover the precise line to modern humans, most theories still disregard issues of sex. While it has been argued that *Homo erectus*, at least in East Africa, was strongly sexually dimorphic, little other physical data clarify this point. It is clear that by the time of fully modern *Homo sapiens*, this extreme degree of sexual dimorphism is not apparent.

What is critical about the emergence of the genus *Homo*, and in fact this is part of the definition, is the development of culture as the major adaptive strategy. Inferring culture, which is an abstraction, is the challenge. Anthropologists have had to ask what the physical remains of culture are. The answer, at least for the earliest forms, has been stone tools. The construction and use of similar tools throughout a group or groups of people are indications of learned traditions for coping with environments. Toolmakers must have communicated and taught their skills to others or the tools would not be so consistent in form. The focus on stone tools is merely a practical issue. These are made of materials that would be preserved over the millennia. People who made stone tools would undoubtedly have made and used other items as well.

Since at least the early *Homo erectus*, the geographical range of humans expanded throughout the Old World. While early African *Homo* fossils are connected with a simple pebble stone culture, the *Homo erectus* finds are often found with far more sophisticated tools. *Homo erectus* sites show evidence of butchered animals and plant use. Also, tools that appear to be awls and needles suggest sewn clothing. While there is little dispute about the gathering of wild plants as a major source of food, some scholars, such as

Jurmain et al. and Klein, question the use of hunting at this point. They suggest that scavenging would produce the same remains. These sites, then, represent either hunters and gatherers or simply gatherers.

During the transitional period between *Homo erectus* and fully modern *Homo sapiens,* regional variations became even more pronounced. More complex stone tool types emerged. During this period, controlled fire was established, shelters were built, and the use of resources from the environment expanded. With the development of *Homo sapiens sapiens,* the modern structure and abilities of humans were set. Undisputed hunting was established, with early *Homo sapiens sapiens* being efficient hunters and gatherers. The ability to use language, a crucial tool for complex culture, was established. The future of human evolution was to be dominated by cultural rather than physical factors.

Does Hunting Make Us Human?

A landmark in American anthropology was the publication in 1968 of a book entitled *Man the Hunter.* (Lee and DeVore 1968) One article, "The Evolution of Hunting" (Washburn and Lancaster), in this highly influential book argued that hunting was the essential economy of human culture and, even in an industrial age, still influenced the workings of human life. Further, as the book's title suggests, the focus of this article was on men and taught gender lessons far beyond the limits of hunting. The article noted, correctly, that almost all of hominid development took place in a pre-agricultural environment. Equating pre-industrial with big-game hunting, Washburn and Lancaster asserted that "In a very real sense our intellect, interests, emotions, and basic social life—all are evolutionary products of the success of the hunting adaptation." (1968: 293) Among the specific developments listed are cooperation, male–male bonding, tools, brain development, sharing, and the family. In a more sinister way, the authors assert that the male need to kill as seen in sport hunting and war is a result of this past hunting culture. Washburn and Lancaster asserted that hunting sets a permanent human sexual division of labor. Men hunt while women gather, and women and their children become dependent on the males. Many interpreted this as meaning that people were destined to live in societies where male dominance was a core tenet.

Thirty years later it is clear that the data do not support the conclusions. Agriculture and big-game hunting are not the only alternatives to gathering. As noted, many anthropologists see scavenging, rather than hunting, as the means by which early hominids obtained their meat. Also in societies that do hunt, big-game hunting is the exception. Meat from small game is far more accessible and reliable. This does not call for the cultural mobilization assumed in *Man the Hunter,* and women, as well as men, often hunt these animals. The most important fact, however, is that it is known today that in most foraging societies the gathering of plants is more important than hunting animals. In many societies, as will be seen in Chapter 3, cooperation and individual autonomy can exist side by side. It could be asserted that humans adapted as gatherers and scavengers. Most scholars today believe that his lifestyle does not lead to male dominance and killer instincts.

Or Is It Gathering?

Theoretically, there were many other objections raised. One of the first, and most important, came in 1971 from Sally Slocum. In one of the pioneer articles in feminist anthropology, she asserted that there were "hidden assumptions and premises" (p. 38) in this argument that were based on a male bias. *Man the Hunter* implied that only men evolved. On the contrary, Slocum demonstrated that there were selective pressures for both men and women present in early hominid evolution. Among other things, the lengthening infant dependency that is part of human evolution increased the intensity of the female–child bond. Women had to gather food for themselves and their children and develop skills of social organization and cooperation in order to successfully rear their children. It is agreed that this, more than hunting, created the selective pressure for larger brains. The first tools could have been containers for gathered plants and devices for carrying babies. Slocum defined families as women and their children rather than as men and their women and offspring. By this approach, when big-game hunting was eventually developed, men would have shared the products of their hunts with their mothers and siblings rather than with their wives.

Other anthropologists[2] elaborated the theme of Woman the Gatherer after the publication of the original article by Slocum. Adrienne Zihlman, notably, focused on a new type of gathering that became possible with bipedalism and tool making that led to human culture as we know it. Slocum and Zihlman presented alternatives to Man the Hunter with a female bias that is as logical as its older alternative. As the strength of the gathering hypothesis took hold, however, a new slant was added. Some anthropologists, most notably Owen Lovejoy, came to agree that gathering was the key economic adaptation of early hominids but then asserted that the gatherers were men. One basic assumption in this train of thought was that females could not be successful both as reproducers and producers, but this would certainly come as a surprise to millions of women, and other female primates, who do it daily. All such theories are highly speculative and share one obvious weakness. Men did not evolve without women and women did not evolve without men. Whatever happened in the Plio-Pleistocene, it surely involved both men and women.

[2]See Linda Marie Fedigan, "The Changing Role of Women in Models of Human Evolution," *Annual Review of Anthropology* 15 (1986), pp. 25–66.

Popular Views

While anthropologists argue in scientific meetings and journals, the general public receives its information from more popular sources. In some of these, exaggerated images of killer apes, naked apes, and aquatic apes[3] take center stage. In many of these forums, the lesson of *Man the Hunter* has become gospel. Many readers concluded that they had male ancestors who were innately killers and that this predestined modern warfare. This conclusion argued that male dominance of women was innately mandated. In a period of anti-war and feminist movements, these lessons had important political meaning. A popular feminist argument of the time was found in an aquatic ape hypothesis that was equally political but spoke to a different constituency. Elaine Morgan (1972), a popular writer, argued, quite to the contrary of any fossil evidence, that humans evolved at the seashore: women became bipedal, their breasts swelled and floated, and they invented tools. Women prevailed without the help of men. Naïve and biased as they appear today, these themes remain influential. Such books remain in print and are widely cited in articles and books outside of anthropology.

In short, it is clear that the fossils of the human past can be used to create a number of origin stories that explain "human nature." It is also clear that the nature of such data is too sparse at this time to prove or disprove most of these narratives. Many anthropologists have refocused their views to look at a different set of data and a slightly different question: What is "primate nature"?

EVIDENCE FROM THE OTHER PRIMATES

All monkeys, apes, prosimians, and humans belong to the same biological order: Primates. This means that scientists can trace the history of all primates, living and extinct, back to a common ancestor. Over time, adaptation to different environments led to diverging branches of primates. One of the most recent splits was that between humans and apes. Earlier the ancestors of apes and humans had split from those of monkeys. What this means is that living apes are the animals most similar to humans. Also related, but more distantly, are the Old World monkeys. These are, biologically, the fictive first and second cousins of contemporary people, and all belong to the primates order. Primates are then divided into two major sub-orders: Prosimians and Anthropoids. Anthropoids include monkeys, apes, and humans. The human family, hominid, is closest biologically to the African apes, including chimpanzees, bonobos, and gorillas. The Asian apes, orangutans, and gibbons are slightly more distantly related. One step

---

[3]See Robert Ardrey, *The Hunting Hypothesis* (New York: Atheneum, 1976); Desmond Morris, *The Naked Ape* (New York: McGraw-Hill, 1967); and Elaine Morgan, *The Descent of Women* (New York: Stein and Day, 1972) for these models.

farther away is the Old World monkeys and then, much farther, the New World monkeys. Genetically the chimpanzees, including the bonobos, are very close cousins to contemporary people.

Primate Studies

The central question is this: What does it mean to be a primate? In addition, then, are there human traits that are the result of being a primate? The answers to these questions can be pursued beyond the fossil evidence of humans and other primates. Studies of living groups of primates, particularly apes and specific monkeys, are used to question whether there are any inborn human traits that we share from our joint primate heritage.

The contemporary study of nonhuman primates has been pursued in three different scholarly arenas:

1. For more than a century, monkeys have been studied in laboratories and zoos, where individual animals and small groups are investigated comprehensively. They can be tested and examined in detail. Monkeys can demonstrate their abilities to open locks, and apes can communicate using American Sign Language. In other words, the capabilities of these animals can be understood. Of course, monkeys do not pick locks in the forest nor do gorillas sign to one another in the highlands. These studies tell what the animals *can* do, but not necessarily what they *actually* do in their own worlds.

2. The second arena for study is captive groups of monkeys. A few troops of monkeys have been maintained, not for public display as in a zoo, but for study in either artificially created communities or protected natural environments. These animals can be observed over generations in a setting that approximates a natural one in many aspects. They are, however, free of predators, diseases, and other animal neighbors. Scientists can study social interactions between animals in these groups in a controlled setting.

3. The third arena is the natural environment of the animals. Since the 1960s scientists have concentrated on discovering how primates actually act in their normal environments. Well-known ethologists, including Jane Goodall, George Schaller, and Dian Fossey (who all studied apes), and other scholars went to the places that the animals lived and observed them there. Even a simple study of this type took years because the primates moved through environments difficult for human observation. The benefit, though, was that these scholars could learn how primates actually act in their own worlds. It should be noted, however, that these studies are better suited to some animals than others. Primates, such as the orangutans, New World monkeys, and gibbons that live much of their lives in high trees, are less available for this study than land-roaming groups such as gorillas, chimpanzees, and baboons.

Mother and child: a chimpanzee portrait.

Primatologists in the past 20 years have completely altered the understanding of primates and what it means to be a primate, but the literature is still limited and biased toward specific species. The theories of gender that have emerged from this literature tend to reflect the type of studies and special biases of these specific points.

Contemporary Primate Models for Sex and Gender

"Studies of monkeys and apes have never been just about monkeys and apes" as anthropologist Susan Sperling (1991: 204) has asserted. When anthropologists study other primates they do so to learn more about innate characteristics of humans. They select the animals to be studied based on two criteria. The first, and most obvious, is *biological similarity*. The African apes, as cousins, should show a family relationship. Perhaps scientists can see in them qualities that are hidden in the cultural complexity of human life. The second criterion is *environmental similarity*. Early humans, it appears, evolved on the ground in a lightly wooded or savanna terrain. Therefore, ground-living primates provide intriguing models for early human life.

While a number of scholars have studied primates in the wild over the last few decades, a few have taken center stage in the debates over sex and gender. The studies by DeVore and Washburn of savanna baboons in 1963 opened the debate over male dominance and breeding strategies. These were challenged by the long-term studies headed by Goodall of the chimpanzees of the Gombe region in Tanzania. Most recently, the study of the bonobo by DeWaal and his colleagues have provided new perspectives. An early assumption was that studies of nonhuman primates would offer a simple base for discussions of human evolution, but just the opposite has proven true.

Savanna Baboons   Savanna baboons are ground-living Old World monkeys. While they are genetically distinct from humans, their adaptation to an environment seemingly similar to that of the early hominids make them an interesting model. They range in a home territory composed of open grasslands with some trees. Living in troops of 50 or more individuals (males, females, and young), they are largely vegetarian, and foraging takes up much of their time. They also hunt the small animals in their areas. Individual baboons gather their own food, and sharing is not common. Unlike contemporary humans, these baboons demonstrate a marked sexual dimorphism, with an adult male growing to twice the weight of an adult female. Also, female savanna baboons have a clear and limited, physically marked, period of estrus when they are sexually receptive.

The studies of Washburn, DeVore, and their colleagues emphasized the dominance hierarchy they observed in the field and their findings became the model for many years, not only for understanding baboons, but also for primate sexual behavior. Focusing on the males, they noted that some seemed to get more food and mated with more females in estrus than other males. They emphasized aggressive displays in these animals and documented changes in the dominance structure over time.

The major group activity for the males is the protection of the females and young. Male baboons have massive canine teeth, fangs actually, while the canines of females are rather small. When predators threaten the troop, the adult males challenge the danger while the smaller animals retreat to shelter. The organization of females and their offspring was not emphasized in this study. DeVore and Washburn did note that females appeared to cooperate and even challenge dominant males in some rare cases, but they did not include this in the larger analysis. The picture presented was of a group dominated by aggressive males who competed to hold this status. Control over food and females was their reward for success.

Later Shirley Strum (1987), a student of Washburn, was encouraged to study the female side of the system. It was known that baboon troops are composed of females and their young, who were born in the troop, and adult males, who were reared elsewhere. Strum found that the adult females had a conservative hierarchy with status that extended to their offspring. High-ranking females could command the best gathering areas and protect their offspring. Adolescent sons, likewise, would protect their mothers and siblings. Strum also emphasized the important role of friendships between females and between males and females.[4] Females often had female friends who stayed nearby, groomed one another, and whose offspring played together. Male–female friendships also were apparent. Adult males stayed near and groomed specific females even when they were not sexually receptive. These males protected these females and their offspring. Babies climbed on and played with their mothers' male friends without fear. Older females often led the troop when they needed to choose which direction to proceed.

In her long-term study, Strum became equally interested in the adult males because she found their dominance pattern more complex than previously suggested. As previously seen, all adult males could threaten all females. Males leave their natal troop when they mature and try to join new troops. To do this they have to compete with older, unfamiliar males. To her surprise, Strum found that the newcomers to the troop were the most aggressive baboons and dominated the older males in the troop. However, counter to what most assumed, these dominant males did not control the females in estrus nor take control of the best food. The dominance pattern of savanna baboons is not as simple as it once appeared to be. Strum found "strong evidence for a complementary equality of male and female in most social domains, including politics and caretaking" and that "male and female baboons are involved in a complicated exchange of favors." (1987: 150)

Chimpanzees of Gombe   The chimpanzees of Gombe[5] have been studied since 1960 and present a very different picture than that of the baboons. Chimpanzees, including bonobos, are genetically remarkably close to humans. If, metaphorically, baboons are cousins, then chimpanzees are siblings. If there were genetic bases for human behavior, these animals would be most likely to share them. Environmentally, however, unlike contemporary or ancient humans, chimpanzees live in forests and spend some of their days in trees and nest in these trees at night.

Gombe chimpanzees show more social flexibility than the savanna baboons. Communities of about 50 individuals range throughout a region. Individuals of these communities move in small, changeable groups that are centered on stable matrifocal units made up of mothers and their dependent offspring. Even adult daughters stay near their mothers. Goodall noted "the close-knit family circle at the heart of a female's web of relationships provides her, as she gets older, with companionship, grooming, play, and—most important—support during agonistic interactions

---

[4]There do not appear to be male–male friendships.
[5]For the purposes of this book unless otherwise noted, *chimpanzee* will mean Pan troglodytes as are found in the Gombe National Park in Tanzania. Pan paniscus, the bonobo, will be referred to as *bonobo*. They are two distinct species of the same genus.

with other community members." (1986: 159) The offspring of high-ranked mothers develop behaviors and alliances from these families that help them establish their own ranks.

Chimpanzees have a distinct hierarchy within the communities. Males compete with one another for status and can be quite aggressive. Male chimps, often brothers, sometimes join together to form alliances against other chimpanzees. Males protect the territory of their group from members of other communities and have been known to kill outsiders. One community in Gombe was destroyed in a five-year period through hostile attacks that approximated human war. Other chimp groups have not demonstrated these patterns, however.

Females also exist within their own hierarchy. High-ranking female chimpanzees, perhaps because they may be able to use better foraging resources, have more offspring who survive infancy and daughters who mature earlier than lower-ranked females (Pusey, Williams, and Goodall, 1997). Regardless of their position in the female hierarchy, however, female chimpanzees are subordinate to the males. Dominant males often try to limit the access of lesser-ranked males from females in estrus, but this is not always successful. Often females in estrus mate with all the adult males in the group. Goodall reported that Flo, an older female in Gombe, was observed copulating 50 times in one day with a dozen male chimpanzees. Other chimps form consort pairs of a single male and single female during her estrus, but these pairings often fail and other males enter the picture.

Chimpanzees are largely vegetarians but also eat insects and small mammals. Termites are collected using prepared sticks, which is a rudimentary form of tool making. Young chimpanzees appear to learn this technique from observing their elders' behavior. The mammals are hunted; a favorite prey is the red colobus monkey. Chimpanzees, unlike other nonhuman primates, sometimes hunt in groups. While many of these hunting parties are all male, significant numbers are mixed-sex groups with a few all-female groups. Meat from these hunts is often shared. When males take possession of prey, they are often approached by other chimps for pieces of the meat, and they generally oblige. Females share with their offspring but rarely with other adult females.

The chimpanzees of Gombe and other research stations have been studied more intensively than other apes. Over the years the picture of these animals has changed from one of an idyllic cooperation to one more akin to human failings. Infanticide, war, incest, and brutality exist along with cooperation, invention, and family ties in the new understanding of chimpanzees. They look more human than they did in earlier studies.

Bonobos Bonobos, Pan paniscus, were first acknowledged to be different than other chimpanzees in 1929, but the first successful fieldwork with the animals did not begin until the mid-1970s as a result of political instability in the area. Two ongoing field stations were established then that continue today. The results of both sites, and the captive studies as well, are remarkably consistent and markedly different than those from the common chimpanzees of Gombe. De Waal and Lanting summarized the differences from the other significant primate studies:

> These apes fail to fit traditional scenarios, yet they are as close to us as chimpanzees, the species on which much ancestral human behavior has been modeled. Had bonobos been known earlier, reconstructions of human evolution might have emphasized sexual relations, equality between males and females, and the origin of the family, instead of war, hunting, tool technology, and other masculine fortes. Bonobo society seems ruled by the "Make Love, Not War" slogan of the 1960s rather than the myth of a bloodthirsty killer ape that has dominated textbooks for at least three decades. (1997: 1–2)

Physically the degree of sexual dimorphism in bonobos is close to humans.[6] Like chimpanzees they live in communities but travel daily in smaller, flexible groupings. Bonobos, more than chimpanzees, maintain mixed-sex groupings, come together at night, and nest in larger groups. The nature of these groups differs dramatically from that of the baboons and chimpanzees.

In bonobo groups, the core permanent relationship is between mothers and sons. Young females leave their home groups and move into foreign ones. The males, however, stay together for life. When females join new groups, they approach a female who belongs to the group and establish a grooming and sexual relationship with her. When that individual accepts her, the new female is accepted as a member of the group. These female bonds, although second to mother–son in some ways, are strong and long lasting. When the newcomer becomes an older mother, it will be her turn to accept younger females.

Both males and females have an informal ranking structure, which is observed largely when one animal charges another as a second backs down. Generally these acts are followed by sexual activity. In other words, if a male charges a male, or a female a female, those animals will mount and rub their genitals together. A calm companionship follows these acts. In major challenges, when male status positions then change permanently, it appears that the mothers of the opponents are key to the outcome. Mothers join the charges, and the sons of higher-ranking mothers, or mothers healthy enough to help, win.

Between the sexes, females appear to dominate males. In situations where limited desirable food is an issue, unlike among chimpanzees, males defer to females. In the sharing of food—and sharing among bonobos includes large fruits as well as meat—the females control the distribu-

---

[6]In bonobos and humans, the weight of females is about 85 percent that of males while in chimpanzees it is 80 to 84 percent; see Frans DeWaal and Frans Lanting, *Bonobo: The Forgotten Ape* (Berkeley: University of California Press, 1997), p. 24.

tion and males remain at the periphery. Male bonobos do not physically attack females, and when a male appears to be bothering a female, other females join together to drive him off. Males have not been observed to join forces against females.

Sexual access that is taken by researchers as a key indication of dominance and submission in other animals is obviously far more complex with the bonobos. Sexual contact appears to be an important part of social interaction among these primates. Rather than restricted, sex appears open. Same-sex and opposite-sex relations are normal and common. As noted, disputes between individuals are resolved and tensions calmed by sexual activities rather than fights. Unlike female chimpanzees, which are sexually receptive about 5 percent of their adult lives, female bonobos are receptive about half of their adult life. Because they are fertile a small part of that period, it follows that much of the sex play has nothing to do with reproduction. DeWaal and Lanting argued that the seeming lack of infanticide among these primates is a result of the fact that no male could know which infants were his offspring.

Primate Analogies

As the investigation of primate behavior matures, generalizations become more difficult. The summaries of primate behavior that come from the first generation of field scholars seem, from a distance, to be caricatures: Baboons as strict patriarchies, chimpanzees as gentle communities, and now bonobos as sexy communes. The second generation of study has shown that female baboons are active players in their communities and that chimpanzees can, and do, kill for food and in aggressive disputes. The second generation of bonobo studies will also bring surprises. This does not negate the work of primate studies, but it does show the importance of long-term studies for understanding complex social animals. This is less a criticism of primatologists, who know this, than of scholars of other disciplines who seize on the initial hypotheses—often long after they have been superseded.

Seeing Our Gendered Selves in Our Relatives

Humans are primates. Anyone who has gone to the primate areas in a zoo has noticed obvious and subtle similarities. These primates, despite cartoons and misreadings of Darwin, are not human ancestors. Evolution teaches that humans and these animals are descendants of a common ancestor in the distant past. Our common ancestor with monkeys lived long before our common ancestor with apes. This does not mean, however, that our ape ancestor was more like a chimpanzee or bonobo than human. In fact, it may be possible that humans may be more primitive, more like the ancestor, than more specialized apes like the gorilla. Adaptations since the last common ancestor have produced offspring that are adapted to different environments. Environment and common biology combine to create a complex picture. A final summary of the major issues that are raised to explain human sex and gender characteristics may clarify the state of the disputes.

The most long-standing argument is over the issue of innate male dominance over the lives of females. In other words, is there an inbred mandate in primates that dictates the domination of females by males? How does a scholar equate elements of primate behavior with this human concept? It is clear that in savanna baboons and chimpanzees, adult males can make females move away or give up food and that females cannot do the same to adult males. It also appears to be true that adult female bonobos can take desirable food from males and can make them change their positions while the males do not do the same to the females. Some primates (gorillas) also show this type of male dominance, while others (lemurs and squirrel monkeys) show female dominance. Still others (gibbons) do not show any type of dominance pattern at all. It is clear that the concept of dominance as it was defined for baboons does not translate easily to other species and, perhaps, even confused the social structure of baboons. This concept about who can control scarce food and mate with females in estrus is both limited and directed only at one gender. In humans, dominance means other things.

A second issue is the development of the human concept of family. Preliminary theories suggested that the savanna baboon system, as it was then known, was a sound model for the system of early humans. In other words, groups would live together with males controlling the females and young and competing to monopolize sex with the females. Only the most dominant males would sire the next generation. This has consequently lost favor with further studies of baboons, other primates, and living human groups. Some nonhuman primate studies have reported cases similar to human monogamy with one adult male and one adult female and offspring (gibbon, lemurs, and some New World monkeys), similar to human "harems" with one adult male and several adult females and offspring (Hamadryas baboons), and dissimilar to humans with no social groups (orangutans in the wild). The one clear generalization that appears in the primate data is one that primates share with all mammals. The core association as Sarah Hrdy noted, is between mothers and their offspring. (1999: 17) In primates, unlike many other mammals, this mother–child unit can continue for years and in some cases life-long. In human groups, as well, the mother–child dyad is the minimal unit in all types of families. The variation in human groups as well as nonhuman primates is largely the roles that adult males play in this unit.

A third issue harkens back to the Man the Hunter hypothesis. In those primates that hunt for meat, what role does this play in the social interaction of the animals? It is clear that primates get most of their food from plants. Some primates also hunt for small animals to eat. Individuals may share their meat with others in their group, and this may help define the relationships between the animals. Chimpanzees, unlike other nonhuman primates, hunt in groups for small monkeys. Most, but certainly not all, of the hunters in these groups are males. When the hunt is over, some of the meat is shared with the hunters and other chimps, including females and the young. Animals with hands outstretched seem to beg for a portion of the meat. The influence of this on longer-term relationships is still unclear. In terms of food, however, there is a clear message. Nonhuman primates do not display a sexual division of labor in normal subsistence activities. Females, like males, forage for their own food. The thesis that our early female ancestors could not care for infants while they gathered their own food is certainly not true for other primates—nor for modern human gatherers and hunters.

Finally, the issue of sexual behavior in primate relationships is actively debated. As mentioned, the role of dominance in the impregnation of nonhuman primates is under debate. Likewise, the extensive use of sex as a social technique by bonobos is not reported beyond that species. The most important caveat when trying to broaden either of these ideas to humans is that human sexual response is biologically, as well as socially and psychologically, different than that in nonhuman primates. Most nonhuman primate females, like most mammals, have periods of sexual receptivity when they are most fertile. There is generally a clear external marking to this period. Many female primates, for example, have a colorful swelling on their hindquarters that make their receptivity apparent from a distance. These females, most importantly, are not sexually receptive outside of this period. In other words, these animals are not available for sex most of the time although the males are. Human females, on the other hand, are sexually available most of their adult lives and give no apparent sign as to the times when they are ovulating. When this difference evolved for humans is highly disputed.[7] This makes analogies from primate data highly problematic.

There is a lot to learn from the nonhuman primates about the nature of being "primatish." The research is clearly still a work in progress, and the future may bring important insights into humans. At this point, there are intriguing possibilities but few clear answers. It seems reasonable to conclude that being a primate provides those animals with neither a patriarchal mandate nor a matriarchal fantasy.

SUMMARY

Millions of years ago humans were very different from their contemporary descendants. Over the years we have become the physical specimens we are today. The development of year-round sexual

---

[7]Helen E. Fisher, *Anatomy of Love* (New York: Norton, 1992); and C. O. Lovejoy, "The Origin of Man," *Science* 211 (1981), pp. 341–50.

receptivity must have had an impact on the relationship between men, women, and their offspring. The development of difficult child-birth and the lengthening period of immaturity in the young undoubtedly influenced the development of gender relations. Most important, the development of culture as an adaptive mechanism made us very different from our ancestors and other primates. One late development, language, allows possibilities of interaction that our ancestors could not approach.

The lessons from our ancestors of that distant time and from our close relatives of other species are important. They help explain some of the differences between humans and other mammals. They set a context for the changes that come. We are not our ancestors or our relatives, however. The best understanding of *Homo sapiens sapiens* must come from a study of Homo sapiens sapiens.

Readings

Ardrey, Robert. *The Hunting Hypothesis.* New York: Atheneum, 1976.

Dahlberg, Frances, ed. *Woman the Gatherer.* New Haven: Yale University Press, 1981.

DeVore, I., and S. I. Washburn. "Baboon Ecology and Human Evolution." In *African Ecology and Human Evolution*, eds. F. C. Howell and F. Bourliére. New York: Viking Fund Publication no. 36, 1963, pp. 335–67.

De Waal, Frans, and Frans Lanting. *Bonobo: The Forgotten Ape.* Berkeley: University of California Press, 1997.

Fedigan, Linda Marie. "The Changing Role of Women in Models of Human Evolution." *Annual Review of Anthropology* 15 (1986), pp. 25–66.

Fisher, Helen E. *Anatomy of Love.* New York: Norton, 1992.

Goodall, Jane. *The Chimpanzees of Gombe: Patterns of Behavior.* Cambridge, MA: The Belknap Press of Harvard University Press, 1986.

Hrdy, Sarah. *The Woman That Never Evolved*, 2nd ed. Cambridge, MA: Harvard University Press, 1999.

Jurmain, Robert; Harry Nelson; Lynn Kilgore; and Wenda Trevathan. *Introduction to Physical Anthropology*, 8th ed. Belmont, CA: Wadsworth/Thomson Learning, 2000.

Klein, Richard. "The Ecology of Early Man in Southern Africa." *Science* 197 (1977), pp. 115–26.

Lee, Richard B., and Irven DeVore, eds. *Man the Hunter.* Chicago: Aldine Publishing, 1968.

Lovejoy, C. O. "The Origin of Man." *Science* 211 (1981), pp. 341–50.

Morgan, Elaine. *The Descent of Women.* New York: Stein and Day, 1972.

Morris, Desmond. *The Naked Ape.* New York: McGraw-Hill, 1967.

Pusey, Anne; Jennifer Williams; and Jane Goodall. "The Influence of Dominance Rank on the Reproductive Success of Female Chimpanzees." *Science* 277, no. 5327 (1997), pp. 828–31.

Slocum, Sally. "Woman the Gatherer: Male Bias in Anthropology." Reprinted in *Toward an Anthropology of Women*, ed. Rayna R. Reiter. New York: Monthly Review Press, 1975, pp. 36–50.

Sperling, Susan. "Baboons with Briefcases vs. Langurs in Lipstick: Feminism and Functionalism in Primate Studies." In *Gender at the Crossroads of Knowledge: Feminist Anthropology in the Postmodern Era*, Micaela Di Leonardo. Berkeley: University of California Press, 1991, pp. 204–34.

Strum, Shirley C. *Almost Human: A Journey into the World of Baboons*. New York: Random House, 1987.

Washburn, Sherwood L., and C. S. Lancaster. "The Evolution of Hunting." In *Man the Hunter*, eds. Richard B. Lee and Irven DeVore. Chicago: Aldine Publishing, 1968, pp. 293–303.

Zihlman, Adrienne. "Women as Shapers of the Human Adaptation." In *Woman the Gatherer*, ed. Frances Dahlberg. New Haven: Yale University Press, 1981, pp. 75–120.

CHAPTER TWO

Histories: Cultural Lessons from the Past?

Were the gender relations of the past similar to those today?
What can we actually know about gender in the past?
What does the past tell us about the present? Or about possibilities for
  the future?

It is clear by now that the lessons of the past can be illusive, at least in terms of the development of behavioral and physical characteristics. But it should be equally clear that knowledge of the past is fundamental to the understanding of the present. Authors who write about gender often refer to a vision of history that forms their view of the present. Some will write that women always were subordinate to men in all cultures and, therefore, sexual hierarchies are intrinsic to human organization. Others write that in the past women were the rulers and men were subordinate until specific social forces intervened to disrupt this natural pattern. By this argument, it is these social forces that have disrupted the natural order and this should be changed. Still others write about a natural equality of women and men in elemental cultures and that such equality is not only possible but the human way. In all these cases, the assertions of history are used to support theories about the present. For many scholars an accurate vision of the past is essential for understanding the nature of contemporary life.

Understanding the past, however, without reference to the present is enormously difficult, if not impossible. Historians and prehistorians recognize this in their research and analysis. When it comes to presenting their findings to the public, however, the prose that is used often hides the problem. Students learn their basic history from textbooks written as if a listing of great men or important political events were the facts of history. These facts, on the contrary, play a minor part in understanding the societies of the past. What these great men (and women) had for dinner and what the common people did on a day-to-day basis are equally important to our full understanding of our human history. It is only logical that the nature of the followers helps explain the nature of the leaders. At the very least, the lives of producers of raw materials and the reproducers of the labor force are central to understanding the greater economy. The outlines of events that are common in public school textbooks are a shadow of reconstructed history. They follow a tradition of presenting facts and emphasizing the elites in societies.

The fact that women only rarely appear in these schoolbooks speaks to this limited view of history rather than the unimportance of women in the human past. This is not to say that there were female presidents, monarchs, or generals who were purposefully left off the lists. Queen Elizabeth I of England, Saint Joan, and the Egyptian pharaoh Hatshepsut appear in these histories. It is the nature of the tradition of writing history, however, that the areas emphasized are those that were most commonly held by men in Western societies. Since Sally Slocum's article in 1975, many anthropologists have pointed to an androcentric bias in Western scholarship. In brief, they assert the fact that most historians and prehistorians have been male, thus their views of the world are those that emphasize male pursuits. When women joined the profession in recent times, this view continued: The traditions of writing history had already been set, and these junior women were trained to follow this pattern to succeed in their profession. Many scholars (Conkey and Williams 1991: 115) have since asserted that history is actually *his* story and that *her* story still needs telling. Still others point to class and ethnic biases in the analysis of the record. The poor and powerless, the darker skinned, and the recent immigrants disappear in the historical literature of Europe and the United States. It is the stories of the most powerful nations that get told while the stories of others do not appear in mainstream histories. To place sex and gender in a useful context, the goal must be to understand the wide varieties of lives that people lived in distant periods in a socially inclusive fashion. It should be emphasized that this goal of socially inclusive history is difficult even for those who seek it the most enthusiastically.

Anthropologists focus on other ways to learn about the past, the chief method being archaeology. Anthropological archaeologists use the physical remains of societies to learn about their cultures. Where there are written records, these are used, but much of archaeological material comes from the incidental remnants of people's lives. In this way these anthropologists attempt to recreate the cultures of prehistorical societies and add to the understanding of historical periods. Like historians, however, archaeologists face major challenges in their search for understanding gender.

APPROPRIATE QUESTIONS

Many people assume that archaeologists discover an interesting site and then proceed to excavate to see what is there. The goal, in this Hollywood movie view, is to find valuable artifacts for museums and self-aggrandizement. In fact this would be the worst type of archaeology. The goal of archaeology is knowledge, not objects. Artifacts are a means to an end, and that end is cultural information. Further, all excavation is destructive and once dug, any unrecorded information that existed about the context of the site is gone. Professional archaeologists work very precisely and excavate only what they must to get the information they need. By tradition, large parts of a site are protected for the future when research methods will allow better excavation.

The ideal archaeological research starts, not with a site, but with a question. Not all interesting questions are appropriate for study. Certainly not all questions are appropriate for all methods of study. First *a question must be of significance.* This means that it adds to the general understanding of anthropology. This may be expanding the understanding of a particular society or theme. For example, the answer to the question "What was the role of women in the religious rituals of Bronze Age Crete?" could add considerably to the understanding of that time. It would also shed light on the role of women in early state-level societies. Similarly, a question about the importance of gathering particular plants in northern Mexico shortly before the development of the domestication of maize might provide lessons about the development of agriculture in general and might also teach something about the roles of Mexican women—if one assumes that gathering was a female activity. Many gender questions fit this first criterion. Information about gender is important theoretically, and many gaps in the knowledge about gender need to be filled.

The second major criterion is that *a question must be answerable.* How do you dig up gender? Archaeological questions have to have some physical base. Questions about abstractions such as emotions or intent are most likely not going to be answered by artifacts. The more technologically based the evidence, the more appropriate it is for archaeological inquiry. The archaeologists must consider what possible evidence could be found that would address these questions. One problem, of course, is that gender is an abstraction. Questions concerning gender must be broken down into elements that can be investigated. The wall paintings at Crete and the physical remains of grains and tools in Mexico make these questions promising. Less grounded questions would waste time and resources. All societies are gendered and, therefore, theoretically appropriate for such questions, but not all cultural sites would offer evidence that clarifies gender differences. Archaeological questions about gender must be carefully crafted and situated in thoughtfully selected settings.

APPROPRIATE SETTINGS

While the site must be selected according to the question, some archaeologists have suggested that some types of sites are intrinsically more appropriate than others. In a recent book about race, class, and gender in archaeology, *Those of Little Note* [Scott (ed.), 1994], several historical archaeologists addressed just this question. Historical archaeologists, who have documents to use with the analysis of their sites, have a special insight into this question. They are able to compare the writing about the subject with the remains they find in their excavations and come to some intriguing conclusions. Three examples from this book should highlight the problem that all archaeologists face.

Archaeologist David R. Starbuck (1994: 115–128) addresses the issue of finding women in military sites of late-eighteenth-century America, where the records show they clearly existed. In fact, the records of the time document that women and even children lived in the forts and camps of both British and American forces. The women acted as wives, lovers, nurses, laundresses, and tailors in the camps. While the women of the common soldiers were sometimes seen as expensive annoyances by the generals, the value of their work was admitted to be significant, and some were paid with rations for their labor. Estimations of the percentage of women in the forces during the Revolution varies, but Starbuck (pp. 123–124) cited a ratio of one female to every four males in British General John Burgoyne's army and a ratio of one woman to every eight soldiers among the Pennsylvania regiments. In most cases, however, the number of women was significant, and a full understanding of military life in this period must include their roles. But as Starbuck noted, "The role of women at eighteenth-century military camps continues to be neglected by most authors." (p. 124)

With any optimism, the reader would conclude that archaeologists such as Starbuck will focus on women and begin to expand the historical record. But, and this is Starbuck's major point, even for those looking for it, the archaeology still does not illuminate the world of the women and children at these sites. In fact, the artifacts that are easily defined as belonging to women or children are rare. Most items were used by men and women alike. It becomes impossible to conclude that a particular button, or pot, or food was used by either a man or a woman. Even those few small items that appear to better fit a woman, such as small rings, could have been in the fort as trade goods. Starbuck, himself, found no clear "women's artifacts" in three sites that he excavated. He concluded that "Undeniably, more gender-specific information will be found within primary documents than will derive from material culture found at archaeological sites, but archaeologists need to make a more deliberate search for contexts within military camps where women are known to have lived, and testing strategies must be devised that will help us to find and identify them." (p. 126)

Other articles in the *Those of Little Note* collection approach their inquiry into gender by selecting a site or an activity in sites that are clearly connected to women. Donna J. Seifert in an investigation of "Mrs. Starr's Profession" explores the lives of prostitutes in the Hooker's Division of

Washington, D.C., in the decades before and after 1890. In this area the homes of working class people and houses of prostitution exist side by side. Looking at the material remains of both types of residences, Seifert observed that in the later period the sex workers lived somewhat better than their neighbors did in other professions. (p. 64) This study illuminates the choices open to those working class women who had little way to be financially independent in this period.

③ Another approach was taken by Louise M. Jackson in her study of Native Alaskan women during the Russian American period of southwestern Alaska. In an extensive review of Russian American records, she finds that Native Alaskan women are most commonly associated with cloth and clothing. They appear as traders, tailors, and recipients of cloth, a major trade good. It is cloth, Jackson asserts, that could be seen methodologically as "a key to gender visibility." (1994: 42–43) Because women are rarely seen in the archaeological material of this era, she advocates a focus on this specific aspect of Russian American trade to bring out the roles that women played. Both Jackson and Seifert argue that archaeologists can find women only if they seriously look at places or activities that were the primary domains of women and where women literally would leave their marks.

THE PREHISTORIAN'S DILEMMA: GENDERING ARTIFACTS

The historical archaeologists just discussed demonstrate some of the difficulties of finding gender in material remains. Each turns to the written records to construct a method to get to the information they want. Elizabeth Kryder-Reid, another historical archaeologist who studied the nature of gender in an all-male community, rejoiced that her project was not thwarted by "the prehistorian's dilemma of assuming universal gender roles." (1994: 102) This "prehistorian's dilemma" adds dramatically to the difficulties of learning about gender relations in the distant past. The methods that historical archaeologists are using for understanding gender in their sites are not available to the prehistorians. How does a researcher know what places or activities in a prehistoric society were female or male focused? How does this researcher know what artifacts would be associated with women and not men, or visa versa? How do you learn about gender in an extinct society that has left no written records if you do not already have some basis of information about the gender system? What is the source of such information?

In prehistoric anthropology, when studying early gathering and hunting cultures, the artifacts and the context in which they are found provide the core data. Feminist anthropologist Alice Kehoe (1992: 28) addressed the problem of interpreting what these artifacts have said in the context of gender. She focused on the "bifacially flaked, symmetrical pointed stone artifacts," which are generally referred to as projectile points. These are among the most common types of artifacts in many prehistoric sites. In the popular literature they are often called spear points or arrow points. Kehoe noted that with modern techniques it was apparent than many of the tools that were so labeled were used as knives or had other, similar purposes. It is reasonable to assume that many were used by women in their work, which must have included cutting and slicing. As Kehoe noted, "The conventional label 'projectile point,' elicited from gross morphology of the artifact, links into the paradigm 'hunter,' normally construed as male. In effect, archaeological convention peoples the past with men and robs women of their artifacts." (p. 28) This convention thus demonstrates a double problem in analysis of such data. First, the general tool is defined by one specific potential use, in this case hunting. Second, the assumption is that hunting is an exclusively male pursuit. In any specific site, neither assumption may be true.

If the artifacts of the distant past are ambiguous with respect to gender, can careful site selection, as suggested by historical archaeology, clarify the situation? As with identification artifacts, this is more difficult in prehistory. In the study of gatherers and hunters in prehistory, the sites are often undifferentiated camps or kill sites. If one assumes that the hunters are male, a kill site might appear gender specific. The nature of artifacts found there may be generalized within the culture to be associated with men. The obvious problem with this is that it works only if (1) all the hunters were male in this specific site and (2) if women would not be found at the site to butcher the meat, prepare the hides, or to perform other tasks. It is possible that this was the case in any specific site, but it is not true that it would be the case in all kill sites. How does an anthropologist discern which type of kill site is which?

Feminist archaeologist Joan M. Gero directly approached this challenge in an article called "Genderlithics: Women's Roles in Stone Tool Production." (1991: 163–193) She also criticized two issues in the traditional analysis of ancient stone tools. First, previous research tended to focus the analysis on the complete stone points, the projectile points to which Kehoe referred. Gero, however, found this focus misplaced. In fact, most stone artifacts were flakes from a core stone or retouched pieces from points. Second, a considerable amount of discussion related to the manufacture of the tools and less to their use. If an archaeologist looked at the uses of flakes and retouched points, it would be difficult not to see them used in the work of women as well as men. The toolmakers perfected their tools for use in leatherworking, woodworking, and plant harvesting. These tasks are not male linked in contemporary gathering and hunting groups, so there is no reason to assume they were so in the past. The more logical conclusion is that women did regularly make and use flake and retouched tools. Further, Gero asserted that there was no reason to assume that women did not make stone points as well. "There are no compelling biological, historical, sociological, ethnographnic, [sic] ethnohistorical, or experimental reasons why women could not have made—and good reason to think they probably *did* make—all kinds of stone tools, in all kinds of lithic materials, for a variety of uses and contexts." (p. 176) As a technique to find these women toolmakers in her archaeological site at Huaricoto, Peru, Gero focused on flake tools made of local materials that were found in dwellings. In these, she asserted, "We will surely 'see' women." (p. 176)

Archaeologists Rita P. Wright and Elizabeth M. Brumfiel focused on other technologies where they expected to find women's work. Wright looked at pottery that she referred to as "an invention of major historic significance, and as one in which women played an active part." (Wright 1991: 195) She found an unwarranted bias, based on modern Western assumptions, about the nature of gender differences in domestic as opposed to commercial production. As a consequence of this bias, the literature assumes that pottery done on the wheel for trade was male-made while more rudimentary pottery made for personal home use was female-made. Applying this understanding to her study of Harappan civilization (6000–1800 B.C.) of the Indus River region, Wright found "no reason to exclude either women or men" (p. 213) from domestic or commercial areas of pottery production. While this type of study falls far short of discovering the gender roles of the prehistoric culture, or even technology in that culture, it did correct misconceptions. There was no evidence or reason to assume that men dominated commercial production of pottery in this case, thus correcting our knowledge of Harappan society.

In another approach, Brumfiel concentrated on technological areas that ethnohistoric evidence suggested were women's arenas. (1991: 224–251) One method to find gender echoed what the historic archaeologists suggested. Even in cultures without records that could help the archaeologist, there can be evidence from outsiders or descendents to suggest that specific activities were performed by a specific gender. Among the Aztecs of Mexico, weaving and cooking appear to be associated with women in art and Spanish reports. As with the pottery in Wright's study, the assumption that weaving and cooking as done by women were domestic activities did not challenge the Western gender assumptions of most archaeologists. Also like the Harappan case, however, both cooking and weaving have commercial aspects that were socially important. Among the Aztecs, food and fabric production were important in the home, market, and tribute systems of political domination. Brumfiel, through archaeology, found a wider variation in women's roles than the period's ethnohistory typically reflects. Their social status, home region, access to markets, and degree of Aztec domination affected the work of individual women. Fabric and food were essential parts of the Aztec system of production and reproduction, and these were the results of women's work. All Aztec women were not alike, however, and the investigation of these products helped illuminate this aspect of early Mexican life.

Another sign that archaeology is coming to the fore in gender studies is that archaeologists are beginning to use their special resources to test

An early Aztec drawing showing a man and woman with two children.

the theories of scholars in other fields where feminist studies have longer histories. A good example of this is another article by Elizabeth Brumfiel (1996) in which she examined Aztec figurines to test theories developed by ethnohistorians. These scholars agreed that the Aztec State developed an ideology of gender that depreciated the status of women, but the effectiveness of this ideology on the local level was in dispute. Did the ideology help subordinate local regions or was there resistance to this ideology of inequality of class and gender? A study of the figurines of different regions at different times led her to support the idea of resistance. While archaeologists have long looked to history and social anthropology for evidence about gender, Brumfiel shows that scholars from those fields can begin to look to archaeology as well.

THE NATURE OF ANALOGY IN ARCHAEOLOGY

The data of archaeology are physical objects and the context in which they are found. These artifacts are the clues used to solve the mystery of the nature of a culture. Perhaps even more than in other mysteries, all the clues needed are rarely present. It is the role of the detectives (in this case, archaeologists) to use the answers they have constructed to create a rational solution. What makes an archaeological mystery even more difficult to solve is that the archaeological detective is not a member of the culture in which the mystery is embedded and, therefore, does not really know what is normal. The common knowledge and hunches that detectives in fiction use to solve the mystery are dangerous concepts in the science of acrchaelogy. With apologies to Sir Arthur Conan Doyle, very little is elementary.

More abstract analysis, however, calls for more problematic methods. How does the archaeological detective conclude which gender used cooking baskets and whether women hunted the animals or men cut the grain? In fact, it is highly unlikely that any archaeologist would make any such conclusions; there is no evidence for them. However, it is possible, even likely, that the archaeologists would assume that women were cooking in those baskets and cutting grain while the men hunted. Of course, there is no more evidence for this than there is for the former conclusions. Why then, does one set of conclusions seem reasonable and the other unlikely? The answer lies in the use of analogy.

An analogy is a comparison, in this case using something known to help explain something that is unknown but similar. It is a simple form of reasoning that is used daily, often successfully, by most people to understand new experiences. In situations of cultural differences, such analogies are often misleading. For example, a naïve Frenchman might reasonably assume on his first introduction to a Scottish kilt that it was a piece of women's apparel. This is a reasonable error because skirtlike garments are women's wear in France; thus our Frenchman is applying the assumptions of his culture in this analogy. It is reasonable but it is incorrect. The more distant the culture, the less reliable this type of reasoning and the more untrustworthy the conclusions are.

In archaeology, analogies are used all the time. Like the Frenchman, an American archaeologist excavating a kilt might identify it as a garment, which it is, and as a woman's garment, which is not. The function would follow from shape and size and, then, by analogy because of its similarity to known garments. The gender of the user would again be based on the archaeologist's cultural assumption that women, and not men, wear skirts. It might be noted that the same garment found in the closet of a teenage American girl might well fit the archaeologist's conclusion. There is nothing in the garment itself that reveals the sex or gender of the owner. Many discoveries are like this.

What would a society that had variable or large numbers of genders look like? How would a society with absolutely no sex roles appear in a site? If any such societies had existed, could they be proven through archaeology? Surely it would be difficult and, perhaps, impossible. Archaeology has come a long way in the study of women and of gender in the past two decades, but some challenges have not yet been successfully overcome.

In general, the assumptions of archaeologists relating to gender have been based on analogies with their own cultures. Some of this is unconscious and some is raised to the level of theory. Western culture has long assumed there were two normal genders and that only one, men, is active in public settings. Men were assumed to be leaders in religion, government, and families. Women were assumed to be helpmates in families, nurturers to children, gardeners, and cooks. Men were dominant and women were subordinate. It was also culturally assumed that this pattern was a human universal. Therefore, it would be safe for scholars to recreate the cultures of the past with this same gender pattern. In recent decades, however, the ethnographic evidence has shown that there is far more variation in gender categories in human societies than was ever expected. The roles once seen as universal now appear to be more unpredictable.

A critique of the concept of a universalistic certainty of the roles of men and women has been deeply embedded in the theories of archaeology. Even in feminist archaeology many studies still focus on the roles of women in specific societies. This is perfectly understandable, and even necessary, given the fact that this information has been missing in the past. A final point must be made. While much of the archaeology is couched in terms of males and females, this should not be taken to mean that archaeologists are not aware of issues of the multiplicity of sexes and genders (see Chapter 11). In more complex societies, physical remains found in cemeteries point to differences in burials between males and females. While this type of information is keyed to sex rather than gender, information about differences between those who appear male and those who appear female can been seen. If there were third genders, or entirely different gender perceptions, they would not necessarily appear. The assumption that there were only two genders in the past and that those were the same as the contemporary, Western conception of gender is more than problematic.[1] The problem here, as in other issues, is this: How can alternatives based on abstract definitions be discovered from a prehistoric past?

Even common patterns found throughout the world are rarely seen in archaeological reports. In many parts of the world, women are the traders in marketplaces. These traders range from women selling produce from their home gardens in village squares to women entrepreneurs in Western Africa trading items throughout regions. Likewise, women healers and religious leaders are often important members of their societies. Where are they in the prehistoric record? With the new recognition of the biases in archaeological analysis, there is hope that these recurrent roles will be found in future work. If analogy is important, there are now clear analogies in the literature that should make the existence of women traders and religious practitioners in past cultures more visible.

---

[1]See, for example, Lynn Meskell, "Running the Gamut: Gender, Girls, and Goddesses," *American Journal of Archaeology* 102 (1998) pp. 181–85; and Cheryl Claassen, "Questioning Gender: An Introduction." In *Exploring Gender Through Archaeology: Selected Papers from the 1991 Boone Conference, Monographs in World Archaeology* No. 11, ed. Cheryl Claassen. Madison: WI: Prehistory Press, 1992.

WOMEN AND POWER IN PREHISTORY

One question about the past has long sparked the imaginations of feminist scholars and readers of scholarly and popular books alike: Was there a time or place when women, rather than men, ruled societies? As you will read in the introduction to Section II, the idea that women were the rulers in the earliest human societies was advanced as a theoretical assertion in social science works for more than a century. A golden age when women held power has also been an ideal allegation in many feminist works over the years. However, other scholars in both feminist studies and a variety of social fields have argued that such societies never existed and are, in fact, impossible. If these societies existed, they should have left a mark on the landscape and archaeology should be able to shed light on this debate. Given the issues raised earlier, however, this would be a serious challenge. What would a matriarchy look like in an archaeological site? Because no societies that mandate that their leaders be women have ever been observed, what would such societies from the past leave behind in the earth that would be an indication of this system?

Two cases represent approaches to answering these questions. Both have been used as proof of the existence of prehistoric matriarchies and both clearly show unusual female representations. However, both have also been subject to strong critical studies that reject them as proof of matriarchal systems. At very least, they present a past where women, or female images, played roles that are absent or unusual in the contemporary world. By examining these cases, the limitations of both archaeological analysis and popular wishful thinking should become apparent.

The first example is a broad examination of late Paleolithic and Neolithic statues and engravings from Europe that have become popularly known as "Venus figurines" or "mother goddesses." These small statues have been variously interpreted as manmade figures of fertility and sexuality or as goddesses in a culture of powerful women. The second example is the variation in the analysis of a particular case, that of Çatal Hüyük, an Anatolian Bronze Age site. This site has been interpreted both as a patriarchal community where fertility is an essential symbol and as an original matriarchy.

Images of Women

One of the most contentious issues involving prehistoric archaeology in the feminist literature involves those female statues and drawings of the late Paleolithic and early Neolithic (Venus figurines or mother goddess images). The artifacts that anchor these disputes are figures of women that have been found in Paleolithic Europe beginning about 30,000 years ago. Many of these figures depict women with exaggerated hips and breasts and diminished heads, arms, and legs. The most famous of these is a fist-sized stone figurine, now called the Venus of Willendorf, that shows these characteristics to the extreme. She has a small, featureless face and a stylized hairdo. Her arms and legs are extremely small; the trunk of her body comprises the bulk of the statue. She has large pendulous breasts and broad and fat hips, and her features are the polar opposite of a modern, European fashion model. To some modern researchers she appears pregnant, to others fat, to others erotic, and to others diseased. For example, Baring and Cashford believe that "The statues are always naked, generally small and often pregnant. Some look like ordinary women, but most of them have the look of mothers, as though all that were female in them had been focused on the overwhelming mystery of birth." (1991: 6) They analyze such a figure as, "weighed down with fertility, so rooted in the earth that she seems to be part of it." (1991: 10)

A different example is a 1995 *Health* article by Chen et al., called "Back When Big Was Beautiful" that argued that this figure was an accurate image of "female plumpness" and, perhaps, indicated the importance of a role of "wet nurse" in antiquity. And again, geographer Jerome Dobson, in a study of iodine deficiency in prehistory, asserted, "The similarity in breasts, abdomen, and body shape between the Willendorf figurine and a thirty-eight-year-old cretin woman is notable." (1998: 10)

These figurines give us a rare human glimpse of the people of the prehistoric past. Along with the famous European cave art, which shows far more animals than people, these figures were purposely made by prehistoric people to illustrate their views of the world. Whether these were created to show realistic snapshots of the artists' world, abstract images of supernatural worlds, or something else entirely is unknown. They do represent a direct connection to the ideas of these ancestors, however, and this is very engaging to many scholars. Many theories have been put forward, and some have become central to the debates. The creators of these figures are speaking to us through their creations, but do we understand what they were saying? Also, are they all saying the same thing?

There are three related questions under debate:

- Who made these artifacts?
- What was their purpose?
- What do they tell us about the cultures of the artists?

Realistically, it is virtually impossible to identify much about the artists from the artifacts themselves. Was it a male hand or a female hand that sculpted any particular piece? Physically, either could do it. Assertions about the gender of the artists then must be based on other indications. LeRoy McDermont (1996) contended that the artists were women who were representing their views of their own bodies.

But the earliest assumptions were that the artists were male and that these men made the statuettes as erotic items or for use in fertility rites. For example, Magin Berenguer, in his book *Prehistoric Man and His Art,* asserted:

Sex and the stomach have always been the dominant idea behind the great majority of philosophies. Directly or indirectly, these two visceral elements have been the driving forces of mankind. This was especially true in primitive society. Man expressed these real material needs directly and unambiguously. When it comes to sex, the exuberant Venuses alone would suffice to prove this contention." (74–75)

Contradicting this view, Bahn and Vertert state the following: "Some Paleolithic depictions of women have been compared with pin-ups in Playboy, and it has been claimed that female figures often appear in sexually inviting attitudes, which may be quite the same as those in the most brazen pornographic magazines." (1988: 165) As archaeologist Sarah Nelson noted, "There is very little evidence in the art to justify a belief in a prehistoric obsession with sexuality or fertility." (1997: 156) That the obvious function of a nude female figure is inherently sexual may speak more to the twentieth-century sensibilities of the analyst than the sensibilities of the artists of the Upper Paleolithic. Bahn and Vertert argued, "The macho view of Paleolithic art is both simplistic and anachronistic." (1988: 182) To assume that these figures were made by women who were devotees of female deities to represent their goddesses or who were making self-portraits may be doing exactly the same thing. In the absence of evidence, any of these assertions resemble inkblot projections more than they do science.

Even more abstract are the descriptions of a wide variety of symbols or objects as female. In many areas of prehistoric art nonnaturalistic lines and forms are found in association with more conventional items. Triangular forms repeatedly appear, and they have been often identified as vulvas with a variety of interpretations of what an image of a vulva might mean. Rectangular forms with crescent-shaped extensions from the top corners are regularly described as bulls with interpretations of maleness, but some, including the premier proponent of the powerful goddess image, Marija Gimbutas (1991: 265–272), considered these female images representative of female reproductive organs. A small number of rod-shaped artifacts with two grapelike extensions along the shaft has been repeatedly defined as a female shape with breasts. Several researchers (Baring and Cashford, Kehoe, Bahn and Vertert) recently pointed out that it can more easily be seen as male genitalia. The reliance on clearly abstract images is even more problematic than reliance on the more naturalistic forms when trying to determine prehistoric gender representation.

Clearly the art of the Paleolithic is a window onto that time. Unfortunately it is not a clear window; it is fogged, and only shadows can be fully discerned. It is the job of the archaeologist to wipe away this fog. At this point, the haze prevails. Gimbutas and other archaeologists have ensured that such figures found in future sites will be well recorded and published. This should mean that the context of the figure would be as important as the figure itself in future analysis.

Until recently, individual artifacts from a wide variety of sites have been grouped and studied as a general, pan-European type. Figurines separated by thousands of miles and thousands of years have been treated as if they are related. Future analysis may prove this true, but the evidence does not support it now. In the absence of rigorous archaeology, these important pieces of antiquity have been used to support the ideas of the time and the orientation of the author. Many have viewed them through male eyes and declared them erotic and fertile. Paleolithic "goddesses," then, reflected a gender role similar to that of early-twentieth-century Europe, with women as sex objects and domestic partners for men. More recently, many feminist scholars rejected that image and saw the reflection very differently. To these scholars, the "goddesses" are powerful reminders of a primitive matriarchy where women were the rulers of society. In these arguments men are not an issue; the figurines represent power for women. Unfortunately, as Pamela Russell succinctly pointed out: "The new feminist authors distort the real archaeological evidence just as much as the early chauvinistic males did." (1998: 265)

Çatal Hüyük[2]

The search for an original matriarchy continues into the Neolithic. During this period, intensive agricultural and early farming communities are found in many regions of Europe. Some would argue that this would be exactly the time when the original matriarchies would have flourished. By this logic, the gathering and hunting societies that flourished earlier would not have been strongly hierarchical, while urbanized societies and states of a later period would have shown signs of early patriarchy. The Anatolian site of Çatal Hüyük, in present-day Turkey, which dates from about 9,000 years ago, represents a people who were at this transitional stage of human development. Economically they used domesticated cattle and plants as well as wild plants and animals and appear to have engaged in trade especially of obsidian. (Wason 1994: 167–168; Todd 1967: 126–128) Their settlement was a compact town with a variety of structures and distinctive art. In this art are female and abstract figures that some have interpreted as goddesses. Even apart from the inferences of matriarchy and goddess worship, this site has important lessons about the prehistory of Europe and western Asia.

Çatal Hüyük was first excavated in the 1960s by British archaeologist James Mellaart (1967), and much of the data come from his work. In the 1990s the site was reopened by an international team led by a student of Mellaart, and new data continue to come to light. (Young 1996: 4–50) While some call this community an urban civilization and others an early form of farming village, all remark on an unexpectedly luxurious standard of living for its residents. (Wason 1994: 154–155) Future research

---

[2]This is currently the most common spelling of the site, but you will also find it as Catal-hoyuk or Chatal Hoyok.

will certainly clarify the real nature of the community, but the current data from Mellaart's excavations suggest a community of people with elaborate burials, highly symbolic art, and a strong focus on religion.

The section of the village that Mellaart excavated was composed of two types of rooms that he defined as houses and shrines. The houses were small rooms with raised platforms but little decoration. The shrines, however, which he felt were not used as residences, were distinguished by their decoration and contents such as wall paintings, statues, figures modeled in the walls, and human skulls. The paintings included hunting scenes, scenes of vulturelike birds with decapitated humans, and a variety of animals. Plaster reliefs and statues included similar images, with cattle horns and deities being prominent. One repeated image is of a female figure, perhaps a deity, sometimes found with leopardlike cats or a smaller male. The most famous version is a sculpture of a rotund female seated on a stool with two large cats posed at each side. While the theology is unclear, it is generally agreed that the art was used for religious purposes.

The burials at Çatal Hüyük are unusual and have been the basis of much speculation. Just fewer than 500 individual bodies were excavated from inside the houses and shrines. In a study of approximately 300 of them, it was found that 136 of the 222 adults discovered were female. (Wason 1994: 156) Burial sites were often found under the raised platforms. The bodies were reburied there after the flesh was removed from the bones. A variety of grave goods were found, with jewelry being common with female burials and tools with male burials, but many grave goods were not specific to either sex. Burials in shrines tended to be more elaborate than in houses, but only a few stood out as extraordinary. Paul Wason, in his analysis of the social ranking of this site, rejected any theory of ruling queens and powerless men but argued that "The fact that women are found among the prominent burials indicates that it was possible for them to obtain what higher ranks there were more or less as readily as men. Further, several female burials involve strong symbolic references. . . . To the extent that these burials indicate central leaders, women were as prominent among them as men." (1994: 162) Of course, the role of kinship, marriage, or achievement in determining such ranks remains unknown.

While the archaeological data are intriguing, if not definitive, the interpretations in more popular literature are far broader and demonstrate no doubts. In many of these works (Stone 1976; Barstow 1978; Gimbutas 1989), Çatal Hüyük appears as an early matriarchy with a religion based on the worship of the mother goddess. Gimbutas lists it as one of the "richest sites" and describes a wide variety of goddess images found there. (1989: xvi) Further, the presumed religion of this site is then used to show the continuity from Paleolithic mother goddess worship through Çatal Hüyük to the goddesses of ancient Greece and Rome and the Celts, and thus, in a disguised mode, into the present. The preliminary work at this one site has become a proof of theories long before a final interpretation is warranted. Archaeologist Sarah Nelson has suggested a reason for the eager adoption of this site by so many nonanthropologists. She interprets the popular interest in Çatal Hüyük as the result of a failure of archaeology to address the issue in a serious way. "While it was heralded by historians, art historians, and goddess worshippers as an example of matriarchy, the site was treated with more reserve by most archaeologists. This is a key example of popular interest filling the void when archaeologists themselves fail to address questions of gender in a sustained and careful way." (1997: 146)

SUMMARY

The study of gender in archaeology is still relatively new. Until recently, gender has not been a major consideration in the analysis of sites, and women in particular have been ignored. Archaeologist Brian Boyd asserted "Of all the social sciences, archaeology has been notoriously slow (reluctant) to incorporate perspectives from the vast amount of literature on feminism and gender." (1997: 14–30) It is also true that in the past few decades a number of archaeologists have begun to turn this around and set a new focus on gender and women's roles in past societies. Historical archaeologists, using historical records, have taken the lead and illuminated parts of history previously ignored. Without such records, the endeavor has been more difficult for archaeologists studying prehistoric cultures, but some of these scholars have also challenged many of the ideas about the nature of the past and introduced new methods of analysis. The importance of analogies from the present and the known past for interpretation of unknowns in the past is a major problematic influence on interpretation. Additional work by ethnographers, ethnohistorians, historians, as well as archaeologists is adding to this information daily. Given the nature of the archaeological method and the relative youth of the venture, we can expect new data and new methods to be published every year. As the cases of Çatal Hüyük and the prehistoric female figurines show, many people appear to have reached conclusions based on limited or exaggerated data. While it is frustrating to be unable to find the truth about the character of these unusual elements of the past, the nature of the evidence makes any conclusions premature. With the recent advances in the archaeological study of gender, however, more reliable theories and answers may come soon.

Readings

Bahn, Paul G., and Jean Vertert. *Images of the Ice Age*. Leicester: W. H. Smith and Son, 1988.

Baring, Anne, and Jules Cashford. *The Myth of the Goddess: Evolution of an Image*. London: Viking Arkana, Penguin Group, 1991.

Barstow, Anne. "The Uses of Archaeology for Women's History: James Mellaart's Work on the Neolithic Goddess at Çatal Hüyük." *Feminist Studies* 4, no. 3 (1978), pp. 7–17.

Berenguer, Magin. *Prehistoric Man and His Art.* London: Souvenir Press, 1973.

Boyd, Brian. "The Power of Gender Archaeology." In *Invisible People and Processes: Writing Gender and Childhood into European Archaeology,* eds. Jenny Moore and Eleanor Scott. London: Leicester University Press, 1987, pp. 25–30.

Brumfiel, Elizabeth M. "Weaving and Cooking: Women's Production in Aztec Mexico." In *Engendering Archaeology: Women and Prehistory,* eds. Joan M. Gero and Margaret W. Conkey. Cambridge, MA: Basil Blackwell, 1991, pp. 224–51.

————. "Figurines and the Aztec State: Testing the Effectiveness of Ideological Domination." In *Gender and Archaeology,* ed. Rita R. Wright. Philadelphia: University of Pennsylvania Press, 1996, pp. 143–66.

Chen, Ingfei; Deborah Franklin; John Hastings; and Patricia Long. "Back When Big Was Beautiful." *Health* 9, no. 2 (March/April 1995), pp. 10–11.

Claassen, Cheryl. "Questioning Gender: An Introduction." In *Exploring Gender Through Archaeology: Selected Papers from the 1991 Boone Conference, Monographs in World Archaeology* No. 11, ed. Cheryl Claassen. Madison, WI: Prehistory Press, 1991, pp. 1–9.

Conkey, Margaret, with Sarah Williams. "Original Narratives: The Political Economy of Gender in Archaeology." In *Gender at the Crossroads of Knowledge: Feminist Anthropology in the Postmodern Era,* ed. Micaela di Leonardo. Berkeley: University of California Press, 1991, pp. 102–39.

Dobson, Jerome E. "The Iodine Factor in Health and Evolution." *Geographical Review* 88, no. 1 (1998), pp. 1–28.

Gero, Joan M. "Genderlithics: Women's Roles in Stone Tool Production." In *Engendering Archaeology: Women and Prehistory,* eds. Joan M. Gero and Margaret W. Conkey. Cambridge, MA: Basil Blackwell, 1991, pp. 163–93.

Gimbutas, Marija. *The Language of the Goddess.* New York: Harper-Collins, 1989.

Jackson, Louise M. "Cloth, Clothing, and Related Paraphernalia: A Key to Gender Visibility in the Archaeological Record of Russian America." In *Those of Little Note: Gender, Race, and Class in Historical Archaeology,* ed. Elizabeth M. Scott. Tucson: The University of Arizona Press, 1994, pp. 27–53.

Kehoe, Alice. "The Muted Class: Unshackling Tradition." In *Exploring Gender Through Archaeology: Selected Papers from the 1991 Boone Conference, Monographs in World Archaeology* No. 11, ed. Cheryl Claassen. Madison, WI: Prehistory Press, 1992, pp. 23–32.

Kryder-Reid, Elizabeth. "'With Manly Courage': Reading the Construction of Gender in a Nineteenth-Century Religious Community." In *Those of Little Note: Gender, Race, and Class in Historical Archaeology,* ed. Elizabeth M. Scott. Tucson: The University of Arizona Press, 1994, pp. 97–114.

McDermont, LeRoy. "Self-Representation in Upper Paleolithic Female Figurines." *Current Anthropology* 37, no. 2 (April 1996), pp. 227–76.

Mellaart, James. *Çatal Hüyük: A Neolithic Town in Anatolia.* New York: McGraw-Hill, 1967.

Meskell, Lynn. "Running the Gamut: Gender, Girls, and Goddesses." *American Journal of Archaeology* 102, 1998, pp. 181–85.

————. "Twin Peaks: The Archaeologies of Çatalhüyük." In *Ancient Goddesses: The Myths and the Evidence,* eds. Lucy Goodison and Christina Morris. London: British Museum Press, 1998, pp. 46–62.

Nelson, Sarah Milledge. *Gender in Archaeology: Analyzing Power and Prestige.* Walnut Creek, CA: AltaMira Press, 1997.

Russell, Pamela. "The Paleolithic Mother-Goddess: Fact or Fiction?" In *Reader in Gender Archaeology*, eds. Kelley Hays-Gilpin and David S. Whitley. New York: Routledge, 1998, pp. 261–68.

Scott, Elizabeth M., ed. *Those of Little Note: Gender, Race, and Class in Historical Archaeology*. Tucson: The University of Arizona Press, 1994.

Seifert, Donna J. "Mrs. Starr's Profession." *Those of Little Note: Gender, Race, and Class in Historical Archaeology*, ed. Elizabeth M. Scott. Tucson: The University of Arizona Press, 1994, pp. 149–73.

Slocum, Sally. *Woman the Gatherer: Male Bias in Anthropology*. In *Toward an Anthropology of Women*, ed. Rayna R. Reiter. New York: Monthly Review Press, 1975, pp. 36–50.

Starbuck, David R. "The Identification of Gender at Northern Military Sites of the Late Eighteenth Century." In *Those of Little Note: Gender, Race, and Class in Historical Archaeology*, ed. Elizabeth M. Scott. Tucson: The University of Arizona Press, 1994, pp. 115–28.

Stone, Merlin. *When God Was a Woman*. New York: Harcourt, Brace, 1976.

Todd, Ian. *Çatal Hüyük in Perspective*. Menlo Park, CA: Cummings Publishing, 1967.

Wason, Paul K. *The Archaeology of Rank*. Cambridge: Cambridge University Press, 1994.

Wright, Rita R. "Women's Labor and Pottery Production in Prehistory." In *Engendering Archaeology: Women and Prehistory*, eds. Joan M. Gero and Margaret W. Conkey. Cambridge, MA: Basil Blackwell, 1991, pp. 194–223.

Young, Penny. "The First Metropolis?" *History Today* 46, no. 2 (February 1996), pp. 4–5.

SECTION II

Making a Living: An Organization of Culture and Society

Cultural anthropology is about how people live together, and most of the data and analyses for the rest of this book come from that field. Because the methods of archaeology and physical anthropology have been reviewed for their strengths and weaknesses, it is important to briefly do the same for this area of anthropology. In many ways, the task of cultural anthropologists is much easier and the availability of data on gender far greater.

METHODS AND ANALYSIS: CULTURAL ANTHROPOLOGY

Cultural, or social, anthropologists study living groups of people and their sociocultural behaviors. This may strike some as counterintuitive since anthropology is popularly perceived as connected with tribes and exotic peoples. In fact, while many anthropologists do study peoples with social systems very different than that of contemporary America, others study aspects of life in urban areas of modern states here and now. Even those who study people living in areas remote from these urban settings tend to study people as they live today. The cultural diversity of the world's peoples is the topic of cultural anthropology.

The hallmark methodology of cultural anthropologists is called *participant observation.* The term is fully descriptive. Anthropologists participate in the cultures they study while they observe them. Anthropologists beginning a new study first read what is written on the people of the region and establish a research question. Many of the research cases in this book are based on questions that have been asked about the nature of gender, or male or female roles in specific cultures. After receiving sufficient funding and appropriate permissions from state bureaucracies and cultural organizations, field research can begin. Field-workers commit themselves to at least a year of concentrated study in the culture of interest. This means moving into the community being studied and learning about it full time. In most cases, the first couple of months are spent getting accustomed to the basics of life. After this the anthropologist focuses on the research question. People studying hunting, for example, will begin to learn from hunters and go hunting. Others studying religion will choose religious leaders as mentors and actively participate in religious ceremonies and meetings. Studying gender issues may lead to a wide variety of activities surrounding gender. Anthropologist Elizabeth Brusco, studying gender among Pentecostal Christians in Colombia, found herself traveling with Bible salesmen and harvesting potatoes as well as attending church services and interviewing numerous Colombians. My own study of gender and politics in a contemporary Native American community in Alaska (Klein 1972) included cooking hamburgers at a basketball tournament, fishing for salmon, picking berries, and serving food at potlatches, as well as attending town meetings, conducting a town census, and conducting hundreds of formal and informal interviews. While a tight research plan is required to begin, it is the rare anthropologist who does not find his or her research being changed and improved by the people in the society being studied. Only in the field do we really learn what the appropriate questions are.

This is a major advantage in the method of cultural anthropology over that of traditional archaeology. In cultural anthropology the people being studied can help set the inquiry. In good anthropology they are active participants in the study. In fact, the anthropologist is the student to local teachers. What this means, for example, is that while an archaeologist, after much study and thought, might hypothesize about the use of a particular artifact, a cultural anthropologist at the same point could further test this hypothesis. First, the hypothesis might be offered to a local person, who would (after controlling the laughing that left tears coming down his or her face) explain the real use of the piece. Second, the cultural anthropologist would then be shown how the artifact is actually used. Finally, several people might explain the meaning of the piece and its place in their lives. More important, people are able to communicate abstractions that are hidden in material remains. The definition of gender itself needs to be established in every culture studied, and this is something that people may articulate when asked. Assumptions that two gender categories were universal stopped cultural anthropologists from asking the question in the past, except in cases where local informants pushed the issue.

After the fieldwork is completed and anthropologists return to their academic homes, the process of analysis takes center stage. What do all of these bits of data and statements by individuals mean? What do they tell us about the culture? What do they tell us about the nature of human culture? While analogies play a smaller role in cultural anthropological analysis than in archaeological analysis, they are still important in the broader analysis of cultural patterns. Scholars do not tend to ask questions if they think they already know the answers. Sometimes in anthropology, the people being studied will tell those scholars that their answers are wrong and open the door to important insights. Just as often, however, the questions that the anthropologist comes with, including academic theories and personal backgrounds, define the nature of the discussion. Sometimes the right questions are not asked, and the answers are not volunteered. So their assumptions and the theories of the day limit cultural anthropologists, like all Western scholars. Anthropologists who are asking questions about gender are largely opening doors for new information and ideas that are still being incorporated into the larger theories.

MODELING THE DATA

To present the volume and complexity of the data that anthropologists have amassed, scholars through the years have created different models for organizing the data that reflect their theoretical interests. The organization of cultures into types or categories is always open to criticism. Cultures are all unique, and any combination into large groups of similar cultures is subjective at best but based on one's research paradigm and focus of investigation. Some particular aspect of society must be chosen and cultures grouped according to that aspect. Clearly this is arbitrary. People of one culture might argue that religion is the most important aspect of society while those of another might argue that art or gender organization were the keys.

American anthropologists have long focused on political and economic systems as the keys for categorization. Theories of cultural evolution are always divided into political and economic stages, and this has become a traditional way to conceptualize cultures in anthropology textbooks. Such patterns have transcended their theoretical beginnings and have become pedagogical models. The structure presented in the next four chapters has its origins in the mid-twentieth-century revival of cultural evolution. By the beginning of the twenty-first century, however, it has shed much of the original meaning and exists mainly as a heuristic device for presenting an array of different societies in textbooks. Here it is used for that purpose but, also, because a recurrent theme in gender studies is that of stratification or inequality. This structure highlights the concepts of equality and inequality while allowing questions about the complexities of these ideas.

Section II employs this categorization and divides societies by their major economic practices and the related political organizations. This structure follows a common pedagogical model and introduces readers to a broad range of cultures through short case studies. Four general categories are used here:

1. Societies that largely rely on gathering and hunting for food resources and demonstrate minimal stratification between categories of people.
2. Groups that largely focus on horticulture and pastoralism and acknowledge some more significant differences in social rank based primarily on age and gender among types of people.
3. Stratified societies that include a small variety of cultures, often including simple agriculture and other techniques in cultures with stronger social hierarchies.
4. The state that represents complex economic techniques and definite social classes.

EARLY THEORIES OF CULTURAL EVOLUTION
AND GENDER RELATIONS

Cultural evolution differs from physical evolution in profound ways. While the concept of physical evolution is a core assumption of the field of anthropology, the idea of cultural evolution comes in and out of favor over time. Physical evolution, of course, is the method of biological development of humans, and other living things, over time. Cultural evolution seems similar on the surface. It assumes that cultures have developed from simple to complex over the history of humanity, and, as such, it is indisputable. However, there were, and are, myriad theories about what this means.

The beginnings of modern anthropology and both concepts of evolution lie in the nineteenth century. While Darwin defined modern biological evolution with the theory of natural selection, other English intellectuals, including many of Darwin's strongest supporters, brought forth the idea of "Social Darwinism." This concept postulated the development of cultures from simple to complex, but, unlike today's cultural evolution theories, it inserted a value to complexity. In a crude way, it was a road map of progress. The most complex modern cultures, modeled after the culture of the author's, of course, are seen as the end points. The question was, "How did we become civilized?" Using the terms of the time, "How did savages become barbarians? What made barbarians civilized?" The value judgment is that the societies of savages and barbarians are inferior to civilization and that those people who live in such societies today are, by logic, also inferior. The theory of human biological evolution does not have these issues because there are no ancestral "less evolved" types of humans living today. In Victorian cultural evolution there are clearly superior and inferior people, and the superior people are Europeans. Additionally, there is no mechanism for change to correspond with natural selection in physical evolution. Change happens, but why or how is not clear. Finally, there was an assumption that all cultures must go through all steps on their route to civilization. This means that savages cannot become civilized without going through the barbarian steps. Looking at this in more acceptable modern terms, this would mean that a gathering and hunting society would have to become agricultural before it could become urban. Herders would have to become farmers. Factually, this does not always happen, and some societies even have historically gone the other way.

It would be easy to reject cultural evolution as an archaic theory of Victorian gentlemen except for two reasons. First, the underlying idea is sound. The earliest human societies were dependent on foraging foods and were structurally simple. Later with the development of farming ideas, societies became more differentiated and stratified. States and urban societies, based on market economies and heterogeneous structures, came later and were more complex. This is historically correct. Contemporary societies of each economic base are not fossils, however, and there are no set rules for progress they must follow. The development of human society, as a whole, however, does follow an interesting pattern and is often used as a heuristic device for presenting data on contemporary cultures.

The second reason is that the Victorian theories of cultural change have had a profound influence on the popular understanding of human development and, particularly, on the popular understanding of human gender. Perhaps surprisingly, the relative societal power of men and women in early societies has been a major bone of contention in the theories of cultural evolution. Further, these theories (as illustrated by the goddess controversy in archaeology) have been used to construct conflicting modern theories on the nature of gender. The three main theories are straightforward to describe. The first contends that the earliest societies were patriarchies and that women gained power as the world became more complex. The second disagrees and argues that the earliest societies were matriarchies and that male-based power systems were part of progress. The final model sees simple societies as egalitarian with inequality, including gender inequality, as a problem of progress.

Sir Henry Maine (1822–1888), who was a pioneer in the study of comparative law, can be seen as a champion of the first model. His "Patriarchal Theory" asserted that the rights of the family unit were superior to those of the individual. Further, "the eldest male parent—the eldest ascendant—is absolutely supreme in his household. His domain extends to life and death, and is as unqualified over his children and their houses as over his slaves." (1965: 72–74) From the beginning, according to Maine, women were subordinate to men and legally just a member of a household.

The most common model was that of the original matriarchy and is most commonly connected with Johann Bachofen (1815–1887) and his 1861 book, *Das Mutterrecht*. He argued that people in the early societies were sexually promiscuous, which meant that the identity of the fathers was unknown. The ties between mothers and children set the structure for the society. With the development of the concept of private property, men overthrew the matriarchy and imposed a patriarchal society and monogamy. It is clear that the concepts of kinship identity and political structure were confused in these models. One of the most prominent American ethnologists of his time, Lewis Henry Morgan, in *Ancient Society*, also spoke to the idea of matriarchy. Morgan studied the Iroquois people of New York and was, therefore, familiar with a culture and system that constructed kinship along female lines and in which women had positions of power and authority superior to those of other American women of the state. The models described by these scholars, while today sometimes used to celebrate a time when women had power, were used in a very different way in the nineteenth century. Matriarchy was the primitive way that progressed to the more desirable patriarchy. Strange though it might be to twenty-first-century sensibilities, these scholars saw proper Victorian womanhood, where women were cared for and kept from the toil of productive labor, as the ideal.

The final model came a few years later in the writings of Friedrich Engels (1942). Using Morgan as a base, he argued that these early societies did allot women important political prestige and power just as they did men. It is clear in these writings that kinship and politics are differentiated. In fact, these societies were truly egalitarian; men did not rule women, nor women men. Moreover, this is considered by Engels, and his frequent collaborator, Karl Marx, as an ideal: primitive communism. With the development of agriculture, private property became possible, men established a patriarchal hierarchy, and women and children became powerless chattel. Their vision of evolution continues beyond the modern state to an ideal communistic state with gender equality that was to follow.

USE OF THE STAGES IN THIS BOOK

These categories allow us to offer an order to the mass of data that exists today. This order, however, must be seen as *a shorthand for learning*, rather than as a list of absolute categories. Outside of the cartoon world, no group of people has ever introduced themselves as "gatherers and hunters." The four chapters in this section are structured in a fashion that echoes the old evolutionary model in a superficial way, but this is not used to prove or disprove that model. Obviously this model has long outlived it theoretical efficacy. However, the categories it produced are useful. The cultural types allow a separation of cultures with different degrees of hierarchy and specialization. Because gender is a primary category in hierarchies, this organization allows a focus on the relationship of gender categories and other social categories. Further, it allows a number of short case studies to illustrate the wide variety of gender organizations found around the globe.

READINGS

Bachofen, Johann Jacob. *Myth, Religion, and Mother Right.* Princeton, NJ: Princeton University Press, 1967.

Brusco, Elizabeth. *Reformation of Machismo.* Austin: University of Texas Press, 1995.

Engels, Friedrich. *Origins of the Family, Private Property and the State.* New York: International Publishers, 1942.

Klein, Laura F. *Tlingit Women and Town Politics.* Dissertation. Ann Arbor, MI: University Microfilms, 1972.

Maine, Henry. *Ancient Law.* In *Everyman's Library.* New York: Dutton, 1956.

Morgan, Lewis Henry. *Ancient Society.* Tucson: University of Arizona Press, 1985.

CHAPTER THREE

Gender Equality? Foraging Societies

Do living foragers fit any of the theories of evolution and gender?
Is man the hunter and woman the gatherer?
Is gender equality possible? Does it exist in foraging societies?

GATHERING AND HUNTING AS A WAY OF LIFE

Far from the theories of academe lie the practical realities of everyday life. Today only a small number of people continue to live a gathering and hunting, or band, way of life. Pressures on the environment of such people by those living in more technologically complex societies have existed for thousands of years. Farmers with expanding populations pushed into the fertile lands of gatherers and hunters, pushing them into the most challenging areas. Most recently, as states established their control over most of the areas on Earth, gatherers and hunters came under the bureaucratic management of central governments. The agents of modernization—teachers, missionaries, physicians, and regional administrators—have brought their skills and ideas, both welcomed and unwelcomed, to all societies. Those few groups of people who live in band societies today do not live like their ancestors any more than any other groups of people do. They are not living fossils. They are modern people who live with a technological system that focuses on the exploitation of wild plants and animals and is similar, in this way, to that used by people since the beginning of humanity.

Anthropologists have studied band societies since the beginnings of anthropology. Many ethnographers have lived to watch the societies they studied as graduate students transform over the decades from foraging ways of life to farming or urban poverty. The data on the gathering and hunting way of life come largely from the fieldwork done with such cultures in the 1900s. As that century progressed, outside influences, and thus dominance, became more intense. The fantasy often seen in the popular press of finding, and studying, a foraging group who had never been in contact with any outsiders is just that. Even though headlines stating

"Stone Age Tribe Discovered" are seen once a decade, there is always a more mundane reality to the event that rarely finds its way to the same newspapers. Freed from these romantic and sensational images, the foragers of recent times have taught the rest of us a great deal about living in face-to-face cultures with simple technology and an art of self-sufficiency.

From studies of a large number of gatherers and hunters in various environmental settings, a general outline of foraging cultures has been developed. What follows is a description from the point of view of the female gatherers of the most common ways of life that accompany techniques of exploiting wild plants and animals. The roles of men and women and the conceptualization of gender are important issues throughout any such description.

THE GATHERER'S VIEW

Foraging

Women in societies categorized as foraging depend, like their men do, on wild plants and wild animals as the major sources for food. A woman's job, in most cases, is to collect the wild plants. She must have learned from her mother and aunts to understand the terrain and plants of her wide area of travel. She has also probably learned to make the tools required for digging roots and cutting and transporting plants. Most often gatherers exploit the areas around their camps, using the tools they have made, until the supply of plants is exhausted. Unlike the men who hunt large game on the move, gatherers have more flexibility in setting their own schedules, which often involve daily periods of gathering. The schedule of the gatherer, then, is routine and reliable compared with the hunter's more sporadic bursts of work and long periods of leisure. Another difference is that gatherers tend to focus their work within a day's walk of their camps, while the hunters may follow their game into more distant regions and be away from the camps for days. Commonly, a woman's work provides the staple foods for foraging peoples that make up the bulk of their diets. Meat, on the other hand, tends to be the more desirable part of a meal.

A woman would generally get much of the meat that she and her children eat from the work of their male relatives. These hunters must find their prey and have the means to kill them. While the image of hunting involves big game and dramatic contests, in fact, in most societies that hunt, small animals provide much of the meat. Even in societies where men are conceptualized as the hunters, women and children often engage in hunting small animals within their gathering ranges. Also, men and women can frequently work cooperatively in gathering plants and small animals. Men who hunt for larger game, however, must be as mobile as their game. This means that hunters use a large amount of land and must move throughout that land searching for food. It also means that the hunters must schedule their time in relationship to the animals. When they find animals, they hunt for as long as it takes to bring in this food. This also means that women, the elderly, and children spend many a day in camps without the men. On the other hand, when there are no animals, or when there is enough meat for the community, hunters have a great deal of time, free from subsistence work. At these times the men can enjoy their leisure while the women work.

Gathering and hunting, as a means of subsistence, places specific demands on the lives of those who rely on it:

1. Both men and women must regularly be on the move. Both the plants and animals of an area are soon used up or change with seasonal shifts, and people need to seek a new area with fresh resources. This means that the women must pack up their few belongings for transport, pack up the children, and walk with the men to an entirely new camp area. Once they arrive, the men build new shelters and the women set up new cooking areas. Obviously their homes must be easy to construct. It makes no sense for these people to put the effort and time into a structure they expect to leave in a week or two.

2. This form of economy does not allow large communities. The number of people who can live and move together is severely limited. Although the environment sets the limits, in many foraging societies, 100 people in a community is too big. As these groups become too large to feed with the local plants and animals, they tend to split into smaller units and move away from one another. Women, like men, have a small number of people with whom they socialize daily, and most of these people are relatives or are married to relatives.

3. It is more efficient to have a division of labor in which some people specialize in gathering while others specialize in hunting. Most commonly, women do the gathering while men do the hunting. This does not mean that women would not kill a small animal they find while gathering or that men would not bring back plants they find; it means that each specializes and has more refined skills in one or the other subsistence method. The simplicity of this division of labor means that boys typically grow up learning to be hunters and girls to be gatherers. No other full-time specializations exist.

Concepts of Wealth and Status

To a contemporary middle-class urbanite, the life of foragers seems exceedingly poor. Food has to be collected daily, homes are impermanent and simple structures, and there is little personal property. Women perform difficult physical tasks to help feed their families. They can own only what they can carry as they move. This limits personal goods to those items necessary for life, such as tools for food collection and preparation and light objects like clothing and jewelry. If people are to be judged by the number of items they own, then these people are poor. However, wealth and poverty are relative to one another in any setting. Within band societies these categories do not make sense. There is no rich gatherer or poor hunter. Women do not compete to have the most jewelry nor men to have the most recent tools. The ideal found in the model of gathering and hunting societies is equality based on rules of communal sharing.

Where the basic exchange ideal is generalized reciprocity, a permanent social hierarchy based on wealth is obviously impossible. It follows that these are classless societies in a profound way. In many societies, the life prospects of an individual are formed by their position in the hierarchy system as much as by their gender. In foraging societies, gender and age are among the few categories that are considered structurally significant in differentiating types of people. Of course, physical traits, force of personality, special skills, and just plain luck differentiate the details of a woman's life from those of others, but there is no structure that dictates these differences.

Generalized reciprocity is what anthropologists call the economic system that rules in gathering and hunting societies. It means that those who have excess give that away to those who do not. They do not expect an equal return for what they give and do not keep records of what was given. What is expected is that each person follows the same pattern. Therefore, if a hunter, or group of hunters, comes home with the meat of a large animal, that meat should be distributed to everyone in the camp. After the next hunt the same people might again bring in the meat and distribute it. The hunters that give should feel fortunate that they are able but should not feel superior or expect any special status or economic gain. They are not great men nor will they be inferior men when they are older or less lucky. Likewise, a woman with better-fed children or hoards of food will not be looked up to for these accomplishments. In fact, if a woman or a man were to hoard things of value, rather than being praised as wealthy, that person would be looked down upon as antisocial. The outcome of this system is that no one goes hungry when others can eat and no one goes cold and unsheltered when others have supplies. All things of value, in fact, belong to the community. No woman or man is rich or poor.

Kinship and Social Relationships

All social rules in gathering and hunting societies tend to be flexible. The nuclear family, consisting of parents and children, tends to be the most important kinship group. Women live and travel together with their husbands and unmarried children, and generally maintain lifelong ties. A woman's children are equally related to both her family and that of their father. More distant relationships are recognized and aunts, uncles, and cousins as well as grandparents are normally treated with great affection. In many such cultures, all members of the society are considered to be family with ties of mutual respect and responsibility.

A young woman marries outside of her immediate family, and often this means she marries a man from another band. After they marry they may live near her family or near the man's family. During their marriage they may move from one camp to another. Marriages are usually monogamous, and divorce is easily obtained. If a woman leaves her husband, she may move in the camps of many family members. As long as she has social and family ties, she can easily be enfolded in a new community. Women often do not have a large number of children. The difficulties of the work, and the problems of food, make it difficult to care for a large family. Among the more painful realities of this way of life is the occasional necessity for infanticide. If a mother cannot find a way to care for a new infant without harming her existing children, and cannot find another woman able to adopt the child, she may smother the infant at birth. In some areas, like the Kalahari Desert, nature intervenes with a biological loss of fertility in women foraging and nursing at the same time. Children are well loved and treated as individuals whose opinions are considered.

Political Organization

The term *band* is given to the political organization of gatherers and hunters. Clearly, this type of system would allow for no tightly organized political organization. There are no offices of leadership, and equality and cooperation are the ideals. In fact, no one has the right to order other people around in band societies; this includes men and women, old and young. The idea, found elsewhere, that men have the right to control women, or that adults have the right to control children, appears absent or weak in most band societies. This does not mean that some individuals may not be admired for their skills or personalities or that others may be considered unpleasant or ridiculous. What it does mean is that there is no structured ideology that accepts such differences as necessary or desirable.

While this is true, in some bands there is an individual, sometimes called the *headman* in the literature, who is the titular head of a group that lives together. Outsiders who wish to use resources within the band's area would approach him or, more rarely, her. This person can represent the band to outsiders but has virtually no power within the band. There is no special way to select this person, although genealogical or kinship principles are typically followed; a band without one could still operate smoothly. If a headman began to act in an authoritarian manner and assumed control over others, the other members of the band were free to pack up and join another band. Thus, the political organization in a band society is far closer to a family than to a government. Although in the early history of anthropology theorists argued questions of matriarchy or patriarchy in these societies, today these arguments are seen as foolish. No one, male or female or group, rules in band societies.

Political organization also deals with two aspects of society beyond the determination of leadership: war and crime. In bands, as might be expected, these took distinctive forms.

Any discussion of wars between bands is short. Bands do not war—they cannot organize to go to war, and there is no benefit to war. Most importantly, war goes against the ideology of cooperation. People who must get fresh food daily cannot afford the time to concentrate on other matters. Plus, as Napoleon is reputed to have said, an army moves on its stomach. This means that supplies are critical to war. Gatherers and hunters have no such surplus to supply anyone for an extended period. There is also no reason to war. Wars in most societies are often over resources and land. Bands, however, do not fight for more land, and their neighboring bands have no more surplus than they do. In fact, these neighbors will share food with them. This means that gatherers and hunters have no war leaders, no military, and no military weapons. Violence is not institutionalized, even in defense.

This lack of structured violence has two important implications for these societies. First, the lack of warfare also means that there is no "warrior" category. In many societies, the role of warrior has significant power in society and is a power position generally barred to women. Where warrior status is important there is an increased differentiation of men's and women's importance. This is not found in bands. A second, devastating consequence has come with the development of neighbors and colonialism. When more complex tribes or even states attack bands, the bands lose. Societies with traditions, and weapons, for raiding or warring that wanted the lands of the gatherers and hunters have never faced any challenge that stopped them from taking them. The consequences of external violence on women and their families have been severe.

Crime is a more complex issue. What does a band do when a person steals or kills? Who do you turn to if your husband is violent or your neighbor hoards his game? The police, courts, or even dictatorial leaders to deal with criminals do not exist. Fortunately there does not appear to be much crime in these societies. There is no need to steal what someone will give you. Disputes between people are often dealt with by the separation of these people; a woman can leave her husband and one neighbor can move away from another. Indisputably, some people in all societies will act badly. When one person, or family, repeatedly causes problems, a simple reaction has been observed repeatedly. The rest of the band simply moves away. One family cannot successfully live alone for a long period. The lesson to the deserted family is that they better live a more socially acceptable life among the next group that takes them in.

Cosmology

Understanding the nature of the supernatural world is as important among foragers as it is in other types of societies. A woman learns the nature of the cosmos and the relationship between her people and superior powers as she grows up. Normally she learns about myriad supernatural powers or beings that reside alongside her people. Rarely is there a supreme god or goddess, and generally the supernatural powers are unranked. Often these supernatural entities are connected with the important resources of the lands. In many band societies, this woman also learns to communicate with an individual supernatural spirit who will guide her through life. Likewise, her brothers and children will have different guardian spirits. All will have their own specific linkage to the supernatural world.

Rituals are important in all foraging societies. The wide variety of beliefs, however, makes it impossible to generalize more broadly. In some, like the Mbuti, their land itself (in this specific case, the forest) was seen as a supernatural being that had to be called upon when things went wrong. In others, like some Inuit (discussed later in the chapter), the resources had specific spiritual guardians (notably, in this specific case, the sea mammals that provided critical food). One acceptable generalization is the lack of full-time religious specialists in these societies. Some men or women may develop relationships with more supernatural beings than others, and these individuals can be called upon for their special knowledge. Anthropologists call the individual who has special skills and the ability to communicate with the spirit world a *shaman*. When trouble comes as represented by death, illness, or threatened starvation, the shamans of the band come together to work for the common good.

Shamans are the physicians in band societies. When people fall sick with normal or familiar illnesses, folk cures are used by elders and shamans who know the resources that are available as medication. Calling on the wisdom of grandma or grandpa, or a knowledgeable neighbor, for minor ailments is nearly universal. When people become severely ill, however, more powerful cures must be sought. In these cases, the community shamans attend their patients by contacting the supernatural beings for help. Major, life-threatening illness is seen as supernatural rather than, or as well as, natural, and the cures can be sought in the supernatural realm. The nature and gender of the shamans differ from society to society, but in most bands they are normal members of the community who are praised for taking time out of their daily pursuits to use their gifts for the benefit of the people. In other words, being a shaman is not a full-time specialization or profession in typical band societies. Shamans hunt or gather like other people, and they use their special abilities whenever they are needed.

While shamans do not occupy positions higher in status than other people, they do possess power and, often, prestige. Their power, however, comes from the supernatural realm rather than a social realm. They are mandated to use their connections with supernatural forces for good by healing or bringing well-being. When they do this, they are admired, like good hunters or gatherers are, but, usually, they do not get special treatment. An exception among the Inuit, where some shamans used fear of their powers for personal gain, demonstrates the potential of having supernatural power. What is particularly interesting is that most band societies do not allow the exploitation of such power.

BEYOND THE MODEL: ETHNOGRAPHIC CASES OF GATHERERS AND HUNTERS

Obviously all gathering and hunting societies are not alike. Gatherers and hunters live, and have lived, in wide varieties of physical and social environments and, consequently, have significant differences in the details of their lives. Descriptions of three different foraging societies are offered to demonstrate these differences. San-speakers[1] of the Kalahari Desert of Botswana and Namibia provide the first case. After 50 years of ethnographic study, they have emerged as the most recognized foragers in the anthropological literature. The Innu, people formerly known as Naskapi, are the second case. The analysis of these foragers of northeastern Canada helped to create one modern understanding of the nature of gender among gatherers and hunters. Finally, the Inuit, people formerly known as Eskimos, present the alternate realities of people who depended primarily on hunting for meat in their unique environment. No three cases could represent the full range of foraging cultures, but these three can offer a flavor of the differences and demonstrate the strengths of the general foraging trends.

San-speakers of the Kalahari

San people have been studied for half a century by a number of anthropologists and other scientists, working alone and in teams. Some became interested in the San because they seemed to represent an evolutionary level in human development. Others saw them as an example of a type of society that could adapt to an extreme environment. Still others reacted to their plight as powerless inhabitants in a hostile colonial world. Within these larger foci are those who found the San concept of gender unexpected.

San culture was adapted to an arid environment. The Kalahari Desert of southern Africa has been home to about 50,000 San people. This traditional San environment is a semi-desert that was home to a variety of

[1]In the past these people were referred to as *Bushmen*, which has now been accepted as derogatory. The term *San*, or the regional names such as *Kung* or *!Kung* followed. The term *Ju/'hoansi* has been offered as preferential to *!Kung*. At this point, there is no consensus about the most appropriate terminology, and, following the bulk of the contemporary literature, I use the familiar San and !Kung with the hope that these terms are not taken as derogatory. The fact that all three of these groups are now known by different names than they originally were reflects the changes in the nature of colonialism. More and more, indigenous peoples, as these all are, are demanding the use of names of their own designation, rather than those that reflect colonial mistakes or prejudices.

game animals and edible plants. More problematic than food, however, was access to usable water. San peoples survived in this environment only by moving throughout a large area and utilizing water sources and food sources in many different places at different times. Knowledge of the environment and skills for exploiting it were the reasons that the San have been able to survive there for so long. These skills include social skills that determine the populations in specific areas and the organization of the foraging activities.

Food Resources The principal source of food came from gathering, which was largely women's work. Richard Lee (1979: 310) calculated that 70 percent of the diet of the Dobe !Kung he studied in the 1960s came from vegetable foods, while 30 percent came from meat. In the region he studied, the protein-rich mongongo nuts were especially important. Besides the mongongo nuts, there were numerous roots, melons, and other fruits that were collected and eaten. Some provided vital liquid in dry seasons as well as food value. While meat was more highly desired, the plants allowed for survival.

When gathering, women traveled far from the home camp for extended periods of work (just as men traveled far when hunting). Women's primary gathering tools were digging sticks and large carrying bags called *karosses*.

A San woman collecting mongongo nuts.

Other tools were used for specific tasks. Women walked miles to areas of vegetation, dug or picked the plants, and carried home their loads, which weighed from 15 to 33 pounds each. In other words, gathering was hard, physical work. It had fewer dangers than hunting, but snakes and accidents had to be avoided. Like hunting, gathering took a great deal of knowledge to be successful. Women had to know the ecology of their terrains and the nature of the local plants. Histories of previous foraging in a region were important, but, with changes in location, new resources had to be regularly sought out. These women also investigated the availability of water sources and signs of animals while searching for food.

The vegetable food that was gathered belonged to the person who collected it, and it was her decision whether to distribute it to others. Because gathering was far less uncertain than hunting, the distribution, if any, was rarely a public concern. Women gathered in groups, and when vegetables were found all the gatherers took their fair share of the resources. Without scarcity, the ownership of a resource bestowed little prestige. The work of women was valued, but it was not glorified.

Clearly, hunters were perceived of as significant and brave members of their communities. Their efforts were admired, and their results were valued. Men's hunting brought in the meat that was the most valued food for the San. Animals from the smaller antelopes and warthogs to the larger kudus, wildebeests, and even giraffes were found and hunted in the Kalahari. In the Dobe area, which has been a center of study for Richard Lee (1993: 27), warthogs, duikers, and steenboks were the most commonly hunted animals. Hunting was a dangerous pursuit. San hunters who used bows and poison-tipped arrows had little protection from the larger animals. The poison could take days to kill these animals, and the hunters had to pursue and protect their kill from other predators, including lions and hyenas. It was this large game that was especially prized by the community.

The San, however, did not allow hunters themselves to claim too much glory or maintain any power from the ownership of their game. Glorifying in a successful hunt was considered improper behavior in San society. In fact, appropriate behavior was for individuals to diminish the value of their own accomplishments. A hunter was required to emphasize the role of good luck, and other hunters' help, as the real reasons for a successful hunt. He was belittled if he claimed extraordinary skill or special effort of his own. In a well-known article, "Eating Christmas in the Kalahari," anthropologist Richard Lee (1993) described his reception when he bought a fat ox for the San he was living with for a Christmas feast. Rather than being thanked or praised he was ridiculed for being cheated and stuck with such a scrawny animal. From the point of view of a Westerner, he was paying back the hospitality of the community with a lavish feast, but from the San perspective, he was boasting about his superior wealth and ability to provide food others could not. As he realized, their ridicule was their mechanism to put him in his place and make him a respectable human being. Because of this equalizing mechanism, talented hunters

could claim no special social prestige over the gatherers or their less successful neighbors.

The other mechanism that limited the importance of successful hunters
was the convention for distributing the game. The hunters could not individually claim the meat of large animals. Among the !Kung, the "owner" of
the meat was the owner of the arrow that killed it. Hunters frequently used
arrows owned by others, including women, and that person controlled the
distribution of the meat. (Shostak 1983: 85–86) Distribution was not easy.
The owner, the hunters, their families, and most individuals living in the
group had claim on some meat. A distribution that all considered equitable
and fair took a great deal of social savvy, and charges of being stingy or
showing favoritism were common.

Men's hunting and women's gathering provided the necessary food
and resources for the San. Both worked hard for their results but, perhaps
surprisingly, did not work excessive hours during a typical week. Lee calculated that women spent 12.6 hours a week in subsistence work while
men spent 21.6 hours a week. When he included work on tools and all
housework, the total came to 44.5 hours for men and 40.1 hours per
woman. (Lee 1993: 58) This is far less than what might be expected for the
working hours of adults in agricultural or industrial societies.

Community   The communities of San were highly flexible. Lee defined a
resident unit as follows: "In essence, a Ju/'hoan camp consists of relatives,
friends, and in-laws who have found that they can live and work well
together." (Lee 1993: 62) At any one time, a group of people who got along
lived together. Certainly husbands and wives, children and parents, and
other relatives often remained together, but they did not have to. Even
children had the right to decide where they wanted to live and with whom.
A core of related elders, often siblings and their spouses, most commonly
defined the core of a group, and they were designated as the "owners of
the waterholes" in the area. Outsiders asking permission to use resources
in the area would go to them; once asked, permission was routinely
granted. The camp was named after one of these elders. Most of the residents in the camp were related to these elders directly or through marriage. As groups moved along during the year, some individuals often
decided to go a different way and some groups came together and joined
for a while. When personal conflicts became strong enough to threaten
the cooperative nature of the group, a split was a good way to ease tensions. This does not mean that there was no violence or argument in this
culture, just that there was an informal mechanism to lessen the damage
of such disputes. Raiding and warfare between groups were unheard of.
Sharing and cooperation were the foundation for survival.

Leadership in such flexible units with a philosophy of equality would
also be expected to be flexible. The San did not have chiefs or any other formal leadership positions. Even the elders in each camp who are the "owners" of resources had no marked power over others in the group. Certainly

they could not order others to behave in a particular way, nor could they judge and punish them for misbehavior. Individuals did win the respect of others who followed their ideas and suggestions but there was no requirement for anyone to do so. According to Lee, "Men and women whom we call leaders do exist, but their influence is subtle and indirect." (1979: 53)

Families were the organizing categories. Parents, who had to search widely for appropriate mates for their children, arranged first marriages. In such a small-scale society even the search for an individual who is not too closely related often proved to be a challenge. The first, and other early marriages, were brittle and often ended in divorce, which the wives frequently initiated. When a marriage came apart, divorce by either spouse was simplified by the fact that there was no joint property to divide nor contracts to dissolve. Young children generally remained with their mothers, and divorced adults generally remarried. Children maintained their relationships with both parents' families and lived with them, or called upon them for support, throughout their lives.

Traditional nomadic San women had fewer children than might be expected. !Kung girls sexually matured at approximately 15.5 years and tended to have their first child four years later. Further, despite the fact that they used no contraceptives, married women usually had a four-year period between children. Theories about why this might be true abound. It is clear that children nursed for an extended period up to four years or so, and nursing seems to lower fertility. Also the level of fat in San women was kept low during nursing by the high level of physical exertion that work and walking entailed. The caloric intake also remained low. Regardless of cause, this low birth rate combined with the death rate meant that the society grew slowly and population pressures were mild. (Kolata 1974)

Cosmology San religion spoke of a high god, lesser deities, and ghosts. Fortune and misfortune, including health and illness, were sent by these entities. The ghosts of recently deceased family members were considered to be especially dangerous. They were able to shoot arrows that brought sickness. Defense against these arrows, and the diseases and bad luck they brought, was in the hands of healers who used an internal energy force called *n/um*. N/um was located in the stomach and was activated through ritual dances. Shamans, whose n/um "boils" while dancing, were able to trance and see the entities and arrows that were causing trouble. In this state, they were able to remove the elements that were causing the sickness and return the patient to the path of health. Not all patients could be healed, but the healers volunteered their skills to do their best, and they were respected for the job they did.

Both men and women possessed n/um. One scholar, who studied healing, quoted a !Kung man who was asked about the differences between men and women's n/um: "Men's stuff and women's stuff is all the same." (Katz 1982: 161) Katz found that while both men and women had the substance, it is clear that men healed more frequently and that more men became healers. Half of the men became healers. Only about ten percent of women became healers while a third learned to trance. Most of the healing, then, was led by men. The women who did heal, however, were not barred from becoming powerful healers. Several anthropologists who have studied the San named specific women healers as being the most powerful, or among the most powerful, healers in their regions. (Katz 1982: xix, 172–173; Lee 1993: 121; Shostak 1983: 299) For people who chose to pursue this calling, women, like men, became more powerful healers as they aged.

In short, in issues of gender, like other social categories, flexibility was the rule in San society. A two-gender system was clear and fundamental to the organization of San society, but this was not a hierarchical system. Men and women were not the same, but neither was better or worse. The roles normally taken by women, like the roles normally taken by men, were valued and necessary for successful group life. The boundaries between the genders were relaxed. Patricia Draper, in a well-known article about women among the San, painted a picture of men and women simply getting along as individuals in their camps: "The sexes mix freely and unselfconsciously without the diffidence one might expect to see if they thought they were in some way intruding." (1975: 93)

Innu: Montagnais-Naskapi of Canada

The Innu, as they are named today, are a northern foraging people in eastern Canada. The classic studies of Frank G. Speck (1935) portrayed a highly structured society in which men hunted big game and all lived in hunting areas owned by men and passed from fathers to sons. Another anthropologist, Eleanor Leacock, entered this field in 1949 and left it with a radically different understanding of precolonial Innu life. Leacock interpreted the owned areas as relatively recent results of commercial trapping and sought to discover the Innu who lived there before. Researching the records left by Jesuit fathers and other early Europeans in Innu lands, she was able to describe a way of life that is consistent with contemporary constructs of foragers and reasonable to the people she studied. Importantly, she questioned the effect of European colonialization on the lives of indigenous people and showed the value of documentary evidence in understanding past cultures. The Innu, as she understood them, lived in an egalitarian and flexible culture.

Food Resources The Innu of the seventeenth century were hunters. The environment of the region demanded significant seasonal variations. The winter environment was cold and snowy, restricting access to foods and making the use of snowshoes and sledges necessary for survival. During this season, residential groups were small and conditions were difficult. During the summer, by contrast, the land was bountiful and the rivers ran clear. Residential groups of several hundred could set up by large rivers and, in later times, at trading posts. Game from the large moose, caribou, and bears to the smaller beavers, porcupines, and hares provided the staples of the Innu diet. Meat from fish and birds were also used. Hunters used bows and arrows, spears, and traps to catch their land game and birchbark canoes to fish. Some meat was dried for more extended use when hunting was bad. Plant food was seasonally limited and consisted of nuts, berries, and roots. (Leacock 1981a: 33)

As in most foraging societies, hunting was largely men's work, and gathering vegetable foods was women's work. Hunting was often done in small groups, and women might help with the hunting. Married couples might well fish and gather wood together. Women generally were expected to care for children, make clothing and tents, and prepare food, although men might help with these tasks as well. Flexibility and cooperation, then, were essential to successful life. Game was shared throughout the residential group, and most was eaten immediately. Leacock cites the problems of storing and transporting the game as a reason for this pattern and refers to the practice as "subsistence insurance," a telling phrase. Likewise, the territories of each band also had to be flexible, "amounting to little more than a tacit agreement to keep bands distributed more or less evenly over the given area." (1954: 6–7)

Community   The smallest community unit of the seventeenth century was the group who lived together within a single lodge. This household, which numbered 20 individuals or fewer, was typically composed of close relatives and in-laws. When a young couple married, the residential pattern was that they went to live with the bride's lodge group. The groups were not permanent, and individuals or nuclear families could change as circumstances did. Not all lodge members were relatives; friendships were also important in residence choices. As much as anything, these residences had to be an economically viable unit since, during the winters, only one or two lodges would comprise the entire hunting and gathering unit.

During seasons when food was more abundant, the villages grew larger with more lodges camping together. As with other foragers, these camps were frequently moved and redefined. The adults who lived there made decisions within the camps. Both men and women made their voices heard, but no one was expected to assert his or her superiority. (Leacock 1980: 29–30) Although French contemporaries referred to chiefs, Leacock believed that these were individuals who represented the native groups to the outsiders but held little power within the camps. Leacock referred to an "ethic" of "never forcing one's will on others." (1975: 608) Like the San, a tradition of bringing people "down to size" through ridiculing was well developed among the Innu. Above all, a respect for individualism, combined with an ethical teaching of cooperation, prevailed.

The autonomous behavior of women was a special concern for the Jesuit priests who were sent to Christianize them. The church's concept of a good Christian family included the pivotal role of a wife and mother, who was obedient to her husband and diligent within her household. While Innu women were devoted to their children and were hard workers, their independence was a concern to the priests. These women, like men, were free to divorce when marriages did not work out and had a considerable amount of sexual freedom within and outside of marriage. They did not fear or follow the orders of husbands or fathers, and they expected their husbands to move to their homes for an extended period soon after marriage. Even their hard work, because it was largely performed outside of the family, was seen as a form of slavery and shameful to the priests. To the Jesuits of this period, being a good Innu woman was not compatible with being a good Christian woman.

Cosmology   The religious beliefs of the Innu of the time are more difficult to know. Certainly the Jesuit priests saw Innu cosmology as pagan, and little of the writing by the priests in connection with these beliefs was positive. Priests were especially disapproving of the lack of "awe" in people's relations to supernatural beings. (Leacock 1981b: 194) Cosmological beliefs that continued into later periods allowed some understanding of that of the earlier periods. Innu looked to their religion to ensure good health and success in life. Hunting was particularly ritualized, and important elements of all hunts were rituals of respect toward the animals taken. Bones of hunted animals were treated with special care. Scapulimancy, which is reading the marks left on the burned shoulder blades of animals that have been hunted, was used as a supernatural guide for finding game animals. Men also ritually drummed sacred songs for help in hunting. (Rogers and Leacock 1981: 184)

Healing, as well as hunting aid, was in the hands of shamans. Many individuals attained the ability to communicate with supernatural spirits as they aged, but some people purposely sought more powerful relationships with spiritual helpers. These people were shamans and were able to perform a "shaking tent ritual" in which spirits and shamans interacted for the well being of the community or community members. In the early period, both men and women became shamans and could perform the shaking tent ritual, but in more recent times this role was restricted to men. (Leacock 1981a: 40; Leacock 1980: 41; Rogers and Leacock 1981: 184)

It appears that the early Innu lifestyle was far more similar to that of the model of foraging society than Innu life after colonization took hold. This is particularly true in the realm of gender. European priests and other colonists saw the autonomy of individuals in this society as primitive and undesirable. The substantial and valued roles of women in the society were particularly problematic. Subservience for women became a critical part of the teachings of civilization that were promoted by the newcomers.

Inuit of the Arctic

Studies of Inuit have been part of the core readings of anthropologists since the early studies of Franz Boas, the "father of American anthropology." The images of Inuit culture are part of the view of the "primitive" world in American popular culture. Elementary school students learn little of the variety of world cultures, but they all can draw an igloo. Consequently, there is an assumption that Inuit culture is simple and well known. However, many anthropologists have studied aspects of Inuit culture, and many pictures of the Inuit have emerged.

The Inuit have been described variously as male dominated, as egalitarian, and as seemingly every other possible level of gender differentiation in the anthropological literature. This is due, in part, because of the variations in cultural traditions and environmental stresses among the Inuit people of the Arctic. While many central cultural traits are remarkably similar in the reports of Arctic peoples, regional variations in others are real. The home range of these people stretched from Siberia to Greenland with major populations in Alaska and Canada. The Arctic, as a whole, is among the least environmentally hospitable regions for human life in the world, but within this area, there are distinct variations in the availability of food resources. Inuit cultures adapted to the environments in which they lived, and part of these adaptations were the definition of the roles of men and women. Also because the Inuit have been studied for more than a century, anthropologists have recorded changes in their societies that are as profound as those in Euro-American society over that time. As in Euro-American society, gender roles have changed significantly. Focusing on Inuit culture before extensive colonization, it is clear that the flexibility in gender roles found in the two other band societies described was more restricted in the Arctic.

Food Resources   Economically, and environmentally, the Inuit were the mirror opposite of the San. Among most of the Inuit groups, meat provided the bulk of the food. Among the coastal peoples, seals, walrus, sea lions, and whales provided the most desirable meat. Among the interior groups, caribou was often the chief food resource. Some groups were able to hunt both groups of animals, and most were able to trade for resources they did not themselves obtain. During the long northern winter, game provided virtually all of their food. Anthropologist Edwin Hall estimated that more than 90 percent of the diet of the group he calls the "Mountain Eskimos" comes from caribou. (1984: 341) Guy Mary-Rousseliere asserted that in Canada, "The quest for game dominated the entire existence of another group she calls the Iglulik Eskimo." (1984: 431) At the other extreme, the Nunivak people were said to acquire half their diet from fish, shellfish, eggs, and plant foods. (Ager 1980: 310) Certainly meat was central to all diets and the key to the economic organizations.

Hunting of large game was men's work. Although there were cases in which women helped in group hunts or, more rarely, hunted themselves, the rule of the Arctic was that men did the large-game hunting. Hunting was both dangerous and difficult. Men left their homes to pursue marine or terrestrial game. During the winter, the harshness of the weather and the scarcity of game made these hunts life-and-death pursuits for both the hunters and their families. Women and children remained at home. When the men returned from the hunt, the women were responsible for the butchering, distribution, hide preparation, and cooking of the animals. There was little distribution of food beyond the households of the hunters as has been found among other foragers. (Lantis 1984: 214) Trade partners of the hunters expected to receive meat, as did partners of women in some areas. (Ager 1980: 309) During seasons when fish, migrating birds, and plants were available, women took a more direct part in the collection of food, but men were still primary in the food pursuit. Ager calculated that among one group of Yupik in Alaska, where spring fish runs allowed a concentrated collection of fish in a short period, men spent two or three days collecting fish. At the same time, women spent almost two weeks preparing and drying the fish for extended use. (1980: 308)

The sexual division of labor was both clear and strong in most Inuit groups. (Guemple 1995: 19; Spencer 1984: 327) Men and women had their own tasks and spent most of their time in the company of others of their own gender. Many scholars have interpreted this economic pattern to emphasize the dependency of Inuit women on men. (Friedl 1975: 40) They point out that the very survival of women and their children in some seasons depended wholly upon the food that men brought home. This control over the most important resources in the society conveyed a clear advantage to men, who could have used it to control women in any variety of ways.

Other interpretations focus more broadly on the process of economic life and find the division of labor to be a complementary male–female partnership as the key for survival. (Balikci 1970: 104; Guemple 1995: 19–20; Spencer 1984: 327; Ager 1980: 308) The time and effort that hunters put into each hunt precluded them from doing other necessary chores. Without the waterproof, warm clothing made by the women, the men could not have survived a winter hunt. Women also secured the homes and prepared food for hunters who had no energy left when they returned. Additionally, the child care that was essential to the continuance of the society was firmly in women's hands. While women could not have survived without the products of men's labor, men likewise could not have continued to concentrate on hunting without the products of women's labor. Both men and women worked in, and got respect from, their work in their own distinctive spheres of activities.

Contemporary Inuit women cutting and dividing the meat from a hunt.

Community   The sexual lives of Inuit have long been caricaturized as a part of American popular culture. Long before the sexual revolution, exoticized images of rubbing noses and trading wives shocked people with more Puritanical sexual mores. The reality of acceptable sexual behavior among most Inuit peoples was far more flexible than in the West. (Giffen 1930: 75–76) Men could take lovers before and after marriage without censure. Likewise, unmarried women could take lovers and have children without damaging their futures as wives. Girls were also sometimes forced into sexual encounters, and this was generally not punished. (Spencer 1984: 331) Virginity was not a requirement for marriage, and children were always welcomed. As wives, however, women were required to restrict their sexual relationships to their husbands and others approved by their husbands. Husbands could, and did, share their wives with trade partners and visitors. While women might have sometimes encouraged such extramarital trading, the control was largely in the hands of the men. Wives were able to reclaim control over their own sexuality only through divorce. Either partner, however, easily obtained divorce.

Marriage was clearly an economic partnership as much as a personal commitment. While parents often arranged early marriages, women had some say in the mates. Marriage by abduction, or capture, which was once widely reported, proved often to be more of a stylized ritual pre-arranged by both parties than a real kidnapping. The economic necessity of each person having support from a member of the other gender, as already noted, made the marriage partnership a crucial part of the cultural survival strategy. This does not mean that marriages were not also emotionally satisfying in many cases.

The lives of women and men in Inuit societies tended to be more separated than in European societies. In normal circumstances, children were welcomed additions to the family. Men, as well as women, enjoyed and socialized with children. In times of economic stress, however, infanticide, most commonly female infanticide, was necessary. In some groups, such as the Netsilik of northern Canada, this tradition led to strong imbalances in the ratio of men to women. (Balicki 1984: 424; one count of 150 males to 109 females) In other, richer, areas, female infanticide was very rare. In either case, the decision to kill an infant was based on a conviction that the family did not have enough food to support another person and that there were no other families with resources who wished to take the child. Male children were future hunters who would provide for the family, while female children would ultimately support their husbands' households. Economically, males were more immediately valuable.

Residence throughout the Arctic was seasonally variable. In times when there were abundant foods in a particular area, many families came together there. Spring and summer fishing areas and winter villages in the area that became the state of Alaska were large settlements. In other parts of the year, one or two nuclear families traveled and hunted alone. During the seasons of larger settlements, old disputes were adjudicated and new alliances were made. Community councils and leaders, to the extent they existed at all, were operative at this level. During other parts of the year, family interactions were the structure of everyday life.

Household types were quite variable throughout the Arctic, with virilocality being strong in the far east, variable patterns in the central areas, and a form of uxorilocality in the west. (Guemple 1995: 20–21) This means that in Greenland and parts of Canada, new brides lived with their husbands in proximity to his family. This strengthened the authority of husbands over wives and left women with little outside support in their households. In some Alaskan communities, however, a very different system was prominent. Men lived in the permanent villages of their wives. In these villages, men lived together in a large men's house. They slept and ate there and visited their wives' houses for family time and sex. Individual households were the realms of the women, and women in these communities had relatives and friends close at hand. These women were largely restricted from the men's house and, therefore, any community debates that went on there, but they did have an independence in their personal actions that many women in the eastern Arctic did not share.

Leadership was largely informal with no structured offices of power. In many areas, specific men—by force of their personalities—were able to focus the actions of communities. In regions where this was possible, wealthier men also claimed some authority. Rather than positions of leadership, however, these men had public influence. Their daily actions enhanced or dissipated this influence. Women never, or rarely, filled these public roles. Those who emphasized the influence of women in Inuit societies point to the influence that women had over men, especially their husbands. (Mary-Rousseliere 1984: 435; Ager 1980: 312) In this way women helped direct the secular actions of their households and communities but only through sympathetic, or pliable, men.

Cosmology   In Inuit beliefs the natural and supernatural world were closely intertwined. Animals and people possessed spirits or souls that had powers beyond their physical hosts. Both men and women sought out spiritual power as a normal aspect of life. Some individuals were able to control more spiritual powers than others and could use these powers for social good, or for evil. In the Arctic societies, as in all foraging groups, there were part-time specialists. These shamans hunted and worked like others except during special rituals. Many reports of Inuit life emphasize the power that such people derived by being feared by less powerful individuals. One anthropologist noted that they were "feared as much as venerated." (Hall 1984: 344) Both men and women became shamans.

Most shamans used their powers in socially valued ways to cure serious illness, improve hunting, control the environment, and foretell the future, among other things. Shamans received songs with their spirits and sang these songs as part of rituals. Although they went into healing trances in some areas (Clark 1984: 194), in other areas trances were rarer in curing. (Lantis 1984: 221) Songs, masks, and the sucking out of disease elements were common elements of curing rituals. Shamans and more secular curers used other remedies, including herbal medicines. As noted, spirits were part of everyday life, and their control conferred a very real power on individuals that was different, but in many ways, more important than secular power.

One other aspect of the spiritual philosophy suggests that gender may not have been a static concept after all. Human souls or spirits continued over time. When children were born, they took the name of a recently deceased relative whose soul was reborn within them. This personality existed again in this new life. An infant boy might have been given the name of a recently deceased female or a baby girl might have taken a name previously held by a man. The innate quality of the soul, or the personality of the individual, was not gendered. (Guemple 1995: 27; Giffen 1930: 57) Being a man or a woman never diminished the essence of the person.

The lives of Inuit men and women were far from interchangeable. Clearly in many areas of the Arctic, Inuit women and children were dependent upon men for their most important food resources. While this could have been expected to lead to a strict pattern of male dominance over women, in fact, the outcome was more complex. In many ways the pattern was characterized more by separation than structured hierarchy. Each gender needed the support of the other socially and economically. It is difficult to make any broad generalizations about gender across the wide expanse of Inuit territory. It does appear, however, that in parts of the Arctic the roles of women were clearly more restrictive than in most foraging societies.

SUMMARY

According to the gathering and hunting model, life in foraging societies differed dramatically from popular views of "primitive man." Cooperation, flexibility, and individualism appear to be the key social concepts that governed these societies. Men, who were hunters, rather than being physically and socially domineering, were typical members of their societies who provided important resources. Women, who were gatherers, rather than being submissive collectors of incidental food, were also typical members of their societies who provided important resources. All individuals were not the same, however, and gender was an important social category. Men and women focused their attentions on different activities. In many such societies, men sometimes gathered and women sometimes hunted, but usually men were expected to be hunters and women were expected to be gatherers as their typical activities. In other social settings, the dress, behavior, and preferences of men and women often differed, but rarely did one gender dominate action or was one gender more highly valued. Certainly there was no strong ideology of male or female dominance in the structure of these societies. The importance of the individual and specific events took priority over larger social categories including those of gender.

The foragers of this chapter show little resemblance to the models that were used for Man the Hunter constructions. While the details of each society are unique, the general picture of foraging societies as based on individual worth and cooperation holds true. The foraging societies of today and the recent past should never be mistaken for the ancestral foragers of human history, however. Inuit, Innu, and San-speakers are as distant from those people as any other society of their time. They have equally lived through a history that involved vast migrations and colonial administrations. Further, as the cases show, many of the foragers of recent times have been pushed into environments that are on the edge of human survival. Ancestral foragers would have lived in the most hospitable climates and would not have worried about extreme temperatures, availability of water, and scarcity of food. The foraging way of life, even under pressure, seems to allow for an appreciation of individual worth. This combination of the value of the legitimacy of the needs of each woman and man with a concept of the value of community cooperation fits well with modern democratic ideals.

Readings

Ager, Lynn Price. "The Economic Role of Women in Alaskan Eskimo Society." In *A World of Women: Anthropological Studies of Women in the Societies of the World,* ed. Erika Bourguignon. New York: Praeger Publishers, 1980, pp. 305–18.

Balikci, Asen. *The Netsilik Eskimo.* Garden City, NY: The Natural History Press, 1970.

————. "Netsilik." In *Handbook of North American Indians,* gen. ed. William C. Sturtevant; Vol. 5, *Arctic,* ed. David Damas. Washington, DC: Smithsonian Institution, 1984, pp. 415–30.

Clark, Donald W. "Pacific Eskimo: Historical Ethnography." In *Handbook of North American Indians,* gen. ed. William C. Sturtevant; Vol. 5, *Arctic,* ed. David Damas. Washington, DC: Smithsonian Institution, 1984, pp. 185–97.

Draper, Patricia. "!Kung Women: Contrasts in Sexual Egalitarianism in Foraging and Sedentary Contexts." In *Toward an Anthropology of Women,* ed. Rayna R. Reiter. New York: Monthly Review Press, 1975, pp. 77–109.

Friedl, Ernestine. *Women and Men: An Anthropologist's View.* Prospect Heights, IL: Waveland Press, 1975.

Giffen, Naomi Musmaker. *The Roles of Men and Women in Eskimo Culture.* Chicago: University of Chicago Press, 1930.

Guemple, Lee. "Gender in Inuit Society." In *Women and Power in Native North America,* eds. Laura F. Klein and Lillian A. Ackerman. Norman, OK: University of Oklahoma Press, 1995, pp. 17–27.

Hall, Edwin S. "Interior North Alaska Eskimo." In *Handbook of North American Indians,* gen. ed. William C. Sturtevant; Vol. 5, *Arctic,* ed. David Damas. Washington, DC: Smithsonian Institution, 1984, pp. 320–37.

Katz, Richard. *Boiling Energy: Community Healing among the Kalahari Kung.* Cambridge, MA: Harvard University Press, 1982.

Kolata, Gina Bari. "!Kung Hunter-Gatherers: Feminism, Diet, and Birth Control." *Science* 185 no. 4155 (1974), pp. 183–85.

Lantis, Margaret. "Nunivak Eskimo." In *Handbook of North American Indians,* gen. ed. William C. Sturtevant; Vol. 5, *Arctic,* ed. David Damas. Washington, DC: Smithsonian Institution, 1984, pp. 209–23.

Leacock, Eleanor Burke. *The Montagnais "Hunting Territory" and the Fur Trade.* American Anthropological Association Memoir no. 78. Washington, DC: American Anthropological Association, 1954.

————. "Class, Commodity, and the Status of Women." In *Women Cross-Culturally: Change and Challenge,* ed. Ruby Rohrlich-Leavitt. The Hague: Mouton, 1975, pp. 601–16.

————. "Montagnais Women and the Jesuit Program for Colonization." In *Women and Colonization: Anthropological Perspectives,* eds. Mona Etienne and Eleanor Leacock. New York: Praeger, 1980, pp. 25–42.

————. *Myths of Male Dominance: Collected Articles on Women Cross-Culturally.* New York: Monthly Review Press, 1981a.

————. "Seventeenth-Century Montagnais Social Relations and Values." In *Handbook of North American Indians,* gen. ed. William C. Sturtevant; Vol. 6, *Subarctic,* ed. June Helm. Washington, DC: Smithsonian Institution, 1981b, pp. 190–95.

Lee, Richard Borshay. *The !Kung San: Men, Women, and Work in a Foraging Society.* Cambridge: Cambridge University Press, 1979.

————. "Politics, Sexual and Non-Sexual, in an Egalitarian Society." In *Politics and History in Band Societies,* eds. Eleanor Leacock and Richard Lee. Cambridge: Cambridge University Press, 1982, pp. 37–59.

————. *The Dobe Ju/'hoansi.* New York: Harcourt Brace College Publishers, 1993.

Mary-Rousseliere, Guy. "Iglulik." In *Handbook of North American Indians,* gen. ed. William C. Sturtevant; Vol. 5, *Arctic,* ed. David Damas. Washington, DC: Smithsonian Institution, 1984, pp. 431–46.

Rogers, Edward S., and Eleanor Leacock. "Montagnais-Naskapi." In *Handbook of North American Indians,* gen. ed. William C. Sturtevant; Vol. 6, *Subarctic,* ed. June Helm. Washington, DC: Smithsonian Institution, 1981, pp. 169–89.

Shostak, Marjorie. *Nisa: The Life and Words of a !Kung Woman.* New York: Vintage Books, 1983.

Speck, Frank G. *Naskapi, the Savage Hunters of the Labrador Peninsula.* Norman: University of Oklahoma Press, 1935.

Spencer, Robert F. "North Alaska Eskimo: Introduction." In *Handbook of North American Indians,* gen. ed. William C. Sturtevant; Vol. 5, *Arctic,* ed. David Damas. Washington, DC: Smithsonian Institution, 1984, pp. 278–84.

CHAPTER FOUR

Seeds of Gender Inequality?
Horticultural and Pastoral Societies

Do settled societies establish stricter gender categories?
Is inequality necessary in farming societies?
Do pastoral societies demand male dominance?
Are women to plants as men are to animals?

While foraging societies have long been prominent in the anthropological literature, the reality is that even in the early days of modern anthropology, most existing societies were more heterogeneous and socially complex. Throughout the world, societies based on horticulture and pastoral ways of life drew the attention of ethnographic researchers. These cultures were more complex in terms of technology than those of hunters and gatherers, although most Europeans and Americans still saw them as primitive. Tall tales that mocked tribes, chiefs, medicine men, and chattel-like women forged a permanent imagery in Western culture. In a world still defined by European colonies, these were people politically dominated by foreigners.

PEOPLES WITH DOMESTICATED RESOURCES

Among those scholars who sought the basis of human culture in the distant past, cultures that depended on domesticated plants and animals were too complex to shed any meaningful light on the first human ancestors. They were seen as links that could take the meaning of the cultural evolutionary story to the next level. They were chosen to represent the earliest beneficiaries of the agricultural revolution, when the domestication of basic resources led to new ways of life. As with the foragers, however, the reality of these cultures is far from those of their ancestors. Some have focused on plants and have become skillful horticulturalists, while other societies put their energy into animal domestication to become pastoralists. As an organizational tool, this chapter divides the two forms.

What can these types of social organization tell about gender? If we take a Marxist line, the seeds of gender inequality are found here. In the theories of Karl Marx and Friedrich Engels, this evolutionary stage introduces social inequality, and all the pain that comes with this, to humanity. They conjectured that the move to domesticated resources led to surplus and private property. Surely a surplus in food that allows the possibility of feeding larger populations is hardly a problem in itself. Engels, and more recent anthropologists who followed his system, however, pointed to a secondary result: Surplus was rarely equally distributed throughout a society. Soon some people controlled the most fertile lands for agriculture and others controlled the largest herds. Those who had less fertile (or no) lands or animals became dependent on those who owned the resources they needed. Private property, particularly economically significant private property, according to this form of evolutionary thought, established a hegemonic distribution of wealth that continues to this day. Obvious among the losers in this development were women, who, according to Engels, became dependent on male property owners at this stage.

Even without this evolutionary model, it is clear that the roles of women in horticultural and pastoral societies differed significantly from those of their foraging sisters. The roles of men did as well. Gender was still an important category for human distinction, but the roles of men and women seemed more separate than in most foraging societies. The fluidity of social interaction had been replaced by formal structures of place and family.

Formalizing the Family

One clear difference that distinguishes foraging societies from those that depend on domesticated plants and animals is found in the definition of family relationships. Children born into a foraging society generally counted relatives from both their mothers' and fathers' sides as their family too. People in foraging societies often have been quoted as saying they were related to everyone. The whole society was conceptualized as a large family. In societies that depended on domesticated resources, new babies were more typically welcomed into a family that was drawn from only one parent. They were born into *clans*, social divisions divided according to kinship groups that were the primary organizing units of society. Such kinship ties were clearly traced throughout a number of generations, and new children were identified and socially located in culturally significant categories that defined them throughout their lives. These extended family groups controlled land, herds, water sources, or specific social privileges. Some families controlled poorer resources than did others. The future fortunes of children from different kin groups were at least somewhat biased from the beginning.

The typical kinship systems of these and more complex agricultural societies tended to be unilineal. This simply means that a child belonged to the kin line of either the mother or the father. If a society were patrilineal, children, both male and female, were born members of their father's kinship group with specific rights and duties. This did not mean that their mother and her group were strangers, to be sure. A mother would have a specific, and generally primary, relationship with her children regardless of system, but in a patrilineal system her kinship group was different than that of her children. These kinship groups, called clans or lineages, often owned critical resources, and the members of the groups had rights to use them. A matrilineal system followed the female lines. Children became members of mother's clan rather than father's clan. The father would have been important to his children but not a member of their group. Kinship relationships always went beyond the clans in all unilineal societies and families of spouses, and both parents played important personal roles in individuals' lives.

Because the logic of unilineal systems was so different than those in Western societies, they often appeared exotic to those who first encountered them. The strength of these systems appears to lie in the matter of private property. If in foraging societies, all resources were shared, then in these societies, there were limitations on common use. Fertile, well-watered lands were valuable for horticulturalists, and their use had to be limited. Overuse would have ruined the fields. Who got to farm where? Grazing lands for herds, and the herds themselves, were likewise controlled. Who got to graze their animals in a rich valley, and who got to kill an animal for meat? A stranger could not be allowed to pick the ripe crops or kill a fat animal whenever he or she was hungry. These resources were owned—kinship groups owned them. A member of the group had rights to the resources and had responsibilities to maintain them.

Permanent Homes

Societies that depended on domesticated plants were, by necessity, more tied to particular lands than foragers. While foragers needed extensive areas of land to survive, horticulturalists needed to focus their efforts in smaller areas and needed to be there at specific parts of the season. In other words, they had to prepare their fields, plant them, weed them, and be there to harvest them; in some circumstances, they may even have had to defend them from others. This means that for some extended time, people had to stay in one place. Permanent, or at least semipermanent, villages became the primary residences for individuals. They moved about at other times to trade, visit, or use other resources, but the economic base of these societies was the village. The way of life of a horticulturalist was far different from that of a forager.

Those who depended on domesticated animals were less "place bound." In fact, most pastoralists, at this level of complexity, moved through a large range in order to feed their animals. Herd animals that foraged on wild plants needed to be moved when the food was depleted. Frequently, seasonal changes dictated specific movements. Herds were moved from high lands to low lands, from seashores to inland, and back as the year progressed. The groups that owned the herds moved with them. This differed from the movement of foragers in significant ways. Foragers did not normally have a yearly pattern, and they often moved as individuals or as nuclear families. The makeup of the group living together in one month differed from that in another. Pastoralists tended to move in a more organized and scheduled manner. They moved in groups so that the people living together in May were the same people who were together in December. Also, the grazing lands that the herds used this December are probably the same ones that were used last December. Thus, pastoralists tended to move more than horticulturalists did, but they had a far more organized system for movement than foragers.

Both horticulture and pastoralism assumed levels of permanence not found in foraging societies. People were not free to pick up and move to a new group or area. The people and resources that were important were localized, which demanded a new scale of social organization with new structures for the definition of human distinctions. Gender remained a primary category for such distinctions.

DOMESTICATED CROPS: WOMAN THE FARMER?

Whether the origins of plant domestication represented a revolution or an evolutionary change, clearly life after the development of horticulture was substantially different than before. Women and men, while still having some autonomy, were part of a larger unit that had authority over individual lives. People were categorized in a new way of living and gender was still the primary category.

Economics

An assertion of many feminists is that women discovered domestication of plants. In fact, this is virtually impossible to prove. Whether the hands of a woman or a man first planted the seeds of specific plants will remain unknown. An educated guess might favor a woman's hands. Because women tended to specialize on plant life in foraging societies, it is reasonable to assume that they developed a more intimate understanding of plants than did men. The observations and understanding of plant life that would be needed to begin selective harvesting and planting must have been more important to women. It also seems likely that once planting became a part of the economy, it would remain women's work. In fact, in horticultural societies, at least, women tended to be the farmers. They frequently called on men for clearing fields and other heavy duties. These men, however, mainly continued to focus on animals through hunting and some herding. They also took on roles in community defense and trade that were not necessary in simpler societies.

Gender remained the most powerful category in determining a division of labor. There were few full-time specialists in these tribal societies. Warriors, traders, and community leaders emerged but they were ordinary people and rarely did their civic duties supercede their economic roles. Similarly, religious leaders might be identified and compensated with gifts for their time spent helping others, but they remained primarily hunters, or farmers, or whatever. A girl might grow up to be a farmer, but not only a farmer, and a boy might grow up to hunt and carry out other duties. The complexity of the economic roles was greater than in foraging societies, but there were no strong structural divisions among people.

There were, however, distinct economic differences among groups of people. Women born into families with better lands or more animals lived easier, more secure lives. They also accumulated enough surplus to allow trade for luxury items. In some cases, those families without adequate lands and resources became dependent on those with more than adequate resources. Long-term dependency without return compensation put these people in an inferior social position as well. Likewise, a woman who did not have the support of an established family was severely disadvantaged. Among foragers, the resources necessary for life were unowned. Hunters or gatherers collected meat and plants as they found them. Family disputes led to people separating with no economic consequences for either side. In horticultural societies, however, an individual's livelihood was vested in the family unit, and this dependency had social consequences. Extended families became economic units that had control over their members.

Social Organization

A woman was born into the fundamental organizational unit of a tribe, the kinship group. As noted earlier, these groups were generally organized around either matrilineal or patrilineal rules. Rights to economically and socially important resources were established at birth. Marriages were generally arranged between families and created alliances between groups. These alliances led to cooperative activities and economic partnerships.

In respect to gender, the rules for residence after marriage were actually more important to the individual than the system of kinship allegiance. In both matrilineal and patrilineal systems, men and women had rights in their natal family. Throughout childhood, most people lived with their parents and lineal relatives on family land. It was at marriage that one spouse was usually expected to move to the clan lands of the other.

In patrilineal systems the most common residence rule was virilocality. This means that a bride moved to live with her husband's family after the marriage. This was often a very difficult adjustment for the new wife.

She was living in a strange environment and working on unfamiliar grounds—often far from family and friends. Support for her husband was strong and she had to prove herself a worthy wife. Many women remembered this period as the hardest in their lives, as one when they were continually tested and criticized. A transition occurred with the birth of the first child. As a mother of a clan member she had more standing than she had as a wife. She had produced something of value for the family and was frequently treated with more respect. As she aged, her position as a senior woman gave her some control over the new wives who married her sons. In cases of divorce or widowhood, a woman was at a disadvantage. A childless woman had no lasting tie to her husband's family and hoped that her family would take her back. A woman with children could not permanently take her children away from their clan homes, but as their mother she had a permanent home with them. A man, in this system, lived in the same residence throughout his life and expected his sons to remain with him there. His wife and daughters had more transitory lives.

In a matrilineal system, uxorilocality was the most common residence rule. This dictated that the groom moved to live with his wife's family after marriage. While this was a difficult adjustment for men, it was rarely described in terms of powerlessness. Men often formed alliances outside of the family and generally had more freedom than did women. At divorces, or the death of a wife, men often returned to their natal families, although their children were bound to their own matrilineal homes. A woman had strong family support throughout her life in this system, and her daughters remained with her. While men were always important in her life, male authority was divided between her father and brothers, and her husband(s). Female authority over her was located in her mother and aunts.

Political Organization

A woman found the leadership and control of their communities in the kinship units of these societies. The elders of clans always had considerable influence over their clansmen and women and frequently wielded power over them as well. In some societies, male elders had more say than their female counterparts, but, in many, women elders had strong voices that had to be heard as well. Often communities with multiple clans had councils of the leaders of these clans that could direct community actions. In a few, like the Iroquois discussed later, formal structures that involved representation beyond the villages, and even nations, evolved. In the Iroquois case, at least, the power of both women and men was significant in the system.

Other categories of people gained power in these societies as well. People who controlled excess wealth often had more influence and power than did others. Religious specialists used their control of the supernatural for secular ends. Most significant perhaps were the warriors. Many societies at this level of complexity had hostile relationships with neighbors. Warriors in such societies became very important. In some, the warriors, or warrior societies, took a significant leadership role in the culture. It was unusual for women to be warriors, and, in many societies, women were not allowed to become warriors. Thus, in societies that carry on extensive raiding, women's positions often were devalued. Of course, as is true throughout the discussion of this category of cultures, there were always exceptions. The Iroquois were among the most feared warriors in Native North America, and the roles of women in these nations were significant.

Cosmology

Religious beliefs among horticultural societies were, in many ways, similar to those among foragers. The universe was typically believed to be inhabited by myriad supernatural beings that had differing degrees of interest in humanity. Spirits, ghosts, and deities were believed to coexist alongside the creatures of the natural world. Humans interacted with these supernatural beings and frequently formed alliances with individual spirits that supported them throughout their lives. Special individuals had more intensive knowledge of and help from such spirits and became shamans. They used their positions to help cure illnesses and created positive relationships between the natural and supernatural beings. Other individuals became witches and used their knowledge of the spirit world to harm others. Different societies tended to gender the roles of witches and shamans differently. Some societies defined shamans as men, others defined them as women, and still others did not see gender as an issue. The same was true of witches. All of this was true in foraging societies as well. In some horticultural societies, however, these roles were more formalized, and organized groups of curers became significant.

One other way that horticultural societies differed in cosmological practice from most foraging societies was in community ceremonies. It was common for horticultural societies to hold annual community festivals that celebrated the harvest, first crops, and first plantings. Other yearly ceremonies, based on the significant occurrences in the economic round or cosmological events, were also common. These ceremonies typically required a great deal of work and organization by members of the society, and honors were bestowed on individuals at these times. The details of such ceremonies, however, were highly specific according to society, as were the roles of men and women in these ceremonies.

CASES OF FARMING COMMUNITIES

Four cases of horticultural and agricultural groups, those of the Iroquois, Sambia, Vanatinai, and Yanomamö, demonstrate a broad variation in gender roles and attitudes. While each follows the model to a great extent, the details of the societies create vastly different experiences for women. Each has been labeled as a matriarchy or a patriarchy in the popular literature, but each demonstrates a far more complex reality.

The Iroquois of the American Northeast

The Iroquois nations are indigenous to the areas that are now New York and southern Canada. The term *Iroquois* refers to the Seneca, Oneida, Onondaga, Mohawk, Cayuga, and later Tuscarora nations, or "tribes," that joined together as a political–military confederacy, the League of the Iroquois. The nations were culturally similar, but each group had its own unique social customs and political system. The case of the Iroquois has become well known in feminist literature because their concept of gender relations was among the first to be described that demonstrated strong roles for women, as well as men. They have even, mistakenly, been characterized as matriarchies because women among the Iroquois had far more access to positions of power and authority than their colonial sisters. (Bilharz 1995: 101–102)

Economics   The land of the Iroquois was a temperate forest with distinct seasons. The Iroquois nations based their subsistence economy on the "three sisters": maize, beans, and squash. These three, combined with venison, provided a sound and nutritious diet. Farming was largely the realm of women with men helping to clear fields. The fields belonged to clans, and clan women farmed their family lands. The crops produced belonged to the women, and they distributed them. Surplus plant food was stored for year-round use. Hunting was essentially men's work, and they brought their meat to their wives to process. Fishing, a male activity, added to the food in the summer.

Clans stored surplus food. The cosmology of the nations demanded hospitality for visitors, and part of the surplus was used in this way. Also, the military pursuits of the nations required food supplies, which also was taken from these stores. Control over these resources was in the hands of the senior women of the clan, and they were known to use them strategically. The longhouse and the village were the permanent realm of women. They spent most of their lives close to the villages. Men, on the other hand, traveled far afield to hunt, trade, and war. The essential place of male activities was outside of the villages. Men could, and did, live comfortably in villages and women did occasionally travel away, but the geography of their normal lives were different.

War was important in the lives of these people. The Iroquois nations were known throughout the east as fierce and efficient enemies. This well-earned reputation continued through the American Revolution, with the European colonial nations vying for alliances with these tribes. The prestige of Iroquois men came from their prowess in battle. Iroquois women were supportive of these battles. There were cosmological reasons why war was so important. Women encouraged men to battle in the name of revenge, but because they supplied the battle groups, in some situations they withheld the food supplies when the men's absences would interfere with the women's interests. Captives from raids were brought to the villages and given to the women for disposition. Women had a number of choices. They were entitled to torture and kill the captives, take them as slaves, or take them as additional husbands. The ideal Iroquois woman was no weaker or stronger, no gentler or more aggressive than her male relatives.

Social and Political Organization   All Iroquois nations were both matrilineal and uxorilocal. Children belonged to the clans of their mothers, and, at marriage, men left their clan houses to live with their wives' clans. Villages consisted of a series of wooden long houses. Each housed women and children of a specific clan and their husbands. Men remained members of their own clans after marriage and could return to their clan houses after divorce or the death of their wives. Women remained in the house they were born into throughout their lives. Clan lands were near villages, and women worked together as clanswomen in their fields. Men worked outside of the village in hunting and raiding groups.

Marriages were arranged by the mothers of the couple and had to be between people of different clans. Divorce was simple. A man left his wife's house or a woman piled her husband's belongings outside of the house. Children remained with their mothers in their own clan houses. Brothers and sisters were important allies throughout their lives. Mother's brother, as the closest adult clansman, played a major role in a child's life. This meant that men kept an active presence in both the houses of their wives and their own clan houses.

The political organization of the Iroquois confederacy has been widely documented. While many decisions were made within the clans, broader issues were brought to village councils where all were welcomed to speak. Under the organization of the Iroquois confederacy, a representative form of political organization was also formed. Selected representatives of clans, called *sachem*, from each nation met annually at Onondaga to debate league issues. Issues of peace and war were determined here. Each nation, likewise, had elected sachem who met to determine national policies. The office of sachem was a male prerogative. While some women are known to have held the position as regents for sons, permanent sachems were men. The electors of the sachem were clan matrons. Further, these matrons could recall, or dehorn, the sachems who did not act or vote appropriately. Thus, sachems were men, but they were elected by and continued office because of women. Likewise, war leaders were men who were selected by the women. This is clearly *not* a matriarchy; instead, a gendered form of checks and balances, or a complementary system, prevailed here.

Cosmology   While the religious world of the Iroquois saw many changes, internal and external, during the colonial period, it is clear that from the early days their world was filled with a variety of spiritual beings and structured community rituals. At puberty some boys sought guardian spirits through a wilderness experience that provoked dreams of supernatural importance. Girls during their first period in a menstrual house sought out their spiritual helpers through similar dreams. People who became shamans demonstrated extraordinary supernatural powers. Both men and women became shamans and used their powers to heal. Likewise, both men and women became witches who brought evil.

Another category of religious person was that of the Faithkeeper. These people had specific religious obligations and prominent roles in the regular ritual events. According to early descriptions, both men and women held this position in "about equal numbers." (Morgan 1962: 186) This role was mandated to uphold the morality of the community and to direct the yearly rites. Annual festivals celebrated the new year, first crops, the harvest, and thanksgiving. At these community festivals, new names were taken, dances were danced, and dreams were discussed and fulfilled.

The dream was an important component in Iroquois cosmology. Dreams were believed to be as real as any natural event. Dreams had to be understood, and the conflicts or desires they involved had to be resolved. Unfulfilled desires were seen as the causes of individual illness, which meant that dreams of sexual desire had to be relieved with actual sexual relations and fears were acted out in ways that relieved the stress. Not all dreams had obvious solutions, and public discussions worked to establish the true meanings of obscure dreams.

The reputation of Iroquois society as women centered is clearly exaggerated. Women never controlled Iroquois society. However, neither were women subordinated to men in this society. In some ways, the roles of Iroquois men and women were clearly distinctive and the means for gaining prestige were likewise different. Men earned their status as warriors and women as farmers. In other ways their roles intertwined in leadership roles in kinship, politics, and religion. What stands out in this case is the valuing of individuals apart from their gender.

The Sambia of New Guinea

New Guinea is an island that has been home to a myriad of different, largely horticultural, cultures. While they shared similar types of economies and ceremonial rituals, studies have revealed a broad difference in the ways that they defined gender and designated gender roles. The Sambia are one such New Guinea culture. Among these people, men and women had distinctly different roles with an extraordinary degree of separation between the two. They are probably best known for their tradition of ritualized homosexuality that is described in Chapter 11 but here the focus is on the roles and identities of men and women. (Herdt 1987) The culture of the Sambia provides a vivid comparison to that of the Vanatinai, which follows next and shows quite a different case from New Guinea.

Economics   The Sambia cultivated sweet potatoes, taro, yams, and other vegetables for their primary subsistence needs. Much of the gardening, especially of sweet potatoes, was women's work. While most New Guinea peoples also depended on large herds of pigs, the Sambia had relatively few. Their meat for food and ritual use came from hunting. Men needed meat to build their prestige. In Gilbert Herdt's words, "Men fell trees and clear brush; women burn off the debris, till the soil, plant, weed, and harvest. Men hunt, women do not." (1987: 18) The sexual division of labor was rigid and allowed little overlap. Even the plants were gendered, with crops like sweet potatoes defined as female and plants like taro defined as male. Tools were distinctly gendered, with axes and bows and arrows defined as men's tools and digging sticks as women's. The economic world was fully gendered.

The important activity that defined men was not that of the economy but of war. Although the days of constant warfare with neighboring groups ended before Herdt met the Sambia, the concepts of war and being a warrior were still fundamental to male identity. Aggression, strength, and competence in battle remained the hallmarks of masculinity. Women were perceived, and derided by men, as being the opposite: soft, shy, and gentle.

Social and Political Organization   Kinship was patrilineal and virilocal. People married into another clan, which meant that women most often were forced to move to another, often hostile, community. Most marriages were arranged when the girl was a child or established as an exchange of sisters. In other words, the families exchanged girls as marriage partners in order to be assured that there would be brides for their men. This solidified alliances. Women had virtually no say in the choice of their husbands. Wives and children established a man as a full adult and provided economic benefits. Women were sexual partners, and multiple wives added to the prestige of important men. Wives, however, were also dangerous to men. The very masculinity of men was compromised through sexual activity and contact with women's menstrual blood.

Villages were constructed to physically separate the worlds of women and men. Nuclear families lived together in the woman's house. Within these small houses, however, specific areas were segregated as men's or women's places. Women also used menstrual houses, where they lived while having their menstrual periods and when giving birth. These were strictly women's areas. In addition, all villages had one or two men's clubhouses. These were the places that men convened to discuss men's business, including hunts, war, and ritual. These were also the residences of young men undergoing the initiation rituals described in Chapter 11. Women were completely excluded from the men's houses. Paths through villages were also gendered with separate women's and men's routes. Women and men were spatially very separate. Boys and girls did not play together, and women and men did not touch in public.

Leadership in this society, as might be expected, was situated in the warriors and male clan elders, who were often the same people. War leaders were the defenders of the village. They protected villagers from outsiders, who were perceived as real and imminent dangers. They were aggressive and proud men, and they used their power to safeguard their communities. Male elders were expected to deal with issues of land, marriage, and rituals that were important for community harmony. Female elders similarly had significant say in issues that were vital in the women's spheres.

Cosmology In the spiritual world, the rigidity of gender roles appeared to weaken. The cosmological world of the Sambia included a variety of spirits and ghosts. Female hamlet spirits and male forest spirits helped protect the villagers, while ghosts were known to be very dangerous. Ghosts were directed by sorcerers to bring evil to enemies. The defenders of people were the shamans, who went into trances to heal individuals. Shamans were recognized as self-sacrificing heroes. Perhaps, unexpectedly, both women and men became shamans, and individuals of both genders became powerful shamans. This was the one public role where women stand out as commanding figures. Herdt commented: "That women are shamans is interesting; that they can be prestigious and powerful in a masculine society seems remarkable." (1987: 196) It was the one arena in which the standard sex stereotypes did not prevail.

More than any of the previous cases, the division of men and women was far more rigidly defined among the Sambia. All of nature was gendered in the Sambia world and, more importantly, hierarchically valued. As among the Iroquois, for example, men were highly honored as warriors, but, unlike the Iroquois, among the Sambia men were dishonored by *not* being warriors. Only in the supernatural world was this differential challenged. Sambia women lived with highly constrained roles in a male-valued world.

The Vanatinai of New Guinea

Margaret Mead in her pioneering work in gender, *Sex and Temperament in Three Primitive Societies* demonstrated the variability in the concept of gender using cases drawn from societies she studied in New Guinea. (1935) While the details of this early work are in dispute, the basic themes of human gender diversity remain, and the diversity of gender concepts in New Guinea appears sound. It should have been no surprise that the Sambia, as recorded by anthropologist Gilbert Herdt, represented a gender reality quite different than that of the Vanatinai, another New Guinea group whose case follows. (1987)

Vanatinai was also a horticultural New Guinea society, but one that had a gender system and ideology that could hardly be more different than that of the Sambia. Anthropologist Maria Lepowsky defined their society as "sexually egalitarian." (1990: 171) Men and women had overlapping economic, religious, and social roles. Rather than separate worlds, the Vanatinai men and women commingled in the same universe.

Economics   The Vanatinai lived on a small island off the mainland of New Guinea. Like most societies in their region, their subsistence economy was based on the gardening of sweet potatoes, yams, and taro and the tending of domesticated pigs. Women were designated as "bosses" of the gardens, but, in fact, both men and women worked in them. Both men and women owned land, pigs, and ritual items. Every individual had the right to distribute the plants and animals they harvested. Hunting was largely the work of men, who were able to use spears, but women also did some hunting. Harvests generally allowed for surplus, and this was used for trade or feasting.

Other subsistence work was gendered but not strictly. Men built houses with the help of women. Men built canoes, which both used. Women cared for young children, but men often played with them and were active participants in the rearing of older children. Women cooked and men occasionally did as well. Men and women were not the same, but their jobs overlapped.

Trade, especially ceremonial trade, was important in the island cultures of New Guinea. Trade partnerships with individuals on other islands were nurtured by journeys to those islands, where they exchanged both practical goods and ritual items. Both men and women in Vanatinai culture were partners with individuals on other islands. The gender of the partners was not restricted. Women were in partnership with women or men, and vice versa. The goal of traders was to accumulate enough goods for distribution at important feasts. This allowed them to be recognized as generous and wealthy—or, in a term, a *giver*. Givers were regarded as important people, and, in a society with no ascribed positions of high status, this achieved status gave individuals, both women and men, prestige.

Warfare was the realm of men, but wars were ended long before Lepowsky's study. Even in war, women accompanied men and took part in hostilities. A woman who declared that a battle be halted expected to be heeded. With the end of warfare in the area, sorcery took the place of actual battle. Sorcery was used by men to attack enemies and to bring death. Women rarely used sorcery, and when they did, they dressed like men during the procedure.

Social and Political Organization   The Vanatinai followed a matrilineal system of kinship. Their residence rule, however, was not uxorilocal. Instead, they followed an ideal of bilocal residence, which in this case meant that a married couple spent part of the year in the home region of the husband and then moved to that of the wife for another period. This repeated regularly throughout the years. Thus, the wife spent extended time on her clan lands and worked with her clansmen and women. It also meant that the husband had the same opportunity. Both men and women, then, maintained their kinship ties and nuclear family relationships.

Sexual freedom was the norm before marriage, and children who were born outside of marriage were welcomed into the clan of the mother. While families discouraged some matches, the married couple made the final decisions. Gifts were given to the bride's family only after the marriage appeared to be permanent. Divorce was also a private decision, but the bride's family was expected to return any marriage gifts. Children remained with their clan, which was also that of their mother. People who divorced typically remarried.

Nuclear families lived in their own houses with no distinction between genders. Unlike other New Guinea societies, there were no men's houses. Additionally, there were no elaborate initiation rites for either boys or girls. Men and women were both highly mobile; they not only moved their home from village to village on a regular pattern, but they sailed to other islands to trade. Clan villages were home, but neither men nor women spent all their time there.

While either men or women served as "hamlet leaders," this designation was not formal. Hamlet leaders were called on for direction in issues of subsistence and ritual matters. Public issues were discussed, and both men and women took part in public debates. The role of "giver" was similar to that of "big man" elsewhere in New Guinea, but here there were both big men and big women, who gained importance by becoming wealthy through competitive trade and donated that wealth to support public rituals and needy townspeople. This meant that poorer individuals became beholden to their wealthier neighbors and owed them respect and support.

Cosmology   The cosmology of the people of Vanatinai involved supernatural beings from powerful gods to ancestral spirits. These entities were responsible for the health and well-being of all individuals. The creator was a male, Rodyo, who also collected and housed the spirits of the dead and was a sponsor of sorcery. Other mythic stories involved females as wise women who were the originators of ritual exchange, magical knowledge, and similar cultural necessities. Both male and female deities controlled the world of the Vanatinai.

Individuals depended on the supernatural forces in their daily lives. Both men and women had to know garden magic that allowed them to call on the help of ancestral spirits in growing successful gardens. Likewise, magic was needed to successfully hunt, gather, trade, heal, and find love. Men knew magic to control magic. In more negative ways, men became sorcerers and used spells to bring evil to their enemies. Women, more commonly, used an innate or learned form of witchcraft to manipulate their environment. Both men and women needed to know the ways to counter evil sent against them. Women were expected to give life rather than kill, but, in fact, women sometimes were held responsible for deadly evil.

Important parts of the rituals of every hamlet were the feasts given at death. The death of every individual was commemorated with a large public feast. Families had to accumulate vast amounts of foods and ceremonial goods to be distributed at the feast. Local givers were expected to give generously to all such feasts. Women, as well as men, hosted these feasts and donated to them. Likewise both men and women were heirs to the dead individual, who was honored by the feast. A woman represented her clan and went into mourning, under the control of the deceased's kin, until the final feast for the death of her husband. This reestablished the normal harmony that was disturbed by the death. At a woman's death, a woman of the widower's clan played this role. At the final feast, long after the death, the mourning was completed and goodwill was continued between the families. In a world of witchcraft and sorcery, this peace was ritually important.

The Vanatinai people represented an unusual case in which men and women interacted in a society where the equality of opportunity was inclusive of both genders. The gender antagonism found among the Sambia, and many other New Guinea societies, was absent here. Further, as Lepowsky observed, "There is no barrier in Vanatinai philosophy and customs to women having socially recognized power." (1993: 80)

The Yanomamö of Venezuela

The Yanomamö are a horticultural society in the southern Venezuela rain forest, best known from the studies of anthropologist Napoleon Chagnon. (1968) During the time he studied them, the Yanomamö he knew survived an epidemic and emerged to be a society apparently focused on conflict. Another anthropologist, Alcida Rita Ramos (1995), studied another group of Yanomamö and wrote about a less violent and slightly more gender flexible society, but even in her descriptions the themes of male leadership and control remain. The Yanomamö peoples as they appear in the anthropological literature to date seem to be at the extreme for male dominance for all the horticulturalists.

Economics   The subsistence economy of the Yanomamö was based on gardening and hunting. The gardens, which were built close to the villages, contained a number of crops. Taro, sweet potatoes, sweet manioc, and plantains and bananas were primary foods. Maize was becoming important by the time that ethnographers visited. Other significant plants included cane for arrows, tobacco for chewing, and cotton for clothing and hammocks. Additionally, some crops were raised for their magical properties. A variety of wild plants were also used. Meat came from hunting, with turkeys, pigs, monkeys, and tapirs being among the animals that were hunted. Insects and honey were also part of the diet.

Men took prominent roles in all prestigious jobs in Yanomamö society, although in one group, Alcida Ramos wrote of more flexibility in carrying out most chores. (1995: 30–31) In that group, both men and women carried out tasks elsewhere allotted to the other gender. Men chose the garden lands, cleared them, planted, and tended the crops. Women helped their husbands in the fields with planting and weeding. Hunting was a male occupation, and men left their villages with great care and concern. When they were absent, the danger of attacks from hostile neighbors became a major worry. Women had one activity, wood gathering, that was critical to the well-being of the villages, but this was low in prestige. Every day women had to collect both wood and water for their families. Each woman had to carry heavy loads of wood for several miles.

Like the Sambia, the most culturally significant activity of Yanomamö men was raiding and defense. The Yanomamö world was composed of allies and enemies. Enemies were expected to attack villages using both physical and metaphysical means. Villages were stormed, and men or small groups taken away from the villages were often killed by these enemies. A successful raid concluded with the death of enemies and no fatalities on the raiders' side. Given a shortage of women in Yanomamö villages, the goal of many raids and a desirable end of all was the capture of women. Captured women were raped by the raiders and then given to men as wives.

Social and Political Organization   Yanomamö society was patrilineal and virilocal. Behind a wooden fence, an individual village appeared to be one large building, or *shabono*, but this structure was in reality a series of houses that were joined together. Men, with their wives' help, built a living area for the nuclear family. When all such segments were completed, neighbors filled in the roofs between units. People slept in hammocks hanging from the house rafters. A cooking fire also marked each family's area. Men lived in the villages of their childhood except for periods spent with their wives' parents when they were first married. Women lived with their husband's kin but sometimes in villages where their families also dwelled. Women preferred this situation because they could more easily call on the companionship and support of their parents and brothers.

Marriages, however, were not regularly arranged for the comfort of the wife. Men took charge of arrangements, and many girls were spoken for before they reach puberty. There was a shortage of women largely due to practices of female infanticide and polygyny, the tradition that men were able to have more than one wife. Many men had difficulty finding wives. A marriageable girl in a family was valuable resource. Men exchanged the rights to marry sisters with other men who had sisters. Ideally, men married women from another specific lineage who lived in the village or nearby. However, exchange of marriageable women was the basis for alliances between villages. Also, as noted, after raids women were forcibly married to enemy men. Prominent men were able to command additional wives from families who wished closer relationships. Some such men passed on these wives to younger brothers. Obviously, the wishes of the young women or their mothers carried little weight.

Within a marriage, the wife was fully subservient to her husband. She was expected to put his wishes and comfort at the forefront of her concerns. Chagnon described wife beating as both frequent and expected. He even asserted that wives believed that minor beatings indicated their husbands' affection for them. (1968: 82–83) When beatings were severe, brothers stepped in to defend their sisters. Physical fights between men resulted from such disputes. Women without such protectors were beaten or killed without penalty.

The political organization of the villages was delineated in the lineages. The headmen of the community were the heads of lineages. These were senior men who had a reputation of fierceness and bravery. They needed to be knowledgeable on the variety of alliances and animosities in their region. They were important elements in alliances between villages. An effective headman kept order in the village by the strength of his personality and the support of his kinsmen.

Cosmology   Yanomamö use of the supernatural reflected their view of aggression in the human world. The nature of the spiritual dimensions of each human was complex. Individuals had souls and animal correspondents. One aspect of a person was the *soul component* that could leave the person. When this occurred, that individual became critically ill. Family members searched for it, and they had to bring it back to ensure the person's health. Malevolent individuals attacked the souls of people, especially children, because they were very vulnerable. People also became ill from the presence of evil spirits. Shamans chanted for these patients and manually attempted to remove evil spirits. They did not use drugs as medicines in curing.

Shamanism was a male profession, and many men became shamans. Shamans used their skills to encourage the *hekura*, or demons, to attack the souls of their enemies and to repel the actions of hekura sent against them. To contact the hekura, shamans used hallucinogenic drugs. They chanted and directed their hekura toward their enemies. In a real way this was a continuation of raiding, but these raids were supernatural. Sickness and death without the physical presence of an enemy was as much a part of a battle as a raid. Women and children were victims, but they were not practitioners.

The Yanomamö can be seen as the extreme case of male dominance among horticulturalists. Men controlled all the socially important economic, political, family, and religious roles. Warfare as a prominent part of life flavored the culture as the ethnographers described it. The shortage of women, due in part to the violence, created a competition over women that made them a commodity. In other societies such a shortage might have increased women's status rather than have lowered it. Unlike the Sambia, where the supernatural countered the negative gender images of nature and culture, here the understanding of the supernatural supported this inequality.

PASTORALISM: MAN THE HERDER?

If horticultural societies focused their subsistence needs on plants that were the foraging expertise of women, then pastoral societies focused on animals where foraging men's expertise lay. As the cases of horticultural societies clearly showed, there is no guarantee that a focus on plants meant a cultural valuing of women. Likewise, the focus on animals did not necessitate the devaluing of women and hypervaluation of men.

Economics

The definitional aspect of a pastoral society was that the use of domesticated animals formed the central activity of the culture. Domesticated animals were "tamed" or genetically altered to remain under the control of humans rather than live independently as a species. This domestication was as simple as selection of the gentlest animals or as complexly modified as the modern milk cow. Every pastoral society, of course, had a need for vegetable food for the animals and people. Ranchers had to grow food for the animals or pasture them. Those who used pastures needed to move to fresh lands frequently or have the use of extensive areas of land around their residences. Those who grew food for animals may actually have had extensive fields for animals and people as well. These societies were defined as pastoral, following a cultural valuation that animals were more important or more prestigious than the plants.

A woman born in a pastoral society was a member of a clan that was deemed to be either richer or poorer than others based on the extent of their herds. A major difference between pastoral and horticultural societies was wealth. While in many horticultural societies, some individuals could become more prestigious through their control of food for gift and feast giving, there was often little permanent capital. Fertile land, the most vital resource, was abundantly available. Most horticultural societies showed weak differences among peoples in relative wealth. In pastoral societies, however, the herds were vital capital, and the number of animals an individual or a family controlled was commonly used to define social status. Those who did not have adequate animals became dependent on those who did. In most pastoral societies where herding was a male pursuit, the position of herder conferred a prestige that the female occupations did not.

When wealth was culturally defined and in the hands of one gender, some gender inequality was to be expected.

Some pastoral societies developed highly aggressive systems. In these the roles of male warriors tended to overwhelm the roles of women. A consequence of accumulated wealth was often warfare, or at least raiding. Protection of animals was a common concern in many pastoral societies. Others increased their own herds by stealing animals from weaker neighbors. Herders had to be vigilant against both human and animal predators in order to deal with this problem.

Social and Political Organization

Women in pastoral societies were born into clan organizations. In most, where men herded the animals, this was a patrilineal and virilocal type. This meant that the men of the group remained together and worked with their kinsmen. Frequently the kinship group and the herd became identified as one. In these societies, life was difficult for the women who married into their husbands' groups. Not only were they in a strange environment, often without the protection of their natal families, but often they moved hundreds of miles a year following the herd. They had to care for their children in dangerous and strenuous conditions, where the well-being of the herd seemed to take priority over their own.

As in horticultural societies, political organization was generally located in the kin groups. Most commonly, the older and richer men took positions of authority but rarely did they become autocratic. In those pastoral societies where raiding was common, the role of warrior was often central. Young men with reputations of bravery and skill challenged the importance of their elders. In some such societies, organized age categories were established, and each age category had its own expectations and rewards. Often in such systems, the age grade of warriors was separated physically, as well as socially, from other age grades. Women were rarely constrained by the same categories, but the difference between a married and an unmarried woman loomed large. In many cases, the warriors remained unmarried, while the women of their chronological age were married to senior men.

Cosmology

In broad terms, aside from the focus on the success of the animals rather than the crops, the cosmology of pastoral groups differed little from that of horticultural groups. A general belief in myriad spirit beings was common. Also, the roles of witches and shamans were almost universal. Of course the particular nature of the spirits and their relationship to people varied with each culture.

CASES OF PASTORAL COMMUNITIES

Two cases of very different pastoral groups, those of the Navajos and Tswana, demonstrate the variations in cultures, especially the gender roles and attitudes in this category. While the model presents a significant general picture of pastoralists, the environment and nature of the specific subsistence resource, as well as specific histories, can make significant exceptions to the rules.

The Navajo of the American Southwest

The Navajo are Native American people living in the Four Corners area of the American Southwest. They are currently the largest Native American group with more than 200,000 people. Despite living in a relatively arid region, for some centuries their subsistence focus was on the herding of sheep and goats and the growing of maize. The Navajo are not "typical" pastoralists in some ways. First, they are historically new to this system. Navajo became sheepherders only after the introduction of sheep to the American Southwest in the seventeenth century. Before this they relied on wild plants and animals for most of their food. Today they depend on majority American-style employment while maintaining herds of sheep and even cattle. Second, the roles women play are highly valued both economically and socially.

Economics Until the mid-twentieth century, Navajo families largely depended on their herds of sheep and goats as their economic base. The animals provided food and wool. A medium or large herd was insurance against hunger in even the worst years and surplus for feasts and rituals. The wool from the sheep also provided the raw material for weaving the Navajo rugs or blankets that were prominent trade objects. Gardens provided maize and a variety of other plants. Silversmithing and hunting added to family economic reserves. The animals were individually owned. Individuals began their herds as children when they were given animals as gifts. Throughout life, both men and women added to their personal holdings. The animals, however, were usually gathered together and cared for in family herds. All family members tended to the animals and the gardens. There was little differentiation from day to day between the sheep of different individuals. Women wove blankets and the men did silverwork. Income from the blankets and jewelry had long been an important source of income. Men did most of the hunting, but women traditionally helped. Obviously, both men and women worked in the important economic activities. Individual men and women were allowed to "cross over" and did even those tasks that were gender linked, such as silverwork and weaving. (Shepardson 1995: 166)

A Navajo woman weaving a basket while her baby sleeps.

The ideology of the Navajo, like that of many foragers, worked against the accumulation of great wealth. Individuals and families were expected to cooperate with others and be generous. An ideal of balance that ensured a healthy and happy life spoke against excessive wealth as much as against excessive poverty. While raiding and warfare were part of the historical past of the Navajo and although Navajo have been prominent in the U.S. military, during much of their herding period they did not value raiding like some other pastoralists did. Male, and occasionally female, warriors were honored but also had to be purified because of their connection to death before they could continue their everyday life.

Social and Political Organization   Kinship and family were the heart of Navajo life. The Navajo were matrilineal and uxorilocal. Children were born in the clan of their mother but maintained a special relationship with the clan of their father. Children lived with their mother and father in a *hogan*. The hogan was a small nuclear family house used primarily for sleeping and privacy. This hogan was traditionally located in a compound with other hogans that housed the sisters and parents of the mother of the nuclear family. A compound was often centered on the hogan of a senior couple and their unmarried children. Their grown daughters, with their nuclear families, shared the area. Other clan members, including divorced sons and widowed siblings, also lived in the camp. This group was the most important functional unit. Residents' sheep were herded together, and they shared in the work of animals and gardens.

Parents and mother's brothers traditionally arranged marriage, but individuals had the right to reject these choices. Men could have more than one wife, but this was complicated unless the wives were closely related. A husband could not compel his wife to accept a polygamous marriage. Divorce was easy and could be initiated by either spouse. A woman would retain the children and her home, while a man would take his possessions and return to the home of his mother and sisters. Even during the marriage, a man was expected to spend some time in this compound because of his responsibilities to his clan relatives, especially his sisters and their children. The relationship between husband and wife was important, but so was the relationship between sister and brother. (Hamamsy 1957: 102)

Political organization was rather fluid; before the colonial organization, there were few decisions that affected the Navajo people as a group. Further, there were no multifamily villages before the reservation structure demanded them. Most decisions were made in family residential units, and all had a say. Elder family members had more authority than younger members, and the voices of senior mothers and mother's brothers demanded respect. In this context women, like men, had authority based on their kinship location and force of personality. In relationships beyond the immediate groups, and in the modern political context, men tended to take the lead. This did not, and does not, debar women from these roles, but men more commonly performed them. What was clear was that no one, male or female, had the right to order others to do anything. In this, the Navajo resembled many foragers.

Cosmology   The world view of the Navajo supported the flexibility of gender roles. Their world was filled with spirits both good and bad. The original gods included notably Changing Woman and her sons, the Hero Twins, who, through their efforts, established the current world. This world was based on harmony. Individuals who maintained peace and harmony lived well. Aggression, anger, envy, and competition worked against harmony and were discouraged. In fact, these were seen as the causes of illness or death.

Some individuals who embraced these characteristics were suspected of being witches. Witches, both male and female, brought evil to others. Navajos strictly avoided all things related to the dead. Hogans where people had died were abandoned and avoided. Witches, alone, broke this taboo and used items from the dead to bring evil. Suspected witches were feared and despised.

On a more positive footing, there were several roles for healers. Navajo healers, both men and women, specialized in a variety of techniques used for diagnosis and curing. Singers, who knew the rituals for healing, were most often men, but there were exceptions. Women typically did not take this role until after menopause. People of the third gender category,

Nadlee, as described in Chapter 11, often excelled at these curing roles as well. Clearly all genders could be good or evil and could serve good or evil.

Shepardson asserted, " 'Sharing,' not 'domination,' was the theme of Navajo life." (1995: 174) The differences between Navajo men and women were seen as complementary rather than competitive. Men and women had different roles but these were not rigidly mandated and the ultimate goal was cooperation. Individuals were expected to work together for the well-being of their families. While women remained together through generations, the men divided their time to be active members of their natal families and those of their wives and children.

The Tswana of East Africa

Among the most famous pastoralists in the anthropological literature were those found in eastern Africa, where many societies focused on cattle herding. Before the colonial period, these societies varied widely in the structured political hierarchy that ranged from acephalous lineage-based systems like that of the Navajo to those with formal positions of leadership. The Tswana have a history of political flux over time and region and were described in the early ethnographies of I. Schapera and the recent ethnographies of John and Joan Comaroff as having clear positions of local and regional leadership. In most of these African societies, domesticated crops provided most of the food, but domesticated animals, particularly cattle, were more highly culturally valued. Much of the early literature ignored the women of the societies, but some of the traditional studies, and more of the more recent studies, write women's lives into the ethnographies. The Tswana of South Africa provide a case where women's lives and men's lives were clearly distinctive.

Economics   Crops provided the Tswana with their staple foods. Women were responsible for fields and did most of the field work. Men helped with heavy work, especially the initial preparation of the fields. Grains grown in these fields (most notably including maize) accounted for most of the daily food. Wild plants gathered by women added to the diet. Additionally, maize was processed into a beer that was an important part of hospitality. The ownership of plant foods, however, was not highly valued and did not directly confer wealth or prestige. Surplus was used by the men of the household to feed poorer relatives and allies and, thereby, establish their support.

Animals, on the other hand, had an importance far beyond their food value. Herds included cattle, goats, and sheep, but the cattle were most significant. Their meat was not used for domestic meals but was important for ritual feasts and for socially important exchanges. People also used the milk, hides, dung, and bones of the animals. Animals, including hunted wild animals, were in the realm of the men. Sons and subordinated men herded the animals, while adult men hunted, did leatherwork, and administered the household resources.

Most importantly, men used their animals, and their wives' crops, to build social networks and establish their prestige and influence in the political world. While women produced the food necessary for daily survival, this food was depreciated as unreliable and trivial. The products of men's herds, on the contrary, were lauded as stable and important and not wasted on day-to-day use. As Comaroff and Comaroff summarized: "Above all, however, male and female 'work' were fundamentally different—and unequal." (1991: 40)

Social and Political Organization   Kinship among the Tswana was patrilineal. Men who shared patrilineal descent were related in a complex political and economic relationship. They were ranked one to the other and maintained a competitive stance in challenging those ranks. Rather than cooperative, the patrilineal male relatives were in contested economic and political relationships. Relatives on the mother's side, however, were equals and offered no such challenges. One patrilineal relationship was very close and supportive. Fathers paired specific sons with specific daughters to form cooperative units. The daughter was expected to care for her brother while he remained unmarried, and the son was to protect and represent this sister. When she married, her bridewealth passed to him, but he was expected to retain it, in part, for her future needs.

Parents arranged first marriages. A preferred marriage was with a cousin, but this was not regularly followed. A man was allowed to have more than one wife at a time, but each wife had to have her own compound. Either partner could seek divorce, and divorced women returned to their parents' compounds until they remarried. Young children stayed with their mothers but returned to their father's compound where they were members when they become older.

Living arrangements were somewhat like those described for the Navajo. Each nuclear family had its own house for sleeping and personal possessions, but most activities took place in an open public area. Beyond the senior couple, other structures housed older children, married sons, and other connected relatives. Each woman had a field nearby to tend, and there were granaries to store the crops.

Like many other African societies, age was an important factor in an individual's identity. The Tswana had an age-set system, which meant that people of similar age identified and worked together. At one time the men's sets formed fighting units. (Schapera and Comaroff 1991: 33) Every four to seven years, a new named set would be open, and all young men and women in their late teens would be initiated together with the others of their gender. These sets lasted throughout the members' lives, and people strongly identified with their sets. Members of a set were expected to show respect to members of senior sets. Age was important in all social relationships and senior members of a family had authority over younger members. The senior son of the senior wife was the heir to a compound.

The political organization, then, was somewhat formal. The senior man of a compound was its leader. Wards, groups of compounds related patrilineally and living nearby, were under the authority of a hereditary headman. Wards also had courts of highly ranked senior men who heard disputes. Seniority and rank structured individual status. None of the persons in these categories were guaranteed to remain there. Rank included wealth, and this was largely calculated in cattle. The chief's herd was the largest, and he expanded his herd through fines and other prerogatives. Chiefs, and other wealthy men, established obligations with others by loans to independent men, who owed general support, and dependent men, who were reduced to service. Inequality between men of wealth and poverty was clearly drawn. Women, other than using their rank over lower ranked women, had little say in the exercise of political power. Men represented their interests in public, and they remained legal minors regardless of their age.

Cosmology   While the Tswana believed in a powerful creator deity, this being was not important to their daily lives. Much more crucial were the ancestral spirits that remained with their living descendents and brought good or evil. Men of the patrilineal were buried in their cattle areas, and their spirits were honored with sacrifices to ensure their goodwill. Correct behavior was also needed because the spirits defended the honor of the family. Women were buried in grain-processing areas, and their spirits became part of a communal ancestral force. (Schapera and Comaroff 1991: 43)

Chiefs and family heads had special responsibilities to appease the spirits and ensure the communities' well-being. They were responsible for the proper prayers and sacrifices from the community herds. They also employed, when needed, specialists such as the rainmaker to ensure weather conditions for successful harvests and herding. Other specialists used their supernatural knowledge for good or evil. Some men, and, occasionally, women would use this knowledge to heal or divine the causes of diseases or other mysterious hardships. Individuals paid these specialists for their help. On the other hand, either male or female sorcerers used this knowledge to bring death or misfortune to others. Wives punished their husbands and men attacked their rivals using supernatural power.

Gender concepts among the Tswana were quite different than those of the Navajo previously described. While both tended crops and raised animals, among the Tswana the animals alone conferred prestige, and men controlled the animals. The association of men with animals supported the social valuing of men over women. Further, the Tswana had formal political and social organizations that were headed by men. Women were not fully devalued among the Tswana, but in many ways they were perceived to be less valuable than the men.

SUMMARY

The societies that can be placed in the categories of horticultural, simple agricultural, or pastoral appear on the face to be very different. Indeed, as the cases illustrate, they were. The place of gender in these societies and the roles of men and women differ dramatically from one case to the other. In some the roles women played could be significant and individual women powerful, while in others the roles of women were defined as subordinate to those of men, making it rare for an individual woman to wield power.

Despite these differences, certain social characteristics both define the category and emerge as significant for gender differentiation within it. The nature of the economy, of course, is most apparent. The emphasis placed on those aspects of the economy that were designated as male or female often reflected the importance allocated to members of those categories. Likewise, the nature of the unilineal kinship groups and the residence patterns that were practiced had immense importance to the daily lives of men and women in these societies. Cosmology, too, played a role in the secular conceptualization of gender, with some societies—otherwise male dominated—defining a value for women in the more abstract, supernatural world. Finally, the ideological importance of war, raiding, and daily violence in these cultures influenced the concepts of gender, with women frequently, but not always, devalued in societies with strong warrior traditions.

Tribes offer a categorization of society in which the variation of gender roles and conceptualizations can be studied and compared. As the title of this chapter suggests, the seeds of inequality have clearly been planted, but not all have sprouted.

Readings

Bilharz, Joy. "First Among Equals: The Changing Status of Seneca Women." In *Women and Power in Native North America*, eds. Laura F. Klein and Lillian A. Ackerman. Norman, OK: University of Oklahoma Press, 1995, pp. 101–12.

Chagnon, Napoleon A. *Yanomamo: The Fierce People*. New York: Holt, Rinehart and Winston, 1968.

Comaroff, Jean, and John L. Comaroff. "How Beasts Lost Their Legs: Cattle in Tswana Economy and Society." In *Herders, Warriors, and Traders: Pastoralism in Africa*, eds. John G. Galaty and Pierre Bonte. San Francisco: Westview Press, 1991, pp. 33–61.

Hamamsy, Laila S. "Role of Women in a Changing Navaho Society." *American Anthropologist* 59 (1957), pp. 101–11.

Herdt, Gilbert. *The Sambia: Ritual and Gender in New Guinea.* New York: Holt, Rinehart and Winston, 1987.

Lepowsky, Maria. "Gender in an Egalitarian Society: A Case Study from the Coral Sea." In *Beyond the Second Sex: New Directions in the Anthropology of Gender,* eds. Peggy Sanday and Ruth Goodenough. Philadelphia: University of Pennsylvania Press, 1990, pp. 171–223.

————. *Fruit of the Motherland: Gender in an Egalitarian Society.* New York: Colombia University Press, 1993.

Mead, Margaret. *Sex and Temperament in Three Primitive Societies.* New York: William Morrow, 1935.

Morgan, Lewis Henry. *League of the Iroquois.* New York: Corinth Books, 1962.

Ramos, Alcida Rita. *Sanuma Memories: Yanomami Ethnography in Times of Crisis.* Madison, WI: University of Wisconsin Press, 1995.

Schapera, I., and John L. Comaroff. *The Tswana,* rev. ed. New York: Kegan Paul International, 1991.

Shepardson, Mary. "The Gender Status of Navajo Women." In *Women and Power in Native North America,* eds. Laura F. Klein and Lillian A. Ackerman. Norman, OK: University of Oklahoma Press, 1995, pp. 159–76.

CHAPTER FIVE

Inherent Gender Inequality?
Stratified Societies

Is social hierarchy necessary?
Do all stratified societies subordinate women?
What role does rank play in the lives of women?
Is a general ideology of inequality the key to gender inequalities?

In this chapter we explore gender in societies whose political structures are based on theories of inequality of power and authority. While bands and simple tribes may have some individuals who are held in higher esteem than others and some families who have better fields or larger herds, neither system values, or establishes, a rigid system of inequality between people. Advanced tribes, chiefdoms, or kingdoms, however, have economies that promote unequal ownership of the means of production or produce surplus wealth that is unevenly distributed. Here, then, the question of equality or inequality is inherent *in* the system. Inequality, if not intrinsically seen as good, is accepted and acceptable. Many scholars have asserted that with this focus on hierarchy, women should be expected to be classified as inferior as a class. While many of these societies do depreciate the status of women as a group, in fact, the issues of gender can be central or peripheral to the ideology of inequality in these societies.

THE NATURE OF SOCIAL INEQUALITIES

Morton Fried, a pioneer in mid-twentieth-century cultural evolutionary theory, defined a stratified society as "one in which individuals of the same sex and equivalent age status do not have equal access to the basic resources that sustain life." (1967: 186) Two people of a similar age, then, may have very different life prospects. Fried believed that gender and age would be significant variables even in societies otherwise more egalitarian. There is certainly room for disagreement in this, but clearly in stratified societies inequality is the rule rather than the exception.

In any consideration of social hierarchies there are basic concepts that must be considered and understood to establish a common vocabulary. These terms are used in considering all forms of societies, but they become especially important in understanding stratified societies.

Types of Wealth

The concept of *wealth* itself makes sense only where there is differential access to valuable resources. In a band society, for example, where people share their resources, the idea of wealth or poverty does not make sense. Wealth, by definition, is inherently relative. In many tribal societies there are people or kin groups who have better lands for horticulture or larger herds, and they appear wealthier than do others. Wealth, in itself, need not be especially significant in other aspects of society, however.

The most significant type of wealth, especially important in the theories of Marxist anthropologists, is ownership of modes of production. Simply, this refers to the ownership of means of the production of crucial materials. Ownership of lands that produce crops, herds that produce future animals, and factories that produce essential goods confer special status. These people can restrict access to vital goods or provide jobs and goods necessary for survival. In other words, those who own these types of wealth hold others in positions of dependency. This form of wealth is embedded in a hierarchical structure.

Other forms of wealth may confer no such power but may confer, or be a badge of, prestige. For example, the ownership of a massive diamond worn in a necklace in the United States marks the wearer as rich and socially significant. It indicates that this person, or someone she is dependent on, has enough disposable wealth to use some of it in a conspicuously nonproductive way. Less wealthy people may be impressed by the display, but they will not become dependent on the owner because of it. The ownership of the necklace does not affect other people's lives like the ownership of a business might. However, in some other societies, for example, the Tlingit described later, this form of prestige ownership has far more social repercussions.

Ascribed and Achieved Status

Social position, or *status*, is an important concept in ranked societies. Who people are is defined, in part, by the social categories in which their society places them. Each person has a large number of such designations. A person can be a woman, a daughter, an accountant, a senator, a grandmother, and a student. Each of these categories defines a set of expected behaviors or roles. Balancing the roles that the status categories mandate is part of life. Social statuses change over time through both the efforts of the individual and circumstances well beyond his or her control. Social scientists tend to differentiate two types of status: *ascribed* and *achieved*.

Gender is largely an ascribed status. It is determined for most people at birth. These are the social categories a person is born to. The kinship categories of son or daughter, brother or sister, for examples, are ascribed. Male or female is also generally an ascribed status. Political positions such as king or chief are also frequently ascribed. At his birth, Prince Charles of England was assumed to be a future King of England. This was based on the identity of his mother, his gender, and his seniority among male siblings, not on his achievements. Other systems might have selected the last born or disregarded gender in this determination. In all such systems, truly inappropriate behavior by the chosen individual may force his or her removal from the birthright, but even minimally competent and moral individuals are destined to hold their predetermined status.

Achieved status is based on individual behavior, but gender can significantly set boundaries on what an individual can achieve. As the term suggests, an achieved status is one that a person has earned. This does not have to mean that all individuals in a society are able to reach this position. There may be some degree of ascription build in. For example, the category President of the United States is an achieved status, but not all people are realistically able to compete for that status. Using history for its clarity, it is obvious that in the period of the election of Abraham Lincoln, no woman, slave, non-Christian, Native American, or the like could become president. President, then, is an achieved status, but some people, regardless of their actions, cannot achieve it.

Classes and Ranks

One final set of concepts must be considered. Anthropologists tend to differentiate between social stratification based on *rank* and that based on *class*. In the former, every individual's social standing is unique, while in the latter social standing is divided into a limited number of categories. The role of gender in the conceptualization of such systems can be quite complex. While it is always artificial to construct absolute categories of women, or of men, in any society, in stratified societies rank always modifies any such conceptualization. A high-ranked woman is different in kind and in prospects than a low-ranked woman, and the same holds true for men.

In a ranked society, all people are categorized as superior or inferior to every other person. For example, a high-ranked elder in a Tlingit community explained to me, "I can line up everyone in town on the beach from the most highly ranked to the lowest and every elder can do the same." She did not talk about groups of people but about individuals. Everyone is ranked and that rank was very important to every facet of life in the Tlingit world of the nineteenth century. Even today, this remains important. While there is a term that translates to "rich person," the strategy for an individual Tlingit man or woman was to move toward the front of the line on the beach, not to enter a category. The role of gender in strategies for movement in rank varies significantly from society to society.

In many other societies these categories, or classes, are more important. Here categories such as "nobles" may be differentiated from "commoners" and perhaps even "slaves." Being a member of that category colors the prospects of an individual's life. States, discussed in Chapter 6, are
stratified in this manner, but even societies with less rigorous political
determinants might use this concept of hierarchy. A person's initial class
standing tends to be ascribed, but men and women, often using diverse
strategies, attempt to rise in the class system through their own actions.
Class systems vary widely in their openness to movement between classes.
In some, individuals may move up and down the class system based on
their own accomplishments or failures; in others, this is very difficult. The
rare cases in which class position is expected to be lifelong are referred to
as caste systems.   *Even caste can be strategically subverted*

GENDER IN STRATIFIED SOCIETY: RICH WOMAN, POOR WOMAN

Economic Divisions of Labor

Women born into stratified societies live in communities with substantial
populations and relatively secure economies. Moreover, they enjoy
economies that allow for surplus. In the economic designations of gender
roles, stratified societies tend to resemble tribes. Generally, women and
men are assigned distinct employment in the economy. Often women are
farmers and men tend the herds, but this need not be true. In many societies men do the farming. In fact, in some rare cases, like that of the
Northwest Coast of North America, the environment allowed for surplus
and stability from wild resources without an agricultural base. All these
economies include men's tasks and women's tasks, which typically com-
plement each other.

While at a high level of abstraction it seems reasonable to discuss
men's work and women's work, it is in the nature of stratified societies to
make such generalizations dangerous. Clearly the work of elite women
and that of poor women are very different in these societies, and the same
is true of wealthy and poor men. In many ways, the lives and work of elite
women resemble those of elite men more closely than those of lower
ranked women. The work of laborers, servants, and slaves has little resemblance to that of their social superiors. Likewise, the remuneration of each
type of work is even more dramatically different.

*Focusing on gender inequality can distract our attention away
from other kinds of inequality*

Concepts of Wealth

As indicated earlier, wealth is a key concept that rivals gender in separating
people in stratified societies. People with great wealth, both male and
female, are literally worth more than those of more modest means. The

case of the Tlingit, discussed later in the chapter, will show how literally this can be true. The social status of wealthier women allows them to live more comfortably than their poorer neighbors and have social privileges that they do not share. Who a person marries, where a person lives, how hard a person works, who orders whom, and what punishment comes with crimes often are determined by issues of wealth and its associated rank.

In many of these societies, wealth and social status are literally worn by individuals. Like the diamond necklace mentioned earlier, special clothing or jewelry often makes the status of an individual apparent to all. Some items such as the tapa cloth of the Hawaiians or the Chilkat blanket of the Tlingit could be worn only by those men and women of the highest ranks. Lower ranked people risked punishment, even death, if they attempted to wear these clothes. In some societies the body, itself, was modified to permanently publicize high rank. Tattoos were commonly used in this fashion. In southern parts of the Northwest Coast, high-ranking babies had their heads molded to form an elongated shape, while to the north the most highly ranked women were allowed to wear large labrets in their lips. Foreigners who came to these societies were often repelled by these traditions, but, to the people who wore them, they proudly proclaimed their superiority over others.

Kinship

In stratified societies, as in tribal and foraging societies, kinsmen and women gain their prestige and power from their positions in powerful clans. In these societies kinship is the central organizing principle. Like tribes, most stratified societies have unilineal kinship systems divided into clan units. Also, these clans may well be considered corporate entities and the real owners of lands, herds, or other valuables.

What sets the clans of these societies apart from most similar organizations in tribes is that clans, here, are commonly ranked relative to one another. In other words, some clans are inherently higher in status than others, and the men and women of those clans are consequently higher in status than people from other clans. These ascribed statuses form the hierarchical structure of the society. Wealth is inherited in this fashion, as are positions of leadership. Often potential marriage partners are determined according to clan alliances and statuses. A woman's membership in her clan situates her life status and opportunities.

In kingdoms, such as those of the Swazi and Hawaiians described later in the chapter, the clans that the kings or queens belonged to were considered to be royal. Other clans of high stature were valued as the clans of royal spouses. These clans of kings and queens made up the elite segment of the culture. The clansmen and women of these units were allowed special privileges and lived comfortable lives. The more distant a clan was from a relationship with a royal clan, the less important was that clan and its members. In other stratified societies, such as the Tlingit, the clans themselves were stratified, with some clansmen and women more highly ranked than their less fortunate cousins. Within the clan, then, some were more important than others. The clans were still ranked against one another, but the high members of one clan were considered equal in rank to the middle members of a higher ranked clan. Marriage, then, was based on individual rank. A high-ranked woman of one clan married her equal, who could have been a low-ranked member of a more important clan. Kinship, then, does not promote equality in stratified societies. In fact, it helps to define inequality.

As in all societies, the relationships of brother and sister, father and daughter, and mother and son are very important. There is an added element to these relationships in hierarchical societies. The behavior of a close kinswoman reflects on the status of her kinsmen. While the behavior of the men is also important, it is frequently the women who are held to higher standards. This can mean that women are carefully limited in their public behavior, or it can mean that women are free to further the fortunes of themselves and their relatives. A woman of high rank, like her male counterpart, is an important member of her society, while a low-ranked woman, like her brothers, is treated as being of little consequence.

Political and Military Control

As might be expected, political power and authority is largely based on rank in these cultures. The highest ranked individual in a clan, male or female depending on the culture, would typically be the clan head or chief. In communities with households from different clans, often the chief of the highest ranked clan is the village chief. The patterns of district and regional chiefdoms follow the same pattern. In kingdoms, the same hierarchical pattern would end with a ruling monarch who was the highest ranked person in the society. The family of the monarch shares in the status and privileges. In most cultures these chiefs and kings are expected to be male. There are exceptions, of course. A few cultures, such as the Lovedu of southern Africa, mandated that their monarch be a woman. (LeBeuf 1971: 97) The Lovedu queen was thought to have a supernatural ability to ensure the rain that brought prosperity to the people. Not only the queen but also the high-ranked women of all the districts of the society held powerful leadership positions. More common are societies with dual monarchs, such as the Swazi described later. In these both a royal man and a royal woman, typically close kin, rule together. In some situations each has a special area of power, but in others each had similar powers. These dual monarchies were most common in Africa but were also found in other parts of the world.

War, or at least frequent raiding, is common in these societies. Regular militaries have been established in the most complex stratified societies. This means that the military becomes a supported specialization and acts as a protection from outside aggression and a support for the people in power. The military is almost always a domain for men and affords men an area of immense power, if not always authority. Rarely are women involved in these groups. Famous stories of the royal guard of the king of Dahomey (now Benin), which was composed of women, is often said to be the origin of the legend of the Amazon warriors. True or not, it is clear that in societies with extensive organized warrior groups, the warriors are given an elevated rank.

Cosmology

The religious systems of stratified society share many characteristics with those of tribes, and even bands. The relationships of individuals to the supernatural realm are generally intimate and personal. Individual spirits, personal connections, and shamanic healers still tend to be important for human physical and spiritual well-being. At this level there is little change. At the more abstract levels of the cosmologies, however, there is considerable variation in stratified societies.

In some stratified societies, however, the image of the supernatural is also stratified. In other words, there are levels of deities and alliances of important deities that reflect the secular realities of the culture. Often the ancestors of high-ranked people or clans are classified as powerful spiritual beings who are evoked for clan welfare. Overall, at this level, the supernatural is seen as supporting the social structure. At one extreme, the high-ranking individuals themselves are seen as divine, or at least as having divine aspects. The royal incest of many of the early kingdoms was justified on the basis that only a deity could marry a deity and have divine offspring. As this suggests, both male and female elite would share in this supernatural power. Another such case is that of the Hawaiians. In that society the supernatural power of the rulers was so powerful that a commoner would die when exposed to it. Not all stratified societies, however, have this connection between supernatural power and high rank. In the Tlingit case, the religious specialist often was not of high rank but could earn enough wealth through his or her curing to become rich and, therefore, comfortable in this society. The place of gender in the supernatural realm, in all these cases, seems to reflect the understanding of gender in the secular society.

CASES OF STRATIFIED SOCIETIES

The cultures clustered under this label share many similarities when it comes to the issue of inequality. They also have many characteristics found in the more complex agricultural and pastoral societies discussed in Chapter 4. The differences between stratified societies and tribes are a matter of degree rather than kind. The differences between stratified societies and states (the next classification) are more fundamental. Many scholars see stratified societies as transitory. Many of these societies historically became even more stratified; some then became states, others became more egalitarian, while many others were enfolded into colonial states.

Given the unusual fluidity of the definition of these societies, this chapter is briefer than the others, and the descriptions of the institutions of the cultures emphasize their differences from tribes. One, the Tlingit, exemplifies a highly stratified Native American culture with powerful elites. The other two, the Swazi and Hawaiians, were kingdoms with more defined political offices. In all three of these cases, women played a prominent role in the society. While other cases could have demonstrated more limited roles for women, the cases presented are in no way unusual or rare. Each demonstrates a different understanding of gender and the power of men and women. Each, also, shows the differences between the lives of women of different statuses and ranks in these highly complex societies.

The Tlingit of the Northwest Coast

The Tlingit are the northernmost of the so-called Northwest Coast Indians. I began my studies of the Tlingit in the early 1970s and have been involved with this culture ever since. My research, both archival and ethnographic, revealed a world where women, like men, were valued according to their individual skills and their social ranking. Much of the description here is drawn from my studies of Tlingit society as it functioned before the time of heavy colonization, which began about 1880. (Klein 1980, 1995)

The Tlingit shared with their neighbors an almost unique environment and economy. This region, with its many islands, was a temperate, evergreen rain forest backed by high mountains. Its many streams have been the breeding grounds of all five species of Pacific salmon. By tradition, salmon and wood have always been the core resources of this region. Wood was the major building material for houses, tools, and much artwork. Salmon, and other fish, were the major foods and a resource for producing wealth and prestige. It is a common claim that the people of the Northwest Coast of North America were the wealthiest preindustrial people in the world.

Economics   What made the salmon industry, before the depletion of modern times, unique was the nature of the cycle of the salmon. Salmon return to the streams of their birth to spawn on a known schedule, which means that fishers knew when and where the resource would be well in advance. Collecting salmon, then, was in many ways like harvesting a crop. In the past, fishers were able to collect enough salmon in three or four months to feed a family for the year plus provide considerable surplus for feasting and trading. Hunting of deer, gathering of eggs, harvesting land and sea plants filled out the diet. The sexual division of labor in

A high ranked Tlingit woman dressed
for a celebration, 1906.

fishing was different than might be assumed. While men did the fishing,
that is, taking the fish out of the water, women immediately processed the
fish into a year-round resource. Fish, unlike grains, were very perishable
and spoiled quickly without processing. To become the valuable resource
they were on this coast, they had to be quickly dried, smoked, and packed
away. Only in this form could they be used months later. It was the combined labors of men and women that allowed salmon to be the staple
resource they were on the Northwest Coast.

Even a large quantity of smoked salmon did not make a person
wealthy, however. This was especially true in a region where everyone was
able to collect salmon. The economic operation that began the development of wealth was trade. The Tlingit traded with Inuit to the north, other
coastal peoples to the south (California), and Native peoples inland on the
other side of the mountains. In this trade, resources such as dentalia
shells, specific furs, and mountain goat horns that were not universally
available and specialized art and prestige pieces such as Chilkat blankets
and fine carvings were important components. The goal of this trade was
not subsistence items, which were plentiful, but items of value, luxuries.
In this long-distance trade, more men than women made the journeys, but
it was commonly necessary for at least one woman to accompany the
men. This was because it was women who were trained for negotiation. As
an elder woman cheerfully explained, "Men are foolish with money."
(Klein 1980: 93) This was not innate but training. Part of a woman's
puberty education at the time was trade and negotiation. (Klein 1995: 35)
Women set the prices for their husband's or brother's goods as well as
their own.

Having many luxury goods did not make the Tlingit wealthy, either. Wealth was calculated not by what one had but by what one gave away. Community feasts, called potlatches, were the occasions for these transactions. Europeans mistakenly thought that these were religious rites, but, in fact, they were formal performances of social relationships. Potlatches were commonly sponsored by a clan or a section of a clan, and people from specific other clans were invited. In the potlatch the guests were feasted and given gifts while they witnessed the generosity and importance of their hosts. Men and women dressed in regalia that reflected their rank and clan emblems. Significant robes, including the Chilkat blanket, were exceedingly expensive and people who wore them thereby flaunted their wealth and rank. Members of the host group assumed new and more prestigious names and gained higher social positions. The more that was given away, the wealthier the giver was considered. Guests, further, had their social status confirmed by the relative value of the gifts they received. Potlatches publicly confirmed current status and provided witness to changes in status. While potlatches were commonly, but not uniformly, hosted in the name of a male clan chief, women in all cases gave wealth, got wealth, and received honors along with men. Important women, like important men, received and gave more than their poorer relatives.

Social and Political Organization   Tlingit society was matrilineal, with clan membership and inheritance going from mother and mother's brother to mother's children. Marriages, especially of high-ranking individuals, were arranged by relatives with rules that asserted that these people should marry individuals of equal status outside of their kin groups and ideally a person in their father's kin group. This so-called royal marriage (Klein 1995: 40) led to a residential group that included men of the same clan with wives and children who were clanmates to one another. What is clear is that rank was important to both men and women and was calculated in the same manner. A husband and wife should be equals. As this implies, there were men of higher rank than women and women who outranked men.

Tlingit lived in large multifamily wooden houses before Europeans came to Alaska. Each nuclear family had its own area for sleeping and storage. Contemporary Tlingits explain that it was similar to an apartment building. The position of the family's area in the house was based on rank with more and less favorable areas. The slaves slept near the door. Small children lived with their parents. When a boy neared puberty, he went to live with his mother's brother in the house of his own clan. A girl remained with her parents until puberty when she would be isolated with other girls her age and be trained in the skills needed by a woman of her position. When she emerged, she was marriageable and soon moved to the house of her husband. In the case of the royal marriage, that house might well be the house she grew up in.

Political organization was invested in the kinship system. The highest ranking man in each kin unit was seen as the head of that unit. He had little actual power over others but had the authority and prestige of his rank, and others were expected to heed his advice. Likewise, his sisters had the same importance of rank. The highest ranking man of the highest ranking kinship group in a town was considered the representative of the town to outsiders. In most things, however, kinship groups acted together in raids and trade groups. In these, individual rank was the base of superiority or inferiority. Disputes between kin groups were also resolved by rank. If an individual from one clan killed or insulted a member of a second, punishment was firmly based on the relative rankings of the victim and the perpetrator. For example, in a murder dispute, if the murderer were significantly higher in rank than the victim, an exchange of wealth would resolve the dispute. If the victim were higher in rank than the murderer, even the life of the murderer could not solve the problem, because the life of the murderer was not equal to the life of the victim. In this case, a member of the kin group of the murderer, who was equal in rank to the victim, was expected to give up his or her life to pay the debt.

It should be clear that ranking affected every aspect of a person's life. The higher the rank, the more severe was the responsibility and the more elegant the lifestyle. Tlingit women, like men, were players in this system and played by the same rules. Gender was not insignificant to the lives of these people, but social rank was more significant. Prestige, authority, and power were vested in the higher ranked regardless of gender.

Cosmology   Tlingit religious beliefs before Christianity became the major faith were quite individual. There were few group rituals, and they centered on the first fish and resources of the year. The major deities of the universe took little interest in the daily lives of people. Raven, the creator of people, was known through myriad morality tales but was not called on for help. Young people were expected to seek guardian spirit helpers to guide them throughout their lives. Some, who became shamans, sought more and more powerful spiritual helpers and became apprentices to existing shamans.

Shamans were called on to heal illness using supernatural help. Most serious illness was seen as the product of witchcraft. Men and women who practiced witchcraft attacked their enemies using supernatural means. Shamans treated their patients by detecting the identity of the witch and using spirits to fight with the witch in a supernatural realm. Shamans built their reputations through the successful treatment of high-ranked patients. Important shamans became quite wealthy. A highly ranked parent paid a successful shaman extremely well. The payment was taken as an indication of the worth of the child. Rather than paying as little as possible as capitalism would mandate, this system supported paying as much as possible. Shamans were not normally high-ranking people, but this wealth could improve their status. Witches, on the other hand, disgraced their families and discovery would hurt the rank of both the witch and his or her relatives. Both men and women became witches and shamans.

Ranking was obviously the central social issue for Tlingit life. What is especially interesting about this system is how gender was not built into it as a criterion for ranking. Quite the opposite, the system mandated that there must be women and men at every level of rank. Furthermore, the rules for increasing or losing rank were centered in individuals, and these rules were the same for men and women. A woman could trade and become richer and concretize this in a potlatch just like men did. An immoral woman could lessen the rankings of her relatives just like a man could. Men and women were not the same, but they were not differentially ranked in this rank-conscious society.

The Swazi of South Africa

The Swazi, studied by anthropologist Hilda Kuper (1963) since the 1930s, were farmers and cattle ranchers living in a semi-autonomous region encapsulated within European South Africa. As a dual monarchy headed by a king and queen mother, they represented a type of centralized chiefdom that could be found many places in Africa. Here, the most highly ranked chiefly role designations were king and queen rather than chief, as they were in some other stratified cultures, but the underlying logic of the system was the same. Kinship and social ranking defined a person's life.

Economics Swaziland was a well-watered country that allowed for rich farms and larger herds for wealthy Swazi. Poorer Swazi, however, lived at a more precarious level and faced regular shortages. The major grain crops of rich and poor were millet and maize, but household fields also included a variety of other crops including sugar cane, groundnuts, and squashes. Both men and women were active in farming. Men helped prepare the larger fields, and both worked in the fields during the intensive summer periods. In the fall both worked with the harvest, and in the winter both worked to prepare and store the crops. Farming, however, was seen as primarily a woman's occupation and not highly valued. Chiefs allocated farmlands to their dependents, and women used lands obtained through their marriages.

Chiefs called on the labor of dependent peoples. The higher status chiefs maintained farms in areas throughout their control and expected local, and lesser, chiefs to ensure their production. They also called on groups of young men from age groups under their command to work their fields. Lower chiefs likewise used the labor of individuals and groups who were dependent on them. The higher ranked Swazi, then, called on the wealth and security of many fields, in different localities, that were tended by others. The poorest could only hope that their own hard work was complemented by good weather and produced enough for their families' needs.

More highly prized than crops were the cattle. Men had the exclusive care of cattle, and women were forbidden to handle the stock. Cattle provided meat and milk. However, few cattle were butchered solely for meat, and milk was primarily children's food. Most importantly, cattle defined wealth and social importance among the Swazi. Cattle were necessary for marriage exchanges, supernatural rituals, and maintenance of alliances. Poor Swazi, before the beginning of wage labor, could get cattle only from wealthier men through gifts for services provided or through loans. On the other hand, the royal herd of Kuper's early studies numbered about 3,000 head. (1963: 44) This included one herd that was maintained for ritual purposes.

Division of labor by sex and age was significant, but both were modified by the factor of rank. High-ranked individuals were "responsible for providing suitable conditions of the success of the efforts of others rather than their own labor." (Kuper 1963: 45) However, everyone was subject to the commands of their superiors, and even the highest ranked had obligations to economic labor. Both men and women organized work parties to complete large-scale tasks and enhance the status of the organizer (who provided food and beer for the workers). While rich and poor ate similar foods and lived in similar houses, the differences between those of high rank and low were apparent in human relationships.

Social and Political Organization   The primary organization principle of Swazi society was kinship. Patrilineally determined, ranked clans formed the backbone of the system. All Swazi were born into their father's clan with its attached ranking. Kuper described five levels of clan ranked according to their distance from the king, ranging from the top clan, which included the king, to those clans who provided queen mothers, to those of local chiefs, to those who had no special social or ritual status.

Marriages were arranged between people of appropriate rank and clan. Only the king could marry within his own clan, and then, none of these wives could become queen mother. Marriages and, more importantly, the right to children were defined through a bride price that was given to the family of the women by that of the man. High-status Swazi men were polygynous, and the king married women from throughout the realm. Kuper reported that during her study, the king had 40 wives by the time he was 35. (1963: 19) Each wife could become queen and bring enormous political power to her people, which then formed alliances and loyalties crucial to the maintenance of the kingdom. It also involved expenses in bride wealth and maintenance of these women and their children that only a king with his royal prerogatives was able to afford.

Husbands had authority over their wives and were the heads of the households. Women had the right to proper treatment, however, and were allowed to return to their own family for support when needed. Fathers and sons were generally not close. Only the oldest son, who could not replace his father, was treated as an ally. In a large household all other sons could potentially inherit their father's position, and the identity of this heir was not announced until after the father's death. On the other hand, the relationship between a mother and her sons was very close. Their alliance was lifelong, and each gained from the success of the other. Daughters, who emotionally were close to their mothers, lived most of their lives far from their parents, but their relationships with their brothers were very important. It is the bridewealth of the sisters that went toward the bridewealth given by their brothers. As adults, these sisters were honored guests in their brothers' homesteads.

Households were composed of a headman, his wives and unmarried children, his married sons and their families, and other dependent relatives. The larger the household, the higher was the prestige of the headman. Each homestead was physically built around a central cattle byre. The main residence, the "great hut," was the domain of the mother of the headman and was the shrine of the family. Wives had to show respect near this hut and were never allowed to enter it. Their daughters, like sons, as members of the clan used it freely. Each wife in a wealthy family had her own hut as well as fields and cattle. She and her children formed a semi-independent economic unit, which she controlled. In a conservative household, the husband slept an equal number of nights in each wife's hut and used his mother's hut as his base of operations. The king and other wealthy chiefs maintained separate homesteads for different wives. This expanded the use of lands and established the physical presence of politically significant chiefs.

The king maintained his principal homestead at the capital. Here the great hut was a spectacular structure where the king and queen mother performed rites that were significant for the entire society. The king's wives shared a common area in the capital homestead. Most residents in this homestead were not family, however. Officials, dependents, and a barracks of guards lived in huts in this homestead where they served the royal family.

The political organization of the Swazi was part of this kinship and ranking pattern. Higher ranked chiefs had authority over lower chiefs and commoners. The royal family had primary authority. What set the Swazi system apart from many other chiefdoms was the dual monarchy. Here, in addition to the king, the queen mother was an important political player; as a pair they represented the ultimate authority. Both were treated with extreme deference, and they appeared in public in elaborate royal regalia that reflected their positions. The king owed his position to his mother. The next queen mother was chosen by the current queen mother according to the position of her clan and her own personality. The current queen mother trained her, and she was not allowed to have other children after she was chosen. When her son rose to the position of king, she took on the role of queen mother. These two people were the heads of all political and religious matters, but they delegated much of the daily running of the kingdom to lesser chiefs and other officials, who were often of the royal clan. Disputes, for example, were heard in the courts of the most appropriate chief/mother based on the position of the litigants and the severity of the disputes. The sisters and daughters of the king did not have chiefly roles but were married to chiefs and became head wives in those chiefdoms.

Cosmology Ancestors played a key role in the Swazi understanding of the supernatural. A spirit world reflected the social realities of the natural world. Male and female ancestors monitored the world of the living and punished clan members who misbehaved through omens and nonfatal illnesses. The head of the family was obliged to petition the ancestors and ensured their goodwill. A woman, although living far from her natal household, maintained her relationship with her paternal ancestors, and they scrutinized her life as well. The ancestors of the king had national importance. A yearly ritual with cattle sacrifice was held in their honor.

The royal family had a special responsibility to the nation through its ability to bring rain. It was believed that only through regular and highly secret rituals performed by the king and queen mother would the climate allow the right amount of rain for abundant harvests and herds. Misbehavior by subjects, or the royal family, worked against the blessings of good weather, and only the king and queen mother were able to counter this.

There were two types of positive ritual specialists among the Swazi: medicine men and diviners. The first, who were rarely women, use physical medicines and rituals to cure ailments and disorders. Some families had special knowledge of such cures, and their designated curers were especially valued. The entire homestead supported the cures and took part in the rituals. Diviners, who were respected for their power, used spirit possession to diagnosis the causes of problems. They were possessed and called to this occupation. Diviners were also trained for their jobs and were viewed as not quite normal. Many women became important diviners after being selected by an ancestral spirit.

Sorcerers and witches were the evil side of supernatural practitioners. Witches, who inherited their potential for witchcraft from their mothers, also had to train and be prepared in order to be effective. Sorcerers used poisons and violence to bring death or disaster to their victims. Jealousy and hatred were seen as primary motivations for witchcraft, and suspects, therefore, came from relatives and neighbors. Both men and women were suspected of such behavior and both were victims.

It can easily be said that the general trend in Swazi society was that men had authority over women. It is equally clear that social rank was a clear mitigator in this. All men (except the king) were expected to kneel before the queen mother and accept her dominance over them. At lower levels a poor man was not superior to a chief's mother in any real way. Even at the top, the relations between the king and queen mother, between chiefs and their mothers, and between headmen and their mothers were seen as balancing one another. Using the category "women" as a way to explain Swazi life would be more confusing than enlightening. Gender was an important factor in daily life and in societal authority among these people, but it was a factor highly integrated with other factors, especially social ranking.

The Hawaiians of the Pacific

Popular culture presents the Hawaiians before European contact as happy and simple people who wore feathers, danced hulas, worshiped exotic gods, and lived in an earthly paradise. The reality of Hawaiians of this period was, of course, far more complex. Their system was an elaborate chiefdom with dramatic differences in rank that were supported by religious sanctions. The direction of the lives of both women and men was determined at birth, and the lives of the chiefs differed significantly from those of commoners. Anthropologist Jocelyn Linnekin (1990), using ethnohistorical methods, investigated the roles of men and women of this period and the changes in gender that came later. She described a culture in which ranking was more significant than gender but where gender appreciably colored life experiences. It was also a culture where women were strongly limited by sacred rules but often important in secular realms.

Economics   Agriculture formed the subsistence base of Hawaiian society. Taro was the major prestige crop with sweet potatoes, bananas, yams, bread food and other plants also cultivated. Fish and gathered foods also added to the diet. Unlike many of the other cultures reviewed, farming here was men's work. While there is disagreement about how much field work women may have done, it appears clear that agriculture and the products, especially taro, were associated with men. Besides domestic food, agricultural goods were exchanged and passed in tribute to chiefly families. As Linnekin noted, "the commoners fed the chiefs" through these tributes. (1990: 78)

Women's primary economic focus was on the making of mats and tapa cloth. These products had great social and economic significance. Common mats and tapa cloth were used for bedding and clothing, but the finest products were displayed by chiefs, who would adorn their homes and dress in a manner that announced their importance. High-quality mats and tapa cloth were also exchanged, and chiefs demanded important tribute items. Even the statues representing deities were wrapped in fine tapa cloth. If the men's production fed the chiefs, that of the women clothed and comforted them. In Linnekin's estimation, "the products of men and women were equally valued" and each had the right to distribute his or her own items. (1990: 46, 55)

The people toiling in the fields, weaving mats, and beating cloth were not chiefs. Chiefs were the overlords; they owned the land. In fact, only the highest chiefs owned land. Lesser chiefs had rights over lands that were granted to them by the higher chiefs. They, in turn, would grant use rights to their retainers. The commoners working in taro fields were there at the will of men and women more highly ranked than themselves. More importantly, these individuals were able to rescind this permission and move the commoners off. Also, some lands were designated as chiefly fields, and the foods grown there belonged to the chiefs. In fact, their chiefs would not normally throw commoners off the land. It was in the best interest of both that the fields be worked. What was socially significant was the fact that chiefs had the *right* to expel their inferiors, and this remained a threat.

Social and Political Organization   Unlike many chiefdoms, Hawaiians recognized both parents' families as important to their social and political identity. For commoners this meant that they had choices about where they would live and with whom they would associate. For chiefs the same choices had societal implications and laid the ground for competition for power and authority. The choice of a wife or a husband or, more importantly, a father or a mother of your child went well beyond domestic affinity.

Marriage, then, was as political as it was personal. Through a favorable marriage, people were able to increase their rank and, more so, that of their children. A form of marriage, called hypergamy, was the ideal. This simply meant that a person wished to marry a spouse of higher rank. Because this was one of the few ways to improve ranking, higher ranked people perceived this as a threat. At the highest level, marriage with women categorized as sisters or daughters was accepted as a way to ensure the highest, unassailable rank for chiefly heirs. On the other hand, chiefly people used marriage with kin as a way to raise the standing of loyal supporters and cemented alliances with high chiefs on other islands by repeated intermarriage at the highest levels. At the higher ranks, then, marriage choices were arranged and maintained as a public concern. Even sexual liaisons by chiefly people could interfere with the balance of rankings. High chiefs restricted the sexuality and marriages of their kinswomen. The marriages of chiefly women, and to a lesser extent men, were far more restricted than those of their commoner retainers.

Marriage for commoners without political aspirations was a far less rigid matter. Sex was a normal part of Hawaiians' lives from puberty through old age. Sexual relationships between men and women were not restricted to marriage. When a couple decided to marry, their cohabitation was openly recognized and accepted but there was little ceremony or exchange. Either spouse could leave the marriage when they wished, and extramarital relationships were common. In fact, a child who was accepted by both a social father (mother's husband) and a biological father was considered fortunate. At the birth of a child families were bound together, and the child was ceremoniously welcomed to the families. Over a lifetime individuals might have multiple spouses and more lovers. These ties were not expected to be the staple core of a household.

At marriage, the couple lived in a household that best suited them. There were no residential obligations to specific kin. Through this residence choice, the couple had rights to use lands and served specific chiefs. Hawaiians were known to move about. Often families moved to visit relatives in other areas in a temporary absence. Also the fragility of marriage ties meant that people were expected to move their residence when marriages came apart. The core of households was not husbands and wives but brothers and sisters. A senior brother and a senior sister were expected to remain in the household of their childhood for much of their lives. With others coming and going with divorce and visits, this pair maintained the claims on land and tribute to chiefs. Related men or women were always allowed to return to this household.

Chiefs did not have a home household like that of the commoners. Chiefs were said to be permanently on the move. They were expected to move from village to village within their areas of control, staying in one and then another. Each village was required to maintain royal homes for the chief and the sometimes large retinue that followed along. The tribute food of the people of the area supported the chiefly guests.

Cosmology   While it might be agreed that commoner women had a general equality with commoner men and that chiefly women could be land owners and authorities over men and women of lesser rank, in the area of cosmology women were perceived as inherently inferior. Women, as a category, were seen as profane as opposed to sacred, and individual women did not take part in important sacred ceremonies. (Linnekin 1990: 13) They were also forbidden to enter temples and men's houses. Men and women were even mandated to eat separately. With men doing much of the cooking, men and women could not eat out of the same dish nor share the same piece of food. Some types of foods, including pork, coconut, and some bananas, were strictly men's foods. Women were severely punished, even killed, for breaking these taboos. The highest ranking women, however, tended to escape punishment. Publicly they appeared to follow the rules, but private infractions were tolerated. Also, at the highest level, female chiefs were allowed to enter and sponsor the sacrifices at specific shrines. Other sacred restrictions were based on ranking rather than gender. Lower ranked people were restricted in their interaction with those of higher ranking. At the highest levels, lesser ranked women and men were required to lay face down on the ground in the presence of an important chiefly woman or man. Although less extreme, the lower ranked were still required to defer to the sacred power represented by the higher ranked.

While these restrictions suggest that religion was purely a male concern, Linnekin suggested that there was a woman's religion that differed

Queen Liliuokalani, the last queen of
Hawaii.

from men's and that this has been largely ignored. (1990: 24–32) Female
gods, including the most universally known, Pele, were significant in the
cosmology and represented sacred females. Some of these, particularly
Pele, were noted as particularly important to women. Women were
recorded making sacrifices to specific gods, but the nature of women's
place in religion was hidden in history. History does record spirit possession by women and suggests a woman's role as prophet. Likewise a
domestic cosmology of many spiritual beings associated with families and
occupations appears to have included both women and men as worshippers. Clearly a formal, male-dominated religion was powerful in Hawaiian
culture, and few women were active participants in it. This religion
imposed restrictions on the behavior of women that many must have
found onerous. These restrictions, however, were mediated, like all other
things, by the rank of the women.

While women were restricted from some sacred activities by virtue of
their gender, they were not restricted from the highest positions of secular
power and authority that were based on rank. Commoners living their
daily lives largely away from the centers of control maintained an easy

form of autonomy for individual men and women. Like in the other cases in this chapter, the concepts of rank and gender intertwined into a complex reality.

Hawaiian culture was based on a highly formalized and supernaturally sanctioned social hierarchy. Here the differences between commoners and those of chiefly rank were significant in all aspects of life. The perceived differences between men and women were secondary and embedded in the larger social ranking system. Like the Tlingit, equality was neither a reality nor a goal. But unlike the Tlingit, a clear class difference existed. The inequality of rank overwhelmed the inequality of gender. Among commoners the relations between men and women were fluid and women had significant autonomy. Among the chiefly ranks, however, gendered differences were significant and formalized. Men, in general, were of greater consequence than women were. However, the rank and power of chiefly women were superior to those of commoners, both male and female.

SUMMARY

The variety of the cultures that are designated as stratified can defy generalization. Some observations about gender in these societies might prove useful. First, the question "What is the position of women in this stratified society?" is clearly misguided. While no society treats all women or all men exactly the same, in these societies the inequality between people is institutionalized. The differences between the life of a woman of high rank in a society and the life of a woman of low rank may be greater than the differences in the lives of that woman and her brother. To be sure, gender is a social category in all of these societies, but the social category of social status or rank could all but overwhelm it. Gender is a social issue, but it may not be *the* social issue that differentiates the life possibilities of individuals.

A second observation is also important for understanding these societies. The individual behavior of women, like men, could reflect on the social standing of the entire clan or social unit. This could be especially crucial when the role of mother was defined as critical for the rank of children. This often meant that higher ranked women were under more constraints for maintaining culturally sanctioned behavior than poorer, or less socially significant, women in the society. Rather than being publicly freer, they may have been more restricted. Of course, there are other cases where the public power of royal or high-ranked women freed them to lead lives that lesser people could not imagine for themselves.

Finally, the issue of power should be emphasized. In many of these societies, specific women had power and authority in their societies that few, or no, men could attain. Whether the power of these elite women was reflected in the lives of ordinary women varies from culture to culture. Stratified cultures often allow for powerful women, but this does not mean that at specific levels of rank women and men are equal. Often men are expected to dominate their wives, but perhaps not their sisters, while at the same time they may be subordinated to women of higher status. The question of gender is always modified by the question of rank in stratified societies.

Readings

Fried, Morton H. *The Evolution of Political Society*. New York: Random House, 1967.

Klein, Laura F. "Mother as Clanswoman." In *Women and Power in Native North America*, eds. L. Klein and L. Ackerman. Norman, OK: University of Oklahoma Press, 1995, pp. 28–47.

————. "Contending with Colonization: Tlingit Men and Women in Change." In *Women and Colonization: Anthropological Perspectives*, eds. M. Etienne and E. Leacock. New York: Praeger, 1980, pp. 88–108.

Kuper, Hilda. *The Swazi: A South African Kingdom*. New York: Holt, Rinehart and Winston, 1963.

Lebeuf, Annie M. D. "The Role of Women in the Political Organization of African Societies." In *Women of Tropical Africa*, ed. Denise Paulme. Berkeley: University of California Press, 1971, pp. 93–119.

Linnekin, Jocelyn. *Sacred Queens and Women of Consequence: Rank, Gender and Colonialism in the Hawaiian Islands*. Ann Arbor, MI: University of Michigan Press, 1990.

CHAPTER SIX

Formal Structure, Formal Inequality? Diversity in the State and Global Societies

Is gender equality possible in the modern system?
Do women with political power in states predetermine high status for
   other women?
Can women have any power in states that deny them legal rights?

A state is very different than the other models of society. Bands, tribes, and chiefdoms may differ in many regards, but they share one central principle: kinship. Obligations and rewards are most commonly couched in kinship terms. More importantly, there is no layer of organization that supercedes the kin lines. This chapter explores gender relations in societies whose political structures are based on territory and centralized governmental authority. While people in states are still born into families and have duties to those families, the center of power in the society shifts from family to government. Further, the focus of authority in government clearly differentiates classes of people who have public power and those who do not. Formal, structured inequality is an intricate aspect of all states. States are heterogeneous, and some categories of people are defined as superior to others. The societies of peasants, and other groups within states that are barred from power, are also often structured into categories of public/private power and gendered inequalities.

Because of the complexity of this category, this chapter is divided into three sections. The first looks at the nature of the state system itself and the implications of this political model for the lives of women and men. The second section focuses on the rural segments of states where peasants or poor farmers live. People in this arena are far from the centers of power but are restricted by the rules of their states. Two cases illustrate the model. The final section focuses on the other extreme of the state, the urban elite. The lives of wealthy and middle-class women in the centers of power are again illustrated with two cases.

NATURE OF THE STATE

Every reader is a citizen of a state. In fact, in the contemporary world system, all people are categorized as members of states and states are autonomous, meaning that no other, larger political systems exist that will peacefully interfere in the internal workings of a country. This does not mean that bands, tribes, and chiefdoms have fully been replaced, but those that continue are now encapsulated, or subordinated, within larger governmental units. In their daily lives, these people may still be largely governed by the rules of kinship and religion specific to their ethnic group, but when they leave their areas, they do so as citizens of a larger entity.

States by definition are heterogeneous. Further, states are also heterogeneous by profession. In these systems people specialize. No longer does everyone produce food while also performing part-time special tasks. In state-level systems, farming becomes a specialization that only some perform. Others may spend their time as religious, craft, or political specialists. Those who do not produce food, exchange the products of their special skills with those who do. Government leaders tax their subjects to provide for the needs of military and political specialists. All states are composed of different types of people united by the power of a common central organization.

Because of the omnipresent nature of the state in our lives, we tend not to question the consequences of such a system. However, many scholars have argued that the state system has rendered human equality, and specifically gender equality, impossible. While many contemporary states, including the United States and Canada, have equality, or at least equality of opportunity, as a societal goal, none have claimed complete success. There are still differences in status and wealth, and these often appear along ethnic or geographic lines. In many of these states "rural," "darker skin tone," "female," and "inner city" are descriptors far more often found with poverty than wealth, with low status than high status, with powerlessness than power.

To understand the effect of state organization on women and men, it is necessary to go beneath the larger structure and look at the lives of people. A review of a few of the hallmarks of state organization and the loci of power may be useful.

Territory   Scale is larger

Most commonly, a woman is a member of a state because she was born within the territorial borders of that state. This is different from being a member of a tribe or a band. In those systems she would belong because she would be a daughter, by birth or adoption, of a member of the community. Where she was born would have been entirely unimportant to her social identity. The child of an anthropologist who was born in a tribal village, for example, would only be counted as a part of that group if his or her mother or father, depending on the kinship system, was a member. On the other hand, children born in a foreign territory to members of a tribe are included as full members of that tribe.

In the state, the first question for the legal identity of a women is, "Where?" And the second is, "To whom?" In many countries, including the United States, all children born within the borders are entitled to state citizenship.[1] This means that a girl born to a mother from another country visiting the United States is a U.S. citizen. This does not entirely settle the question, however, since the children of citizens are not immediately disenfranchised by their place of birth. In many states, including the United States, children born to U.S. mothers, regardless of place of birth, are also born with U.S. citizenship. Those born with U.S. fathers, however, may or may not be granted immediate citizenship. The rules for this have changed with circumstances. During wars, for example, states have often been wary of accepting as their citizens the children of male soldiers born to women in the war zones. In other words, the rules for territory are clear, while the rules for kinship are variable.

What should be clear, regardless, is that the rights of a woman in a state are legally based on citizenship rather than kinship. It does not follow that all citizens of a state have equal rights. In many states, historically and in the present, women have not enjoyed the same rights as men. They are, however, equally under the control of the state in the sense that they must follow the laws that pertain to them and must suffer the legal consequences when they do not. They may be categorized as wards of fathers or husbands, just as children are wards of their parents in the United States. The final assertion of authority for women, and for men, is in the hands of the state.

In the model of state autonomy, patriotism is primary. Ultimate loyalty is owed to the state rather than a family group. A woman should not put the needs or beliefs of her family above those of the state. For example, a parent cannot ignore paying taxes in order to pay medical bills for a child nor kill a neighbor for dishonoring a daughter without expecting state sanctions. Likewise, a mother or father cannot prevent a son from being drafted into an army in wartime. People might understand the feelings of the parent who acted in any of these ways, but the good of the state takes priority. Family ties, like ethnic and religious ties, may be important to individuals in a state, but, unlike every other system, the state places the authority of the government first.

Defending Borders

States go to war. Because territorial boundaries define the legal boundaries of the state, defense of those borders is essential to the continued

---

[1]Here, we refer to "state" in the larger sense of "country," not in the U.S. sense of individual "states" such as Illinois, Florida, or Nebraska.

existence of the state. Surely not all states are at war all the time, but it is in the nature of the state system to war. In addition, it follows that expansion of the state lies in the expansion of its borders.[2] Since the earliest states of Mesopotamia, Mesoamerica, and Asia, states have had to defend their borders and have attempted to capture new lands. To be ready to do this at any time, states developed permanent military organizations.

The development of a military can have profound social implications for life in a state. It sets up a unique professional category within society. This means that some people—until recently, almost exclusively men—hold full-time employment as warriors. When they are not at war, their job is preparing for war. The ability to physically overwhelm others and kill, or subdue, them becomes socially valued and honored in the context of protecting the state and the citizens. Military men are honored for their willingness to endanger their lives for the cause. As heroes, such men have often become political leaders as well. Men in this profession are expected to be physically strong and are taught to be aggressive in battle. Often, the image of men as the stronger, more aggressive gender is socially validated in the existence of a military.

While a military in its essence functions to protect, history has shown that without loyalty or strict control it can also threaten the state. The concentration of weapons and the skill to use them in an organized force can work against the government of a state and its citizens. Military leaders who do not fit into the political system have tried to change the system. Many a coup d'état has been successfully led by military units. Women, although rarely combatants, are often victims in such civil conflicts. Additionally, an organization of young men, trained to be physically aggressive and who live in largely all-male settings, can, if poorly trained, be threatening to those around them. A tactic in many paramilitary forces today is to kidnap or recruit young boys and train them in antisocial chaos. Ten-year-olds are encouraged to drink, use drugs, and to show their worth by fighting. Without education and social controls, they become a danger to themselves and others. In many countries, areas around military, and especially paramilitary, bases are particularly dangerous for women.

A final way military situations threaten women is by taking their sons and husbands away from home. During wars, states have often conscripted young men, forcing them to leave family responsibilities to serve the state. Others volunteer, seeing that duty to their states also serves their families. Their absences leave voids at home, however. Their roles must be filled by those who remain behind, often older men and women, who add these to their own duties. Further, many of these young men never return, creating permanent holes in the lives of their families.

[2] Certainly many states have strong influence beyond their own borders by means of international businesses, control over vital resources, crucial alliances, and military threats, but legal authority is still vested within their own lands.

Law

The rights and obligations of women and men in a state are codified into laws. This means that individual actions are judged by preexisting rules that were often written far away and, perhaps, long ago. Because states, by definition, are heterogeneous, laws are seen as necessary to ensure that different types of people are all functioning together for the common good of the whole. Certainly, these rules have been written by an elite and, for the many, who must follow these rules, by an elite from a different ethnicity and a different gender. Even in those fortunate democracies where such things are voted on, rarely can all people vote. According to the rules of the original American constitution, which Americans honor for its democratic principles, only white, land-owning, male citizens had the vote. In fact, the legal practice of slavery defined many Americans as property. Class, perceived race, gender, and place of birth were criteria for voting. Despite this, all people were required to follow these laws.

Laws, therefore, codify the state's idea of correct behavior. This also means that laws codify national concepts of inequality as well. In many contemporary states, women do not have the vote and may not have an equal voice in court procedures. The same is true for ethnic and religious minorities. This means that the concerns of women and minority groups are only heard through the filter of others. Moreover, the only way they, themselves, can be enfranchised would be through the vote of those already with that power. Even then, in a phenomenon that has been called the tyranny of the majority, the interests of larger voting groups overwhelm unique interests of smaller minorities. In more autocratic states, this is even more pronounced, with only the defined elite of the state making the decisions. It is virtually impossible to find a state today where some group of people is not disadvantaged in relation to others. The stated ideal of many democracies—and of the United Nations— of human equality has not yet been realized, and some fear that inequality is so deeply embedded in the state system that it may never be realized.

Laws that relate to gender issues differ widely throughout the world. Some states, such as Saudi Arabia, require women to be fully covered by fabric in public while others, such as the United States, require that breasts and genitals be covered. Such laws reflect ideas of female modesty held by the majority, or, in some cases, the religious authorities in power. Walking down a main street fully naked in either country would be illegal and entail a penalty. Of course, in one case it would undoubtedly be a fine and public ridicule, while in the other it could quite likely end or ruin a life. Each rule is culturally determined. Each can also be changed when societal attitudes or the nature of the people in power change. It should be remembered, however, that change can occur in many directions and that the women of Afghanistan, for example, had fewer restrictions on their behavior in the 1970s than in the 1990s.

In the twenty-first century, movement between states has become common. Immigration and transnational communication is part of the reality of modern states, which means that women and men from a variety of cultures are coming under the laws of states distant from their original homelands. This can also mean that people are subject to restrictions of traditions that are important to their gendered realities. For example, in some cultures multiple wives for one man is an ideal. In the United States, a person may have more than one spouse in a lifetime but not more than one at any time. The status of second wives in women who immigrate to the United States is legally revoked. Polygamy is illegal and punishable by law. Likewise, in other cultures, genital surgeries on men or women are considered necessary for successful lives. In the United States, male circumcisions are legal, but female surgeries are not. Women of such societies who wish to see their daughters have these surgeries must go outside the law and find illegal practitioners. Members of such cultures who may have immigrated to the United States may well find these laws unjust, arbitrary, and discriminatory. Most Americans, however, accept these laws and tend to view those who break them as not only criminal but immoral. It is difficult for those in dispute over such issues to see that the argument is based on cultural differences rather than universal concepts of good and evil.

Religious Authority

A state religion confers moral authority on the state itself. In some states, local religious diversity is allowed, but most states have an official religion or, at least, a privileged religion. In other words, the laws of the state, and even the leaders themselves, become more than legal; they become metaphysically right. In some states, especially theocracies, the difference between secular laws and religious laws is slight. This means that when a citizen disagrees with the political leadership, that person can be seen as defying the god or gods as well. It should be of little wonder that religious leaders could sometimes be as successful as military leaders in overthrowing political regimes.

Religious concepts of gender frequently favor the secular laws of a state. Many states today have predominant or state religions that are rooted in the Old Testament. The teachings of Islam, Christianity, or Judaism heavily influence countries throughout the world. Even states such as India, where none of these predominate, the colonial history leaves a model for laws heavily influenced by Christianity, although in this case certainly modified by Hinduism. Historically embedded in these Old Testament religions, beginning with the story of the creation of humans itself, is a concept of male superiority that has been used to justify secular laws.

Just as military service became a full-time specialization in states, so did religious leadership. Also just as military service was gendered as male, so most often was religious leadership. Religions became hierarchical in states, and the hierarchy was often bureaucratized. What this really means is that religious leadership became formalized and tasks within religious units became differentiated. Issues of organization, economics, and obligation of membership had to be resolved at the same time as cosmological issues. The religious leaders located both physically and ideologically in the urban, state center were mandated to ensure that a common theology and structure united local temples or churches throughout the state. Folk religions and local healers were seen as detrimental to this. Women's roles, which were often prominent in these realms, were further diminished. Formal training by members of the religious hierarchy, restricted to those they considered fit, became a credential for approved religious practice.

ON THE PERIPHERY: GENDER IN RURAL AREAS OF THE STATE

States are composed of both cities and rural areas, but states are ruled from the cities. The city, itself, is unique to state organizations. The ability to feed a large, non-food-producing population is found only in this complex form of social organization. The central political, religious, and administrative leaders and their organizations live and work in the main cities. Others who work in these organizations and the other businesses that spring up to serve them and their workers also live there. Many cities are also home to the landless citizens who come hoping to find whatever work they can to feed their families. For the most part, people in cities provide services and products but not food. Control over rural, food-producing regions is critical.

States are fed by producers in rural areas. Women and men in these regions tend to live differently than their city counterparts. Most farm or provide necessary services for farmers. They are far from the center of public power, but they are affected by the decisions made there. Rural and urban dwellers often see themselves as very different kinds of people, but their symbiotic relationship is essential to the functioning of each and of the state itself. In many contemporary states, such as the United States and Canada, rural farmers are small business owners or work for larger agribusinesses. They are educated in the same manner as urbanites and can move easily between the city and the countryside. In much of the world, however, the life of the rural dweller remains closer to classical peasantry, where the local community is far more isolated from the town and the people are far more distant socially from their city cousins. Many scholars, who have studied the issue of gender in peasant and urban settings, describe very different roles for men and women. To understand gender in a state setting, then, both urban and rural societies must be considered.[3]

---

[3]There are other categories in cities. Ethnic enclaves that are based on tribal or even band configurations can still exist within states.

Peasantry as a Gendered Way of Life

Anthropologist Eric Wolf, in his class book *Peasants,* described peasants as "rural cultivators whose surpluses are transferred to a dominant group of rulers that uses the surpluses both to underwrite its own standard of living and to distribute the remainder to groups in society that do not farm but must be fed for their specific goods and services in turn." (1966: 3–4) He pointed out that the "peasant dilemma" was "balancing the demands of the external world against the peasants' need to provision their households." (1966: 15) While peasants, then, like tribal agriculturists, based their economy on farming, they fundamentally differed from them by being inextricably subordinated to another segment of society. Peasants did not only have to worry about growing enough food for their families and perhaps enough to trade for special items and services, but they also had to have enough additional surplus to pay the rents and taxes they owed to the elite.

Peasant life has been perceived in two apparently opposite ways in American popular culture. In the first, men are seen as toiling in fields, while women and children are confined in shacks; all are barely coping with the difficulties of their lives. In the second, men and women are colorfully dressed dancers celebrating at agricultural festivals and enjoying the simple pleasures of country life. While each image simplifies and warps the complexity of any person's life, there is a small truth at the core of both. Peasant life is difficult, and, by definition, peasants are not wealthy. Economic concerns are real and deep. Men do hard work in fields, and women do care for children and live in simple homes. Their lives are not limited to these dimensions, however. Likewise, peasant communities do have celebrations and dances. The men and women, often those young and unmarried, socialize and have fun at community events. Men often gather after work in public places and enjoy the company of their friends. Women may gather in homes and enjoy the company of their friends there. This is also a small part of more complex lives that coexists with the more subsistence-based activities.

Anthropologists, like the general public, have sometimes described peasants from both extremes; consequently, there has been considerable dispute over the nature of peasantry. In these days of theoretical reflection, even the validity of the category itself is reasonably in dispute. Certainly, in many parts of the world, communities that were until recently highly self-contained have now built ties with urban areas and even other countries. Working in cities and immigrating to places with better work options have become intrinsic elements in the reality of this group of people. They maintain their ties, and perhaps identity with their natal homes, and many plan to return there when they have the resources to do so comfortably.

When scholars began to look at gender issues, the disagreements took on a new context. The original view of gender in peasantry was one of extreme patriarchy. Married women were seen as limited to homes, where they toiled for their families and were bossed around by their husbands, other adult males, and even mothers-in-law. Men, on the other hand, were giving orders and were free to go wherever they wished for work or fun. Women were trapped in their domestic domain. As anthropological research revealed peasant women who were neither cowering nor resigned, the original patriarchal concept was challenged. First, as the definition of peasantry itself suggested, no one, male or female, really had societal power in a peasant community. Such power was located in the elite. Local public power was somewhat limited as well. Most important decisions were tied to households and, therefore, were domestic. Uses for a family field, or animals, or changes in the household were domestic issues. Who made domestic decisions became an important issue. Field work has shown a number of such societies in which women's voices were heard loudly along with men's voices in these discussions and a number where they were not. A key difference between these societies appeared to be ownership of land.

Because farming is the heart of the peasant economy, it follows that land ownership or, at least, rights to use land are essential for economic security. In some societies, like many in India, land is passed from father to son. This means that land ownership is vested only in men. Women are dependent on their fathers and husbands for this basic resource. In peasant communities elsewhere, like many in Spain and Greece, both sons and daughters equally share in the lands of their parents. In a marriage, the lands given to the husband are joined with those given to the wife into a new family estate. In some cases, the wife's land comes as a dowry at the beginning of the marriage, while the husband's is added at his parents' deaths. For many years, then, the family land comes from the wife. In such cases, the wife has a recognized interest in the land and its uses, and decisions about the land must include her. Also, daughters, as well as sons, have an interest in land issues and must be educated about care and use by their parents. Along with decisions and ownership, the amount and type of work in the fields that are done by women vary greatly.

Households are the most important units for peasant life. The nature of the households varies widely from the patrilineal extended family households of northern India to the bilateral nuclear family households of rural Spain. In any case, the household is the principal residential and work unit. Household members share the work and share the resources, although specific roles may well be gender defined. Women often bring dowries to their new households. In some cases, as noted, this can be in land and can provide the new wife with an important position in her new home. In many other cases, the dowry is paid in a more liquid form. In other words, dowries may be paid in money, precious metals, animals, or other items that can be traded or used for household expenses. In these communities, the men tend to provide the land while the women provide the cash. In successful families, the school fees and dowries of the next generation are often drawn from these funds.

In recent years, such dowries have been used in ways that are far more sinister. In areas as far removed as India and Greece, dowry deaths have become an issue for federal governments. Men marry women for their dowries and then kill them. The men retain the dowries from their late wives, remarry, and collect new dowries. Some men have apparently killed more than one wife in an effort to become wealthier. The women are typically said to die in household accidents such as "falling into the fire," and often no investigation takes place. As the number of such "household mishaps" increased to an unbelievable number, families, officials, national groups, and even international interest groups began to protest. As these dowry deaths became an international embarrassment, the federal elites passed laws and increased police activities to curtail the practice. It is ironic, and tragic, that the dowry that can secure a woman's status in one family can be the reason for an early death in another.

On a surface level, peasant communities share the religion of their urban, elite countrymen and women. In Christian states, priests and ministers from among the more educated elite are sent to rural communities to head churches. Their authority comes from the church itself, and these religious leaders frequently come with little understanding or sympathy for the people they will serve. Islamic and Hindu states often follow the same pattern. Only recently has it become likely that a peasant boy might become educated enough to be eligible for formal positions of religious

A bride and groom ride in their wedding celebration in rural Greece.

leadership or for a girl to gain the less lofty positions open in these religions for women. Outsiders, then, commonly hold religious authority. Within some peasant communities, however, there are local practitioners of what is often called folk religions, or little traditions. These people, who may be male or female, are ideologically rejected but may be passively tolerated by leaders of the urban "great traditions." They, unlike their urban colleagues, come from the local communities and understand the local culture. While they may be taken as symbols of the backwardness or superstition of peasants in urban areas, on the local level they are often highly regarded and called on in times of health or economic crises.

Cases of Rural Life

The cases of peasant Greece and rural Spain provide both contrast and continuity. The peasant life of Greece in the 1960s represents a classic picture of European peasants with additional emphasis on the gender implications of such a system. The case of Spain begins in a similar setting but continues through long-term field research to demonstrate the changes that modernization has brought to such communities. The changes in gender expectations are dramatic over time. Some of these changes limit the possibilities for poor, rural-born women, while others widen them.

Peasant Greece   One of the earliest articles that questioned the concept of women's powerlessness and argued for the utility of the private-public distinction focused on the lives of women in a Greek village. Ernestine Friedl (1967) argued that observers had been reporting the appearance of male dominance in such communities without looking under the surface to the reality of people's lives. The prestige that men and their work received in the public arena was only part of the story. She asserted that "the women in a Greek village hold a position of real power in the life of the family, and . . . the life of the family is the most significant structural and cultural element of the Greek village." (1967: 97)

In the village of Vasilika, the public space was predominantly male space. Adult women did not shop or eat there except during religious festivals. This was a place where men stopped to drink beer or coffee and visit with their friends. Even the church, as a public gathering place, was gender segregated with women and girls expected to stand behind the men in most circumstances. In public celebrations for saint's days when homes were open to guests, men took the central roles as hosts, and women of the family served; women guests were served after men.

Men, likewise, held all significant public positions. Only men could be priests, and no women held positions in church councils. Men held political offices, although women had the vote and could have, theoretically, been elected. Women were allowed to become schoolteachers or doctors, but none were. Beyond the village, the officials and representatives from the state or region who came to Vasilika were also male. When a represen-

tative of a household dealt with people outside of the house, that representative was male. In public, other than in rare festivals, women appeared as
subordinate, or they did not appear at all. The "appearance" of women's
subordination was strong.

Within a household men and women lived more complementary lives.
Men did much of the field work, tended the horses, and took care of the
farm equipment. They also did the grocery shopping in the stores located
in public areas. Women performed most of the indoor chores. They also
grew tobacco, vegetables, and cotton in gardens near the houses and
tended the small farm animals. Men sometimes helped with these chores.
The household labor was necessary to the lives of the family, but held little
prestige or honor for either men or women. Men's work was neither better
nor worse than women's work in the household, but neither brought prestige to the workers.

Where Friedl found the reality of power was in land ownership. Women
brought land to the household through their dowries, and that land
remained largely in her control—it was not her husband's to sell or to use
in ways that she did not approve. Ideally, the husband expected to inherit
land equal to that of his wife, making the couple equal landowners within
the household. Discussions and decisions about the use of this land had to
be made in private within the home. Issues dealing with the land and the
crops grown on that land were women's issues as much as they were men's
issues. For the same reason, the marriages of children involved both their
fathers and mothers. The dowry that went with a daughter was taken from
the lands of both parents. In addition, the lands brought to a son's marriage by his wife affected the futures of these lands. The questions of consequence to the domestic lives of most families were those that women, as
well as men, decided as a family in the household. Here Friedl found the
"reality" of women's powers. She did not argue that the women of Vasilika
dominated men in any situation. Women had their own work that they
managed, as did men. In household settings where men and women interacted, however, she found dominate a gender complementarity that other
scholars had ignored: Women did not dominate, but they were not dominated. Outside of the family, however, the ideology and the practice of
male superiority were clearly the rules.

The research challenge that Friedl posed for others studying peasant
societies is that gender can be far more complex than it appears and that
scholars must look for the complexities of such societies rather than the
surface appearances. Real power is not always situated in public places
nor is it always apparent. She also suggested that it is not always stable
either. Men in Vasilika were having trouble finding women with equal
amounts of land to marry them at the time of this study. Wealthier women
were marrying men who could offer them more comfortable urban lives.
In these lives, however, their land might not have the same importance as
it would in the village. Also, local men were marrying poorer women who
came with less land and potentially less potential say in the family. The

observation that gender relations were dynamic in even the most apparently static communities proved important for future studies.

Rural Spain   The changes that Friedl saw beginning in Greece were not unique to that country. Jane Fishburne Collier (1997) studied a dramatically changing community she called Los Olivos in the 1960s and again in the 1980s. During the earlier study, she found a village where agriculture was the central industry and families operated to succeed in this arena. By the 1980s, agriculture no longer could provide a comfortable livelihood for most people, and other economic strategies were sought. The families, as well, changed dramatically in their efforts to provide for the future. While both realities reflected on the nature of life in a state for rural Europeans during the twentieth century, the agricultural base presented not only an economic base but also an ideological norm that has now disappeared. The changes of the later study speak to contemporary efforts of such people to cope with new challenges. Both ways of life had different expectations for gendered behavior, and whether the new way of life improved or limited the lives of women is open to debate.

During the 1960s agriculture was central to the way of life of the people of Los Olivos.[4] The livelihoods of virtually everyone who lived in the village were tied to the success of the fields. With relatively few class differences in the community compared with the state, those who had enough land to employ others to work were considered local elite. Those who had enough land to sustain their families made up the middle class, and those with insufficient land to satisfy the needs of the family and who worked for others to supplement their income were socially at the bottom. Neither large landowners nor landless workers lived in this town. A variety of produce was grown on the farms with olives, vegetables, and chestnut, and fruit trees found in fields around the village. Small animals including donkeys, goats, and chickens were common. Nonfield wage labor was available in shops and services, and emigration to wage work in the urban areas had begun, but local agriculture remained the base of the economy. This meant hard work and long hours for farm workers, but life in the community appeared relatively stable.

Men worked on the farms. The wealthiest men managed their farms and hired workers to do the manual labor, while the poorest labored on others' land. Self-sufficient landowners worked on the land for their families' well-being. Women also did some farm work, but the work of women and men tended to be separated on the land. Additionally, women had to work in their homes and care for their children. In these tasks they also commanded the labor of their older children and, if they were wealthy, hired domestic servants. The poorest women and their daughters worked

---

[4]While agriculture was long the major economic base of the region, political and economic upheavals in Spain earlier in the century affected this area deeply. The situation in the 1960s was not "traditional" in the sense of having a seamless continuity with the past.

as domestic workers in the community or in urban areas. In the 1960s only the poorest people commonly left the village to take work in the cities. Men's work and women's work was clearly differentiated, with men being in public positions of authority.

The focus of economic and social life was the family land. Both men and women inherited land, and a marriage created a family estate that was maintained for the children. A successful man managed his farm in a manner that enhanced his children's inheritance. This meant that spending for the increased comfort or well-being of the parents was seen as somewhat selfish. The household furnishings that the couple's mothers prepared for their wedding were expected to last throughout their lives. New household goods would go into their daughters' future homes. This also limited men's possibilities because sale of land or other valuables would be socially unacceptable since it represented a cut in future inheritance. Women had some security in the knowledge that the land and its resources would be protected.

In the 1980s, the economic world of Los Olivos was entirely different. The bottom had fallen out of farming, because they could no longer compete in the market with the more technologically advanced farms elsewhere. While farming was the occupation of choice in the 1960s, it now was a low-status position. The security of family farms and the focus on inheritance were gone. Instead, wage labor in cities became the dominant preferred work. Men and women became wage earners and brought their salaries to the family. Regularly redecorated apartments in the cities and modern and fashionable dress indicated success. Children's inheritances were less in land and more in education. They needed to be prepared to earn good wages. The family security of productive land was replaced with the fear of losing a principal wage earner.

The conjugal ties and those ties between parents and children seemed to be the essential relationships that defined this society. In both the 1960s and 1980s, husbands and wives were united in their expectations of sacrifice for the successful futures of their children. The nature of the husband and wife relationship, however, changed in those years, as did the formal rules for courtship that preceded it.

In the 1960s, men and women led very separate lives in many ways, but these lives were intimately intertwined. The activities of a woman reflected on the reputation of her father and husband, and those of a man reflected on his mother and wife. The activities that would bring disgrace to a family were different for a man and a woman. A woman, most of all, had to be chaste. Even the suspicion that a woman may have had sexual relations with a man other than her husband brought shame to the family. In a society where inheritance was the basis of social position, any question of disputed paternity endangered that position. Only undisputed chastity supported the position of a man as the true heir of his father and the true father of his heirs. The issue of family honor or shame was seen here, as in many societies, as invested in the proper behavior of the women. Men, on the other hand, were expected to make sexual conquests outside of marriage with little consequence for the integrity of their families. A man who impoverished his family through unwise management of the property and resources brought less shame to the family than would a perceived indiscretion of a woman.

The maturing girls of Los Olivos were strictly reared with little unsupervised access to young men. Courtships were very public and very ritualized. In their mid-teens, boys and girls began to meet publicly for Sunday walks and chaperoned dances. As they paired off they might walk toward the girl's home and talk. Talking in front of her home was the next step, and parents, fully aware of their child's attachment, would break up undesirable pairings, especially with a person without sufficient inheritance. After about a year, when the courtship became serious, the boy would ask the girl's father for permission to enter her home. At this point the couple were formally seen as engaged to be married, and the boy was expected to visit with his fiancée for a few hours each night. These meetings were closely chaperoned, and no physical contact was allowed before marriage. This would continue for several years with many marrying in their middle and upper twenties (a bit earlier than the previous generation). Courting was a period before family obligations defined the hard work of providing for the future. Before marriage, sexual activities were forbidden for women and restricted to prostitutes for men. Marriage and children redefined life.

After marriage, the success of the new family property became the paramount economic concern. Men worked much harder than before marriage. They worked on their farms all day and often socialized with male friends in bars at night. Their time at home was limited. Women, on the other hand, became focused on their homes. Their work was there or nearby, and they rarely went to public events. While they could visit relatives and friends during the day, they were expected to limit their socialization. While they worked hard, they were no longer at the call of their mothers and older sisters for help with chores. In fact, newly married women could call on unmarried relatives for help now. While their husbands held authority in the family, their separate interests left the women with control over most of their activities and those of their children.

By the 1980s, with less emphasis on land and inheritance, much of this changed. Unmarried couples now were allowed go out together unchaperoned and had the privacy to talk about emotions without audiences. They also planned to marry much earlier than their parents did. They could now rent apartments, and both could earn money. Earlier economic restraints were gone. A continued value for virginity in a bride was challenged by the increased intimacy between couples. Marriages, with acceptable sexual relations, became desirable and practical.

After marriage these modern couples maintained a much more integrated life than their parents did. Before they had children, both held jobs and could socialize together in public. After they had children, the wife would either leave her job for child rearing or keep the job and hire child care. If the women gave up their jobs, they lost the independence of an income and the status of earning for the family; if they did not give up their jobs, they were seen as neglecting their children. Men spent more time at home and with the children than their fathers had. Men spent more time with their families and less in public recreation, while women spent more time in public than had their mothers. Women could now use money for themselves and their homes. Fancy clothes, once restricted to young courting girls, were available to married women as well. On the surface, the choices and opportunities for women had opened up. At the same time, as Collier illustrated, they became more economically dependent on their husbands than their mothers had been. The loss of a husband in this period, by death or desertion, was economically disastrous to a family, while in the past the family landholdings provided economic security. At the same time, the value of housework and child care was socially depreciated. In the earlier time a woman's work at home was respected as an integral part of the family's position; now, only work valued by earnings was considered important.

The shift in kinship expectations between the 1960s and 1980s was dramatic. The farming family with strict expectations for the behavior of men and women transformed into an urban, wage-earning family with choices that were more fluid for men and women. Further, children who had been obligated to their parents for use of their lands during their lives and inherited only after their deaths were now obliged to get a good education that would allow them to find good jobs. Where they held these jobs and what they would do with their lives was out of the parents' hands. The freedom of these many choices, however, was bought with a loss of security for all—perhaps especially for women.

CITIES AND THE URBAN ELITE

Cities make up the political and administrative core of a state. Practically, a number of cities may play different roles in a complex state. Washington, D.C., is the political capital of the United States, while New York City is the economic capital, for example. State power in any form is located in urban areas. This means that the elite of the state tend to live and work there. This does not mean that *only* the elite live in cities. The poverty of cities can rival the deepest poverty in rural areas. In fact, in many modern states, poor people from rural areas move to cities. Squatters' camps and urban ghettos are part of the landscape in many cities.

Most people either love cities or hate them. This fits the dual image of cities that most Westerners find familiar. One image shows the rural area as pure. It is where honest people work hard, raise healthy families, and live honest lives. The city, on the other hand, is dirty, manipulative, crime ridden, and phony, like the people who live there. You can trust rural folks but not city folks. The city is, at best, a necessary evil. A city "eats up" a naïve rural child who seeks his or her fortune there. The people of Los Olivos and Vasilika who continued to work on their farms were secure in the knowledge that they were living a worthwhile life.

The other image depicts the city as a place of opportunity. Max Weber, a classic social theorist, quotes an early European principle: "City air makes man free." (1958: 94) This originally referred to the freedom from lords of manors, but it also later referred to the freedom from the demands placed on individuals born into small communities. The expectations of families and the community on an individual and the demands of state taxes and laws on the households were stifling to many. The promise of the city was that a person could act as an individual and choose from the many opportunities that existed there. There were personal choices to be made, and mistakes from the past could be forgotten. The people of Los Olivos and Vasiliki who married and took jobs in cities followed this road.

Living in Cities: Middle and Upper Classes

The focus of the model that follows is on the urban elites who make up the upper and middle classes of many states. These are the leaders of government, the military, economics, education, and religion and those who support them in administrative and service positions. This category also includes the families of these people. The governmental leaders determine the policies that affect the lives of people throughout the state. The economic leaders are also the owners of much of the property and many of the businesses that provide jobs and create the wealth of the state. As the leaders of the ideology and bureaucracy of organized religion and the institutions of higher learning, they are in a position to define what is considered moral and what is considered rational. Finally, the leadership of the military provides the insurance that these powerful positions will prevail.

Obviously, the number of people in these positions in states may vary widely. In some states, one family may dominate all the important offices and may be supported by a small administrative staff. In many developing countries today, the upper and middle classes comprise a very small percentage of the total population. The distance between these people and the mass of urban and rural poor in wealth, education, health, mobility, and, of course, power is so staggering as to suggest different worlds. In other states, Australia or Norway, for example, class differences are far less extreme, and class mobility is far more common. It is difficult to generalize too broadly about elites, but in all states a wealthy element of the population has the ability to set the standards for others.

Urban elite families often live in nuclear family households but tend to socialize with kin and others in their social class. Marriages are often arranged within this set, and, in some places, marriages between cousins or more distant relatives are preferred as a way of keeping the wealth and power of the upper class concentrated. The household duties that poorer

like
Hawai'i

odd that she makes no mention of women with careers

women perform/in their own homes are done in the most elite homes by hired servants. Wealthy women manage the work in their homes rather than do it themselves. In many states, the elite women are well educated, which means they can be useful in the public arena in charity or paid work and/or in the private arena as interesting wives who can manage important households. Those in the middle class see such education as a doorway into a more prosperous lifestyle.

The lives of women of this urban elite can differ dramatically from the lives of peasant women. They differ not only in the obvious category of wealth but often also in gender rules that apply to them. For example, the peasant woman in India must cover her face when she ventures out of her house in her husband's village, and she is expected to follow the orders of her husband and his mother to the letter. Women of the urban elite, however, can aspire to be the prime minister, whose orders are followed by men and women and who can debate men and women from India and abroad. Indira Ghandi, her daughters-in-law, and many other elite women have sought and held public offices. This is possible for the city woman but not the rural woman. On the other hand, the women of urban Saudi Arabia are expected to veil in public and exercise authority only in the context of single-gendered activities. Rural areas have similarly gendered rules, but they are more relaxed in some ethnic conclaves.

Cases of City Life

The variations in urban living and the differences in gender possibilities in different social settings within cities are as great or greater than those in rural areas. Two cases illustrate different worlds for women in cities. The first is that of elite Saudi Arabians in Jiddah and the second is that of the Japanese middle class.

Saudi Arabian Elite Women   While the lives of peasants have been of interest to anthropologists since the beginning of the field, city dwellers, especially the elite, have only rarely been studied. It is still unusual to find a study of elite women. One anthropologist, Soraya Altorki (1986), did just such a study in the city of Jiddah in Saudi Arabia. Altorki, a Saudi woman who left the country as a small child, was able to return as a native ethnographer with the access and limits that that category placed on her. She was welcomed into elite families, who thought it natural and important for her to learn more about her culture. She was, however, an unmarried woman and, as such, was bound to the rules of modesty and segregation that that status entailed. Consequently, she had wide access to women and their activities in the homes but virtually no access to unrelated men and the public life of the city. Her study of domestic life among the urban elites, however, filled in a massive hole in the knowledge of Saudi life.

The elite women of Jiddah lived very privileged lives compared with peasant women anywhere in the world. These women were economically well off and had no realistic fears about future economic hardship. According to the law, they inherited from their parents but at a rate that was half that of their brothers. As widows, they inherited one-eighth of their husband's property. Although a man, father, husband, or brother managed this money for them, they had access to their money and were encouraged to spend it on themselves and their children. A woman with luxuries reflected well on the status of the family.

These women were never called on to perform heavy labor or work outside the home. Within their homes, they had servants to do the housework and nannies to watch the children. The elite women were responsible for the house and children, but they worked in their homes as managers or administrators rather than as laborers. Few worked out of the house. While there were respectable and professional jobs, such as physicians, open to Saudi women, these jobs involved tending to other women. In a recent U.N. survey, less than 10 percent of Saudi women worked outside of the home.[5] (World Statistics Handbook 1995: 162) In wealthy houses, it was the responsibility of the male head of the household to take care of the needs of everyone in the family plus those nonfamily retainers who lived there. The idea that a woman needed to work for wages would only shame the household.

The dichotomy of public/domestic, with one specific exception, works well to describe the rules for gender in this community. Within Saudi Arabia, these women lived their lives in a domestic world.[6] When they left their homes, their freedom was notably restricted. In public they were required to wear black overcoats over their dresses with a shawl that covered their heads and faces. Younger married women could sometimes leave their faces uncovered in cars and other semisheltered areas but only with their husbands' approval. Older women and unmarried women were held to much stricter codes. Women were required to have the permission of their husbands or fathers before they left the house. Women were not allowed to drive their own cars, so servants or male relatives drove these women.

Most commonly when women went out, they were visiting female friends and relatives. Older women, especially, had visiting networks to ease the isolation of their households. It is through their female friends that women obtained information about the world outside of their households. One critical piece of knowledge from such visits had societal importance. The women of the house learned about the marriageable girls in other households within their class. Because a proper marriage was necessary for the honor and continuance of a family and because the men of the family were restricted from meeting eligible brides, it fell to the women to bring information and suggest matches. A bride and groom

---

[5]In this same survey more than 84 percent of the men were "economically active."
[6]These families travel internationally. When in other countries, the women often, with the permission of men, followed the gender rules of the other country. They could unveil and travel in public as long as no unrelated Saudi man was present and their husbands and fathers agreed.

were not expected to have seen one another until their wedding night. In some households, an opportunity for a glimpse of the bride from a safe distance might be arranged. It was the families that arranged the marriages; the couple had little say.

At marriage the wife came to her new household with a dowry of furniture for several rooms that the couple would occupy and clothing for herself for a year. If she moved into her husband's father's household, her mother-in-law became an immediate authority over her, but, if she and her husband established an independent household, she became the head of the domestic unit. In either case, her chief responsibilities were to care for her husband and be obedient to him. She was expected to have his children and to tend to their needs as well. If she failed in her responsibilities, her husband would take a second wife or divorce her. Either brought shame, and divorce evicted her from the household. Her children, except those very young, remained with their father. Unlike the fate of many poorer women in this situation, a divorced woman was likely to be taken into the household of her father or brother and be cared for. If she had maintained a good relationship with her father, her return home would be very comfortable. Even without close personal relations to take her in, it would be shameful to the husband's family to have her disgraced, so to uphold its own honor, a comfortable lifestyle would be established for her.

Only a woman who publicly shamed her own and her husband's families would be in serious danger, and Altorki described no such cases in the families she studied.[7] Women, however, threatened the honor of the family far more than men did. Morality dictated that women had to be modest and create no gossip. They were required to appear veiled in public and quietly obey their men. They could not gamble or drink alcohol and, when unmarried, must not be seen at functions with men present. If any of these rules were publicly broken, the family of the offender was severely shamed. A woman's bad behavior reflected on the men in her family, who had not properly controlled her. Men also could bring shame to the family but only when their behavior became so extreme and public that it caused a scandal.

A moral woman's standing in the community depended on her male relatives. As the daughter of an elite man, men and women of lesser status and wealth deferred to her and were able to call on her for help getting work or loans. If she was well educated and had a profession, this did not define her social position, although the education and profession of her husband did. She had some authority over her children, her servants, those to whom she gave charity, her daughters-in-law, and, perhaps, by force of personality, some others. If she accepted and followed the rules imposed by her society, she lived a very comfortable life surrounded by family and friends.

---

[7]A very public case of the lengths to which this can go, however, occurred in the 1980s, when a woman of the royal family who had left her family to elope with a foreigner was executed.

Japan: Middle-Class Women at Home and Work Japan is among the most urbanized and industrialized states in the world today. Despite this, it has maintained a unique cultural core that flavors the cities and businesses. Metaphorically, the entire nation is seen as a family, with the royal family at its head. Likewise, this metaphor of family pervades the smaller units of the state as well. A paternalistic business system, where loyal and obedient lower status individuals work tirelessly for superiors who care for their needs and reward them with lifelong employment, has been studied by Westerners seeking the secrets of their economic success. The system does not translate well to the West, however, because it is based on a uniquely Japanese cultural sensibility that is very different from that of the West. Gender concepts, likewise, are drawn from this cultural core with the centrality of family relations. Consequently, the shared lives of urban Japanese men and women often appear exotic from a Western perspective.

Japanese women of all social strata are responsible for the well-being of their homes and children. This obviously means different things according to the economic and social position of the woman. For this case, the focus is on urban, middle-class Japanese families. Japanese middle-class women live comfortable lives but are burdened by a concept of family duty that leaves them little autonomy. While many urban Japanese women work outside their homes, the responsibility for the smooth running of the home remains theirs. Their husbands' and fathers' responsibilities are situated in their outside economic pursuits as "salarymen" who provide financially for the family. Sociologist Anne Imamura, who conducted an ethnographic study of urban Japanese housewives, described a world with "Very little overlap . . . between the two worlds of home and work. The husband has his friends and colleagues, and they tend to gather in bars or restaurants after work or on the golf course on weekends. The wife's friends are mainly in the neighborhood, and often they do not know one another's husbands." (1987: 13)

While there are surface similarities to the situation in Saudi Arabia, there are far more differences. Japanese women and men are allowed to be in each other's company in private and public without shame. Their separation is based on a demanding division of labor that creates separate social cohorts. Also, Japanese women are expected to manage their households. They control money and make major decisions. They may often be too busy to leave their house or children, but they do not need the permission of a man to do so. Additionally, the husband's role is similarly confined. His heavy workload may keep him away from his home for extended periods. He cannot choose to stay at home and neglect his work any more than she can choose to go out and neglect her children.

One of the central tasks of Japanese housewives is the promotion of her children's education. An elite education is the key to economic and social success. It is the obligation of mothers to help with homework, prepare children for examinations, and prepare them for a successful school day. This preparation can be time consuming. In a study of the preparation of school lunches for nursery students, anthropologist Anne Allison

(1997) described the time and energy spent by mothers in preparing the daily *obento*, a traditional box lunch, for nursery school. The lunchboxes were expected to include several small courses, each of which was separated and decorated. The box had to be beautiful as well as efficient and nutritious. Magazines directed at women featured elaborate instructions for creating appropriate obentos for young children. The children were required to eat their food swiftly and completely, and teachers kept watchful eyes on their eating habits. When a child failed to follow the rules for eating lunch, both the child and the mother were brought to task. Mothers were informed of better ways to make a proper lunchbox through meetings or notes sent by the teachers. Additionally, mothers were expected, on a teacher's request, to create appropriate containers for a variety of school supplies and obtain new supplies for the next day at school. They also had to be available for meetings with teachers, school field trips, and mothers' association meetings. One result of this as Allison reported was, "Few mothers at the school my son attended could afford to work in even part-time or temporary jobs. Those women who did tended either to keep their outside work a secret or be reprimanded by a teacher for insufficient devotion to their child." (1997: 308) Allison saw this as preparation for both mother and child in appropriate behavior for success in the Japanese educational system but also as promoting a state-supported, gendered economic agenda in which women do all domestic work in order to allow men to concentrate on work in the public domain. An additional benefit to

A Japanese obento: presentation of
the food is as important as the taste.

businesses was that women who had to work to afford high education costs were relegated to low-paid, part-time jobs.

Families traditionally arranged marriages, but this has begun to change. While families still have the desire to ensure an appropriate daughter-in-law or a hard-working son-in-law to carry on the family business or social standing, young men and women are claiming more authority in the process. In Imamura's study, 43.8 percent of her sample said their marriage was arranged, and 46.5 percent said they chose their own mates. (1987: 30) A significant number of Japanese men and women still have their marriages arranged and hope, as do others around the world in such marriages, that affection will grow as the couple lives and works together. Dorinne Kondo, who studied gender in the workplace, reflects that "Individual preference need not be entirely ignored, but it should be a secondary consideration." (1990: 132) In any case, the divorce rate in Japan, although generally increasing, remains low.

Alice Lam, in a case study of women in management in Japan, asserted that "Sexual inequality in employment appears to be a universal phenomenon, but evidence seems to indicate that Japan represents an extreme case among the advanced industrialized countries." (1992: 17) For the most part, the lifetime employment opportunities that the Japanese economy was known for until very recently were offered only to men. Women were relegated to part-time employment, family businesses, and small, temporary assignments for less prestigious companies. Before 1985, open discrimination against women in employment was both legal and accepted. In that year, the Equal Employment Opportunity Law prohibited unequal treatment of women in training, benefits, retirement, and dismissal issues. It only "exhorted" companies, however, to show equity in recruitment, promotion, and job opportunities. (Lam 1992: 3–4) Discrimination in the latter categories was legal but seen as morally wrong. While progress in the first set of categories has been marked, it has been less impressive in the second. Some corporations have added all-female work teams or hired the most elite female graduates, but this has not greatly benefited most women workers. Alison Davis-Blake noted that "By 1995, only 6 percent of first-level managerial positions and less than 1 percent of top management positions in large Japanese firms were filled by women." (2000: 164)

Because the system of salarymen demanded total devotion to work and the role of housewife demanded equally total devotion to home, the two roles remained incompatible. Even the best educated women were expected to give up their professional work when they married. The world press followed an example of this in the early 1990s when Crown Prince Naruhito married an accomplished Oxford- and Harvard-educated Japanese diplomat, Masako Owanda. It reported that her reluctance to marry was based on her hesitancy to give up her career to retreat to the confines of the royal household. Although now a well-integrated member of the royal family, for years she was pitied for being childless and, therefore, not fully performing her proper role. When a daughter was born to her in 2001, calls for return to earlier inheritance rules that allowed women to ascend to the thrown were widely heard. Her sister-in-law, Princess Sayako, has remained single into her thirties. Elite, nonroyal women are clearly beginning to make different choices than did their mothers as well. Many women have begun to marry later or not marry at all. The total fertility rate in Japan decreased from 2.14 in 1973 to 1.43 in 1995 due to the growing percentage of unmarried 20- and 30-year-old women in the population.[8] (Raymo 1998: 1023) Women who were economically independent and held university degrees were more likely to be unmarried than those with less education and wealth. If these women are marrying later, or not at all, their life choices could portend dramatic changes in Japanese society.

SUMMARY

States are the most heterogeneous sociopolitical system humans have developed. Inherently different lives are led by different segments of the population. While it is true that all women have different lives regardless of the societies in which they live, the variables that separate different people would be less extensive in more culturally and socially homogeneous settings. In states, however, the differences between people can be immense, and the differences in opportunities between women of different classes, ethnicities, and regions can be as great as between two independent societies. It would be foolish to assume that anyone could describe *the* Japanese woman or *the* Indian woman or *the* woman of any state.

For most of the world today, public positions of power are still held by men. There are, of course, exceptions, with the Scandinavian countries being the most outstanding examples. Even countries largely viewed as male dominated, including India, Sri Lanka, Israel, and Bangladesh, have seen women in the highest political offices. More widely, the ability for women, especially married women with children, to work outside of the home in wage labor has expanded greatly among the urban elites. However, while the opportunities for wealthy and middle-class women have expanded in some places, it must be remembered that most of the poor in states are women and children, and it is not a given that having a woman or women in high office improves their lives. Poor women can rarely choose whether to work outside of the home or not. They must seize any opening to work for the well-being of their families. Students in the United States often ask when women first came into the work force and expect a date in the mid-twentieth century. The fact is, of course, that

---

[8] It is unusual for Japanese women to choose to have children outside of marriage, so low marriage rates and low fertility rates fit more closely here than they might in other populations.

while middle-class married women began to enter the work force at that time, poor women toiled as servants and factory workers as long as those jobs existed. African-American female slaves, the immigrant women who worked in factories and sweatshops, and the female sex workers on urban streets were women who worked hard, under horrific conditions, to keep themselves and families alive. The story of the state, and women in the state, is a complex one, and the challenge to any scholar is to avoid oversimplifying it.

This complexity, however, is key to understanding the nature of gender definitions and the varied lives of women in states. It is important to understand where a woman, or collection of women, is situated in the complexity of rules and expectations that is their state. Do women have power? Over whom or what? Which women? Undoubtedly the most elite women have more power than the lowest class man does, but what does this mean? Are women defined into a domestic domain while men are defined into a public domain? If so, how are these domains defined, and what do they mean in this society? In the end, there are far more questions than answers, but there may be a better understanding of what the useful questions are.

Readings

Allison, Anne. "Japanese Mothers and Obentos: The Lunch-Box As Ideological State Apparatus." In *Gender in Cross-Cultural Perspective*, 2nd ed., eds. Caroline B. Brettell and Carolyn F. Sargent. Upper Saddle River, NJ: Prentice-Hall, 1997, pp. 298–314.

Altorki, Soraya. *Women in Saudi Arabia: Ideology and Behavior Among the Elite.* New York: Columbia University Press, 1986.

Collier, Jane Fishburne. *From Duty to Desire: Remaking Families in a Spanish Village.* Princeton, NJ: Princeton University Press, 1997.

Davis-Blake, Allison. "Review of *Office Ladies and Salaried Men.*" *Administrative Science Quarterly* 25, no. 1 (2000), pp. 164–67.

Friedl, Ernestine. "The Position of Women: Appearance and Reality." *Anthropological Quarterly* 40, no. 3 (1967), pp. 97–108.

Imamura, Anne E. *Urban Japanese Housewives: At Home and in the Community.* Honolulu: University of Hawaii Press, 1987.

Kondo, Dorinne K. *Crafting Selves: Power, Gender, and Discourses of Identity in a Japanese Workplace.* Chicago: The University of Chicago Press, 1990.

Lam, Alice. *Women and Japanese Management: Discrimination and Reform.* London: Routledge, 1992.

Raymo, James M. "Later Marriages or Fewer? Changes in the Marital Behavior of Japanese Women." *Journal of Marriage and the Family* 60 (1998), pp. 1023–34.

Weber, Max. *The City,* trans. and eds. Don Martindale and Gertrud Neuwirth. New York: The Free Press, 1958.

Wolf, Eric R. *Peasants.* Englewood Cliffs, NJ: Prentice-Hall, 1966.

World Statistics Handbook. New York: United Nations Publication, 1995.

SECTION III

Issues of Gender

The chapters in this section shift the focus from specific cultures and types of cultures to issues that appear to affect gender definitions across all cultures. All of these issues have been introduced in the previous chapters because they are profoundly important to the understanding of gender in the societies discussed. In fact, we shall return to some of the cases from the previous chapters to explore further the topics of family, politics, religion, and creativity as they apply to gender.

Such a cross-cultural examination of issues should be entered with some words of caution. While it is necessary, it is very difficult to examine broad topics across manifestly different societies. Definitions of terms must be clear and so must the limitations of those definitions. Even the basic definitions of sex and gender are questioned in the final chapter with examples of the diversity beneath these basic terms. Often it is the most obvious terms that need the most scrutiny because we think we know what they mean and, therefore, so must all other people. For example, what is marriage? Anthropologists have long asked whether marriage is a universal human trait. The answer to that question is located in the definition of "marriage." If marriage is a lifelong sexual, economic, kinship union between two, and only two, people of different genders that is publicly entered into with a religious ceremony and is socially/legally binding, then marriage is not universal. In fact, if this were the universal definition of marriage—which is clearly based on an image of American middle-class marriages in the 1950s—such a marriage is incredibly rare. It is even rare in the United States today. If an anthropologist wants to compare marriage in the United States, among the Yanamamö, and among peasants in Greece, for example, what core definition would make sense in each society? On a commonsense level, it is clear that marriages exist and are important in each society but the internal definitions of marriage in each differ from one to the other. Whose definition do we use? If we choose one, how do we apply it to the others? How do you translate cultural concepts across cultural lines?

Anthropologists through the mid-twentieth century attempted to create broad and scientific comparisons of cultural traits. In these, a trait, such as "monogamous marriage" would be listed and then each culture in the survey would be coded as having this trait or not. The hope was that by creating large databases of such information, correlations between traits would show larger patterns of human behavior. For example, if monogamous marriage regularly was present when "patriarchy" was and both were also regularly absent together, a scholar might hypothesize that there is a logical link between the two. Of course, this would be the beginning of a study and would require more research. However, these surveys lost favor with the realization that often the definitions were culture-bound, and generally, American-culture-bound. What is monogamous marriage: One spouse during a lifetime? One spouse at a time? One legally sanctioned spouse at a time or over a time period? What is patriarchy: Men have more public power than women? Men have all power, women have none? In the same class, men have more power than women?

An important dichotomy that illustrates the difficulty of universal categories is that of public and private domains. The rules and structure of a society are important to all who live there. People are not free to do what they want without considering the laws. Laws can designate even the clothes they wear. In reality, however, most aspects of a person's life are not dictated by a state or formal authority. Family, neighbors, and friends play far more important roles than politicians do in daily lives. This difference between private lives and public lives has been an important one in feminist literature and this private-public dichotomy has encouraged many debates.

In the landmark work, *Woman, Culture and Society* in 1974, Michelle Rosaldo argued that because women were always subordinated to men in society—an assertion that seemed real at that point, if not now—looking for women's power in the public arena would be futile.[1] However, to assert that in society X there are no women chiefs, or leaders, or prime ministers and, therefore, women had no power there, ran counter to what was known by researchers in those societies. Women were not totally powerless. At least not all women were powerless. Mothers-in-law had considerable power over their daughters-in-law in some societies, and mothers had authority or at least influence over their adult children in others. As the examples in the previous chapters have shown, specific women or women in specific roles in many societies were far from helpless. Understanding this, scholars suggested that looking for power only in public offices missed an important part of the power dynamic. Looking for power in private lives, or the domestic domain as it was also called, would shed light on women's sources of power. The recognition that power and authority went beyond the confines of public offices allowed studies of aspects of women's lives that had been ignored.

One insight that came out of these studies, however, challenged the public-domestic dichotomy itself. In most non-state societies, the dichotomy does not make sense. As an example, people had to ask what part of San life was public and what private? Was a Tlingit potlatch a private (family) or a public event? Clearly, where kinship was an essential organizational framework, differentiating public from private was imposing a Western

---

[1]Michelle Rosaldo. In *Women, Culture and Society*, eds. Michelle Rosaldo and Louis Lamphere. Stanford, CA: Stanford University Press, 1974, pp. 2–3.

urban concept where it did not fit. The larger concept was valid and useful: Power is found in many places other than governmental offices. The division into public and private is not universally useful. In states, where the use of the dichotomy originated, "person as citizen" and "person as family member" are not identical categories. Thus, where these two categories are often in conflict, the differentiation can be a valid conceptual tool for understanding political issues. Feminists in the United States have rallied behind the slogan "the personal is political," and it may also often follow that "the domestic is public."

The problem is clear. The solution is less than perfect. Because there is no common language or vocabulary that people in all parts of the world speak, there can be no perfect universal categories that all people would accept as correct. It is the work of the researchers to define their terms and understand the cultures they are studying well enough to apply these terms sensibly to those cultures. The unforgivable intellectual error would be to assume that the working terms and definitions are more than that. Those scholars, who assert that marriage, or patriarchy, are universals, are using very different definitions of the terms than the equally good scholars who declare they are not universal or even widespread.

The following chapters explore some of the more important definitions and arguments that anthropologists have developed and that inform our understandings of gender and gendered lives cross culturally.

CHAPTER SEVEN

Wife, Mother, Sister, Daughter: Gender in the Family

Does kinship drive gender relationships?
Is the role of mother the same across the globe?
Are the roles of wife and sister in conflict?
Does the institution of marriage subordinate women?

Men and women do not function simply as men and women in any culture in the world. In most societies, primary identities include husband, brother, father, son, wife, mother, sister, daughter, and other kinship categories. Most kinship categories are gendered. They do not encompass all gendered categories, but these are certainly core categories. Students of gender in anthropology have both embraced and grappled with the concepts that traditional kinship studies have offered. While this chapter focuses on the topics of kinship and family, it would be little wonder if the reader finds familiar themes and data here. Kinship has taken a central role in each societal model and each case study presented in Section II. Sisterhood is surely powerful as feminists have taught, but it is also overlaid with powerful kinship assumptions.

Anthropology has studied kinship as long as there has been an interest in anthropology, and theories of kinship have come and gone. It is certain that kin relations are central in most societies and that there are a limited number of models that can illustrate most kinship systems. Some of these models have included positions for women that challenged key Western assumptions about the nature of women, in general, and women in specific family roles, in particular. Some elaborate theories have been constructed to resolve these apparent contradictions.

KINSHIP AS GENDER: GENDER AS KINSHIP?

In 1987 Collier and Yanagisako edited a volume entitled *Gender and Kinship: Essays Toward a Unified Analysis* in which they proposed the idea that gender and kinship, at least as they are defined in a European and American informed scholarship, are inherently linked. As they wrote:

> Although gender and kinship studies start from what are construed as the same biological facts of sexual reproduction, they might appear to be headed in different analytical direction: kinship to the social character of genealogical relations and gender to the social character of male–female relations (and even to male–male relations and female–female relations.) However, because both build their explanations of the social rights and duties and the relations of equality and inequality among people on these presumably natural characteristics, both retain the legacy of their beginnings in notions about *the same natural differences* between people. Consequently, what have been conceptualized as two discrete, if interconnected, fields of study constitute a single field. (p. 34)

Americans, of course, assume the concepts of male and female to be biologically defined, and they also assume that the construction of kinship is biologically based. Families are begun with the sexual intercourse of a male and female to create a child. Genealogies are reckoned by tracing these children from genitors to genitors. Obviously, we allow adoptions as part of the pattern, but these are folded into the format of "natural" births. Anthropologists, however, pointing to the variety of kinship structures around the world, have always argued that kinship is inherently cultural. This apparent contradiction is resolved by separating levels of analysis. Anthropologists affirm that the forms of kinship that a society chooses are culturally constructed, but, at a deeper level, the definition of what would be defined as kinship is based on biological models. These deeper biological models at the same time are inherently gendered. A less culture-bound anthropology needs to question the universality of these deep assumptions and to search for the underlying cultural models of each society's kinship and gender models. It should also ask how, or if, they intertwine.

Another connection between gender and kinship should be obvious. Gender definitions and gender roles are initially learned in kinship contexts. Not only are children taught how to be good little boys and girls by family members, the role modeling of their family members also provides the templates for their future behavior. They will not only be categorized by gender, but they will be expected to live their lives as members of that gender and that family. In other words, the roles of a woman in one family and those in another of different traditions and classes may be quite different. Collier and Yanagisako phrased it most elegantly: "Families in our society both reproduce and recast forms of gender inequality along with forms of class inequality at the same time that they nurture children." (1987: 3)

SOCIAL STRUCTURE: THE SOCIETAL MODELS

The structural logic that organizes societies is referred to as the social structure, and, as has been seen, the heart of that structure is often kinship.

Because the differences among the three major kinship structures are based on gender categories, they have sometimes been seen as pivotal to the understanding of larger gender issues in societies. In fact, this is often overstated. Patriliny, matriliny, and bilineality, as systems, all leave room for considerable variation when it comes to the lives of men and women in the societies that employ them. They construct different routes for men and women, but they do not determine how individuals will navigate them. Other factors such as rules for residence and marriage, which vary within these larger structures, are often more critical for the limits and goals of men and women.

Unilineal Systems

Unilineal kinship systems are those that choose to link a child with one, but not both, of his or her parents. Every child, then, belongs to one, and only one, kinship group. Individuals may well feel a connection with the groups of their other parent, and their grandparents as well, and may find affection and support from many people, but they *belong* only to their own group. Regardless of which parent is determined to be the link in any specific society, there are important structural elements that are constant and very different from those found in bilateral societies. Unilineal systems create unique groups of kinsmen and -women that can function as units. Simply, every person in a particular lineal group (a lineage or clan) is related to every other member of that group and not lineally related to people outside of that group. The only way to become a member is to be born or adopted into this group. Practically this means that unilineal groups can own property as a whole and there will be no dispute over the ownership. A clan can communally own farm property, herds of animals, or an apartment house in a city. The death of any person in the clan does not confuse the ownership. Inheritance is between the deceased and his or her lineal descendents, who already are group members. This type of organization is sometimes called a corporate kinship group because it can act as if it were a single entity. This, in part, explains why these systems work so well in horticultural, simple agricultural, and pastoral societies, where group ownership is efficient and successful. The gender of the parent who provides new members does not change this basic structural strength, but patrilineal and matrilineal societies do have differences.

Patriliny   Patriliny, or patrilineal kinship, is a system in which children belong to the lineal kin groups of the fathers rather than the mothers. So if father belongs to clan A, then his sons and daughters will as well. The children of the sons will carry on the line to the next generation. The gender of each individual determines whether his or her children will belong to his or her group. In the case of patriliny, a family tree would descend only from males.

Popular writers have often jumped to erroneous conclusions about the nature of patriliny:

1. Patriliny does not mean that there is no relationship between children and their mothers or the maternal lineages. In fact, the mother is virtually always a potent force in the child's life, and her clan or line can also be significant. Patrilineal systems do vary strongly in the role the mother's side will play.
2. Both men and women are members of every clan or lineage. The men pass on this membership, but women are, in almost every case, lifelong members of their natal line. Women as sisters, father's sisters, and daughters often have significant roles in clans.
3. Patriliny is not the same as patriarchy. Patriarchy refers to the rule of men over women. Men may have more public, and perhaps private, power than women in specific patrilineal societies, but this is not mandated by the patrilineal model. It is reasonable to argue that men in a patrilineal system, particularly when combined with virilocality (described later), would have an easier time in establishing and maintaining positions of power than their sisters. However, there are enough examples of women with influence and power in such systems to reject any blanket statements about absolute power.

Matriliny   Matriliny by definition is the logical opposite of patriliny. Matrilineal kinship traces the line of kin from mother to child. In other words, a child becomes a member of his or her mother's lineage or clan at birth. The father, and the father's clan, may be very important supporters of the child throughout his or her life but cannot be clansmen or clanswomen. In some matrilineal societies, the children may live with their fathers' clans for a period during their lives.

Many people are even more confused by matriliny than they are by patriliny, and some of the earliest descriptions of matrilineal societies by Westerners were almost unrecognizable. This system almost defined "the primitive" to some Westerner observers. They hypothesized that this system must exist because the people in these societies did not understand the concept of biological paternity. Others suggested that they understood the biology but were so sexually promiscuous that they could not know the actual biological genitor of any child. In either case, maternity was always known, so the link between mother and child was built on. Needless to say, neither was true. Most people in matrilineal societies are quite clear on paternity but do not use that knowledge in the cultural creation of their kinship groups.

The confusions about patriliny were also carried through to popular descriptions of matriliny that described societies composed of women with men in peripheral, or lesser, roles. In fact, fathers and fathers' clansmen and women are very important to individuals. Among the Tlingit and Navajo, for examples, the identity of the paternal line is an integral part of the identity and social standing of a person. Of course, matrilineal societies do have both men and women members. Men as brothers, mother's brothers, and sons are crucial individuals in the workings of their lineage groups. They have clear roles and often are seen as leaders. Finally, just as patrilineal societies are not patriarchies, matrilineal societies are not matriarchies. In no known matrilineal society do women, as a class of individuals, rule over men, as a class. There are clearly significant women in matrilineal societies but there are also significant men, and often those men can take positions of power.

A significant difference between patrilineal and matrilineal societies with regard to the potential importance of men and women may be that in a matrilineal society, men and women owe their position in their lineages to women. It is difficult to depreciate the status of your mother when your own is linked to it. In a patrilineal society, on the other hand, the status of mothers often reflect less on the status of their sons. Women can be depreciated without an immediate effect on men's positions, which is considerably less likely in a matrilineal system. This is far from asserting the priority of women in power positions in matrilineal society, but there is a structural reason the status of women generally appears to be important in matrilineal societies. All too often, however, matriliny is confused with matriarchy, and strange, but erroneous, theories appear.

Theories of Matrilineal Puzzles   European cultural assumptions have vividly colored the way matrilineal systems were described and analyzed. Scholars found the idea of matriliny unsettling and debated the position of father in such groups. The classification of matrilineal systems was seen as particularly problematic and needful of explanation. Because European systems tend to be bilateral with local biases towards men in inheritance and naming, societies that favor the mother's side appear more foreign than those that favor the father's side or show no favoritism.

Among the founders of social science, matrilineal structures were assumed to be characteristic of the earliest stages of human evolution. Lewis Henry Morgan, for example, hypothesized stages of evolution where kinship systems moved from primitive promiscuity, to matriliny, to patriliny, to modern European-style families. He, and others, suggested a primitive logic that created a system that depended on obvious and reliable links. Biology dictated that everyone knew the mother of the child while the sire of the child was disputable. Following kin links from mother to child, therefore, was natural logic. In Morgan's scheme, it was at the point where private property (ownership of herds of animals, homes, and agricultural lands) was established that inheritance became a problem. The problem was, as he defined it, that men could not leave their property to their sons. "With property accumulating in masses and assuming permanent forms, and with an increased proportion of it held by individual ownership, descent in the female line was certain of overthrow, and the substitution of the male line equally assured." (1877: 345) The assumption that women did not hold this property or that their property was unimportant is inherent in the logic of seeing this as a problem. If women owned herds, or lands, then they could easily leave them to their daughters in a matrilineal system; they could not do this in a patrilineal system. This hypothesized change from matrilineal to patrilineal was necessary because it served men better, and men would have not allowed the previous system to continue. In addition to the fact that there are no historical materials that suggest that this actually occurred, the theory suffered from its cultural assumptions about gender that may, or may not, have existed in the situation being considered.

If this gender bias ended with the first generation of anthropologists who studied kinship, it could be considered only an historical oddity and passed over. The reality, however, is that until very recently, kinship studies in anthropology rest on the same types of gender assumptions. For example, a landmark article in anthropology by Audrey Richards (1950) introduced the concept of the "matrilineal puzzle." The puzzle concerned male authority in matrilineal, and particularly, uxorilocal societies. It also raised an interesting issue of the conflict of a man's role as brother with his role as husband. As she presented the problem: "An individual of the dominant sex is, initially at any rate, in a position of subjection in his spouse's village, and this is a situation which he tends to find irksome and tries to escape from." (p. 246) While the context in which she raised the issue was suitably limited, the idea of a matrilineal puzzle went beyond her use to be used to show that there was something inherently wrong in matriliny itself. The argument focused on the tensions between men and the split loyalties to husbands and brothers by women that were assumed universal in these societies. As anthropologist Linda Stone noted: "Matrilineal systems were thus seen as beset by special strains, as fragile and rare, possibly even doomed to extinction." (1997: 117) One famous anthropologist, Mary Douglas, however, asserted in 1971 that not only was it not doomed but that it was an advantageous system for expanding the economic system.

One of the curious facts about the matrilineal puzzle is that the strains of patrilineal societies were rarely addressed with the same depth of inquiry. There is no patrilineal puzzle in the anthropological literature. Many societies show that the situation of women in patrilineal, virilocal marriages can be more than "irksome," but this has rarely been considered theoretically interesting because it is seen as personal rather than structural. In other words, women may be unhappy, but because they are not seen as playing important roles in the public spheres of a society, this fact is not seen as theoretically interesting. The tensions in women's roles as sisters and wives and men's roles as husbands and brothers have only recently been addressed in studies of patrilineal societies and others.

Bilateral Societies

In bilateral societies both mother's kin and father's kin are related to their offspring. A child, then, has equal ties with a large number of relatives who can offer support and identity. These relationships may be very informal and opportunist. A person may call on the relative who is best able to offer help. In band societies, for example, families may visit relatives in areas with better hunting, and in states they may call on influential relatives for jobs or connections. This flexibility is the strength of such systems. Wide-flung family ties can be insurance in times of need. On the other hand, they do not work well as corporate units. A bilaterally constructed family has difficulty in jointly owning land or other nonliquid resources over genera-tions without limiting rules of inheritance. Land-owning families in parts of Europe used the rule of *primogenitor* to keep wealth intact. This meant that the oldest son inherited the entire estate and other children were left as dependents. The reason for this "weakness" is that in bilateral systems only full siblings have exactly the same set of relatives. A father is not related to a mother's family, while children are directly related to their par-ents' in-laws, and cousins have whole sets of relatives that other cousins do not even know. Each generation calls for complex inheritance rules and, all too often, family breakups. In other words, bilateral society favors flexibil-ity over permanence.

What does this mean for gender relations? It really means that it is dif-ficult to make any definitive statements about how the structure affects specific aspects of society. The flexibility may lead to societies that value gender equality and others that mandate extreme gender differentiation. Either could be constructed in a bilateral system. The system does not favor one gender over the other, but neither does it demand gender blind-ness beyond the rules of kinship construction. Other rules—including those for the construction of households, marriages, economic ownership, and political leadership—define gender relations.

MODELS FOR LIVING: HOUSEHOLDS

The organizational system of kinship in a society obviously has repercus-sions well beyond the reckoning of kin connections. On the domestic level of society, the rules for who lives with whom have far more importance for the daily lives of everyone in the culture than the broader structural rules. The most important relationships and the rationale for work are found in households. The essence of gender relationships are also taught and played out in this domain. Societies have developed different rules for residence. Each form solves some problems while creating others. In some cases, these problems appear to affect one gender more than another.

Neolocality

Most readers are accustomed to the residence pattern that anthropologists call *neolocality*. All this means is that a newly married couple sets up house-keeping in a new location rather than moving in with a relative. Often these new homes are near the families of either the bride or groom but not considered part of them. When they have children, this new nuclear family unit (parents and children) has a distinctive existence beyond that of their relatives. This form of household is becoming even more widespread with the growth in migration and urbanization. Land stress and family separations often encourage the establishment of these smaller households. Also the confusion of Westernization with modernity has sometimes made American and European styles appear more desirable. As seen in the cases in Chapter 6, some families in Saudi Arabia, Japan, and rural Spain are establishing neolocal, nuclear family units where extended family households had been the rule of previous generations.

The lure of these new households for young couples is obvious, especially to Americans. This type of home allows autonomy from family constraints and the freedom to create a personal space. Senior relatives may still have authority over the younger relatives, but it is no longer evident in every detail of daily life. Mothers-in-law, and fathers-in-law, especially have less say in the lives of daughters-in-law and sons-in-law. There is far more freedom to make decisions in this form of residence.

The other side of freedom is responsibility, and neolocality increases the load of responsibilities that men and women carry. A mother-in-law may order her daughter-in-law around in extended households, but she also shoulders much of the work of the house. A young woman in her own house usually is expected to manage the home, feed the family, care for the children, and do whatever other responsibilities she has in the community. Her mother is not there to help her nor are her male relatives. The case of the urban Japanese woman described a person who was expected to spend so much time on her house and children that she did not have time to work outside her home. If she wished to continue a career she had begun, she was assumed to be neglecting her children because there was simply too much work in her household role designation for one person to do. In extended families with other adults present, the work is shared. Likewise, in a nuclear family household, a man shoulders responsibilities for supporting this family that could be shared in bigger households. The Japanese husband had to work away from home an inordinate number of hours a week to financially support his wife and children. This Japanese couple was free from the constant demands of their elders, but they had little time to enjoy this freedom.

While neolocality may free husbands and wives from an immediate dependency on their elders, it creates a powerful dependency on one another and a degree of isolation from other family members. As several cases have already shown, the bond between married couples is not universally strong. In neolocal, nuclear families, the successes and failures of the husbands and wives are immediately important to the whole family. A weak or abusive husband in this type of household threatens his wife more than he might in a larger household. She has nowhere to turn for support or protection without going outside her household, and this may not always be possible. If her husband dies while her children are dependent, she must find some way to support herself and her children. In urban societies, the number of women and children living in poverty or living with abusive men appears epidemic. Without extended families to protect them, effective societal programs to support them, or personal wealth, it is no surprise that these conditions exist. Neolocal, nuclear family groups that are headed by competent, compatible, economically comfortable spouses may take hard work but be happy and successful. The main problem is that when things go wrong, there is nowhere to turn within the household.

Virilocality

Virilocality, or *patrilocality*, is a system in which a newly married couple lives in the household of the father of the husband. In other words, the man remains in the household of his birth while the wife leaves her natal household to join him. Patrilineal societies generally use this system, but so do some bilateral systems. The men in these households are closely related while the married women generally are not.[1] In such extended families, a senior man will be head of the household, and his wife will frequently be head of the women in it. The rest of the household will be comprised of the married and unmarried sons, their wives, children, and the unmarried daughters. In some large households, the senior generation may be comprised of brothers and their wives rather than one married couple, and in these the eldest brother usually is the family head. Such families are typically engaged in a shared economic enterprise, such as farming, and the family jointly owns the resources, notably land or animal herds, necessary for success. The men of the family who work together also live together in this system. Such families are then often corporate economic entities as well as assemblies of kin.

The benefits of this form of household should be obvious from the discussion of more isolated families. There is security and sharing in extended families, either patrilineal or matrilineal. When a mother wants to concentrate on a task without worrying about her children, she can ask another woman in the family to care for them. This can become quite organized, such as in some African groups, where women who trade in the community markets share their profits with other women who perform the household tasks. If a man wants to take a job outside of the family business or farm, he may do so as long as the money he earns is shared with the family. If a particular economic enterprise does not prove profitable for a time, the economic wealth of the whole unit supports those who worked on it. School fees, taxes, marriage gifts, and ritual offerings come from the common treasury. If a husband or wife dies, the remaining spouse and children

---

[1]In cases of brothers marrying sisters or cousins or polygynous marriage of sisters, the women may be related to one another but not in the lines of the men or children.

normally remain a part of the household and are supported by it. As people age, their physical tasks are taken over by younger members of the household, and they continue in positions of authority as elders.

Of course, there are problems in a virilocal extended family, and these problems fall heaviest on the women. The life of a new bride is the most unenviable position. Virilocal extended families in northern India present an example of the problems that such a bride can face. Women must marry men from different villages, and because they do not travel or visit with strange men in their villages, they often have arranged marriages. The bride and groom are virtual strangers on the day of their marriage. The bride then leaves her parents and siblings to move into a household of strangers—all of whom have more status than she does. She is expected to obey and care for her husband, follow the orders of all men senior to her husband, and follow the orders of her mother-in-law. The mother-in-law assigns her work and scolds her when she does not work up to expectations. The relationships between daughters-in-law and mothers-in-law in India are notoriously difficult. Only after a woman gives birth to her first child, preferably a son, does she earn some respect in the household. Her relationship to her children, who are patrilineal members of the household, gives her a permanent place. Even then, her husband and mother-in-law still dominate her. Her only opportunity for authority over others comes later in life, when she becomes a mother-in-law to her son's wife. With her husband's death, her own son may be head of the household, and he is expected to honor his mother. Her daughters will leave the village when they marry, and she can expect to see them only when they visit.

If a woman wants to leave her husband's virilocal household or her husband rejects her, her options are limited. If her father or brothers are willing to take her in, she can live with them in her natal home. She is unlikely to remarry and, if the breakup were thought to be her fault, she would dishonor her birth family. In an extreme case, such as the case recorded by Stanley and Ruth Freed (1980) of a woman named Devi, who was returned by her groom who said she was not a virgin, she might even be killed by her father to save her, and them, from suffering. With the apparent increase in the frequency of dowry deaths in this society, it is clear that many husbands solve the problems of an unsuccessful marriage by murdering their wives. In any case, men may remarry, and they keep custody of their children.

Uxorilocality

A *uxorilocal,* or *matrilocal,* extended family permanently includes a senior woman, her husband, her married daughters, their husbands and children, and unmarried sons and daughters. Married sons are expected to visit often and spend some time in their natal household. Adult sisters and their families can also head a household, with the eldest sister often acting as the matriarch. At marriage the groom leaves his natal home and moves in with his new wife and her relatives. As in virilocal households, the newcomer has few allies and never becomes a full member of the family. However, men in this situation tend to be treated differently than women in corresponding patrilineal situations. While they are expected to respect the household, they are not expected to act subserviently to their wives nor to take direct orders from their fathers-in-law. Further, they have responsibilities to their sisters and mothers in their natal household and are required to fulfill them as well as duties to their wives and children. Divorces appear to be less problematic in such households, and the husband can leave or be sent back to his natal household where he is welcomed. Children remain with the women in the household of their clan or lineage. Daughters remain with their mothers throughout their lives, and sons leave at marriage but often remain important in their mothers' affairs.

Matrilineal, uxorilocal extended families work especially well when the primary economy of the household keeps women working together. A good case of this is among the traditional Navajo of the American South-west. After their import by the Spanish, sheep became a central part of the Navajo economy. Women and children herded the sheep, and women made Navajo rugs from their fleece. Women owned their own animals that they herded together with those of their sisters. Men's herds were sometimes joined with their wives' or sisters' herds. In either case, all peo-ple knew which animals they owned. Small farms of corn and other veg-etables were also cared for close to home. The homestead was composed of a number of small nuclear family homes, called hogans, and separate structures for cooking and animals. Every married woman had a hogan that she shared with her husband and children. Men were required to avoid their mothers-in-law, and the separate houses facilitated this. Men were clearly pulled between two households. Loyalty to their sisters and mothers in their own clan was balanced against loyalty to their wives and children in their wives' clan. They had a little authority in the household of their wife and some authority over decisions made in their clan home. In both settings, however, the women also had authority and considerable say over what happened in the households.

Avunculocality

What happens when a matrilineal society has an economy that requires men to work together in groups? What happens in some of these societies is *avunculocality*. Avuncular means "uncle-like" and avunculocal means to live with an uncle. Because this is a pattern found in matrilineal societies, the uncle in question is the mother's brother. In fact, a young man will live with his mother's brother. Most matrilineal systems follow uxorilocal rules. Because this mode of residence is relatively rare, it is best to return to the Tlingit, who historically had an avunculocal system of residence. (Klein 1975: 80–83) Fishing, of course, was the heart of the subsistence economy. Men fished together in streams that they had rights in or on the fjords that separated the many islands. Uxorilocality would divide the men who formed these fishing teams. Fishing with nonrelatives would bring into question the rights to fish in an area and the responsibility for retribution in case of "accidents." Avunculocality solved these problems but created others.

Tlingits, until the twentieth century, lived in long, wooden, multifamily houses. In the traditional Tlingit system of avunculocality, a boy approaching adolescence would leave the house in which he had lived with his parents and siblings to move to the household of his mother's brother. This was the house of his own clan, and he lived there for the rest of his life. He needed to go at a young age in order to acquire the knowledge of his clan, which only his uncles could teach him. His sister remained with their parents until she married. At that time, she went to live in the clan house of her husband. A woman, then, never lived in her own clan house. While this solved the problem of fishing teams, it seems like an odd solution for a matrilineal system. The women, and their young children, were not protected in their clan houses. The women of a clan, who had strong roles in trade and wealth accumulation, were separated.

The Tlingits had another rule, applied most strongly to the elite, that addressed this concern. The ideal marriage, called by some the "royal marriage," was between a man and his mother's brother's daughter. (Klein 1975: 81) They are not related by Tlingit law because the bride belongs to a different clan than her father while the groom belonged to the same clan as her father. When this rule was followed, a young man moved into the clan house where his future wife was born. This meant that she did not have to move at marriage and stayed with her mother, and father, as long as they lived. In fact, if her sisters and female cousins married the same way, the women and young children in the house all belonged to the same clan. A house, therefore, would have two clans living in it: one of the women and one of the men. In this rather complex way, the men of a clan remained together and the women of a clan remained together. Of course, not all marriages followed this pattern, but clearly many elite marriages did.

While anthropologists have labeled the systems for postmarital residence according to a small number of patterns, it should be absolutely clear that no society chose their rules for residence off a prepared menu. Each society developed its own traditions. None of the rules solved all the problems that a society faced, and household rules changed with other changes in the societies. Gender was always an issue as were the questions of the nature of marriage and child rearing. People created these rules, but the lives that people lived were also constructed around the rules.

BALANCING ROLES: FAMILY FROM DIFFERENT ROLES

In all societies, people are reared to have specific expectations about their relatives. These relationships can be very deep, and inappropriate behavior can be seen as an unforgivable betrayal of trust. It should be no surprise that news of abuse between parent and child or husband and wife, relationships seen as protective in American culture, is received as far more severely than the same criminal behavior between strangers. As must be abundantly clear by now, in different societies the expectations are different; even the definition of who is a relative is different. However, a certainty about the importance of essential kinship relationships does appear virtually everywhere, although the details of their identities will be different.

Mother–Father–Uncle–Aunt–Children

Because the rearing of children is a primary duty vested in kinship groups, we could expect to discover the categories that are most similar in this realm. In a broad scope that is true. The obligations to teach, protect, and nurture children are largely, but not solely, vested in the roles of the parental generation.

Mother–Child   This dyad may be the true universal of kinship. All societies recognize the mother–child bond as deep and enduring. While there are myriad cultural reasons, the biological base cannot be ignored. The fact that the woman gives birth to and nurses the child has to be built into any kinship equation. Of course, there are adoptions, wet-nursing, servants, and infant formula that allow flexibility in specific situations, but largely, the woman who gave birth to the child feeds and cares for her or him during the period of infancy. During this period, the relationship of the mother and child is unchallenged. As the child grows, however, other roles may take equivalence or priority.

Many anthropologists have come to define the nuclear family as a mother and her children rather than a father, mother, and children. The sense of this may resonate with Americans who see more mother-headed families than ever before. In the past, such families were assumed to be temporary at best and aberrant at worst. Now it is clear to most that, while perhaps not preferable to a father-and-mother–headed family, the mother and child family can be long term and successful. Anthropologists see such female-centered families in a variety of diverse cultures. One such situation is found in families in which a man has several wives. In some polygynous families, the husband is a temporary visitor to the home of each wife, and each individual unit of wife and children tends to operate as a unique family. While there is a larger family that includes the husband, other wives, and children, the core of daily life is lived in this smaller social unit.

A very different situation is found in what is now called *matrifocal households*, which have been most extensively studied in the Caribbean (including the Garifuna described in Chapter 10) and are more widespread in modern states. Matrifocal households tend to be extended families that are kept together through the ties of mothers and children. These families include men, but not primarily as husbands or fathers. The mother–daughter, mother–son, and sibling ties take priority over marital ties. Unlike uxorilocal households, the philosophy of kinship is bilateral. The pragmatics of the social and economic setting, however, makes this a viable way for people to cope with the short-term jobs and relationships, complexity, and mobility that define their lives. Mother's home is always a base to which to return.

In very different circumstances, where strong male dominance is the rule, the mother–son relationship can be crucial to women. In a household like those of the Northern Indians discussed earlier in this chapter, the woman's identity as wife to her husband does not ensure her a significant standing in the home. Her identity as daughter or sister is even more tenuous because she lives in a different village than they do. Her identity as mother of a son, however, is the one that brings her respect and some authority. As an adult, the son is expected to respect and defend his mother and put his wife in her service. Similarly, in polygynous cultures, the observation that a man may have many wives but only one mother has been used to explain the difference in status that wives and mothers are sometimes accorded. Of course, in the same system, it is often the planning and work of the mother that makes her son the one, among many, to inherit his father's wealth or position.

Father–Child   In most societies men have a minimal role in the rearing of very young children. Even in American society, where men are just beginning to be encouraged to take a role in child rearing, a man who takes the primary role of caretaker for his children is still considered rare enough to invite comment. The concept of a househusband or a "Mr. Mom" remains the premise for comedies. As the latter term implies, this role is still seen as the mother's regardless of the gender of the actor. The father's role is different. He is expected to economically support and protect the family. He is also the male authority in the nuclear family and has the role of teaching his sons to become adult males as defined in the culture. On a general level, these duties are common in the role of father throughout the world. There are major variations, however.

The most obvious differences lie in matrilineal and matrifocal societies. In the former, many of the expectations that fall on the status of father in the United States are defined here in the role of mother's brother. Where father is not lineally related to his sons and daughters, he has less authority over them. In such societies, however, he often has a close personal relationship with his children. Without the obligation to discipline them, he often has a more informal relationship that is commonly more loving than the one the children have with their stricter mother's brother. Daughters are likely to live with their father throughout his life and care for him in old age. In a matrifocal setting, the father is often absent much of the time or is an occasional visitor. Other men, often mother's brothers or family friends, act as role models for the boys and offer support for both boys and girls. More than one or two men may share the "father" role here.

The relationship between a man and his sons in a patrilineal society might be expected to be as close as that of a woman and her daughters in a matrilineal society, but that often is not the case. In many such societies, a man does not become fully autonomous until his father dies. Even then, his brother or father's brother may take the role of head of the family. In cultures with rules such as primogenitor or ultimogenitor (where the oldest or youngest child or son inherits), the decision is essentially made at birth, and children unlikely to inherit are prepared for other pursuits. In many societies, however, the decision of who inherits is left in the hands of the father, who makes the decision near his death. This system allows for the children, or more likely, sons to compete for their father's favor. In polygynous societies, such as the Swazi discussed in Chapter 5, this can take a particularly aggressive turn, with mothers actively taking part in the competitions. The relationship between fathers and sons in such situations is rarely comfortable. Even in societies where a clear heir is drawn, the father–son relationship can be problematic. Anthropologist Doren Slade (1992) described the agonies of a Mexican farmer who had nightmares that reflected an underlying wish that his father were dead. While he, the only son, loved his father, he could not inherit the farm nor act as a land-owning adult man in his community until his father "retired" or died. Because his father was unwilling to give up the status his land gave him, the son remained a legal minor and emotionally conflicted.

In cultures where there is little competition for scare resources, such as band and some tribal societies, the relationships between fathers and their children can be more informal and mutually supportive. Daughters often rely on their fathers and brothers for support when they live in their husband's homes. It is the father's role to challenge the husband and his family if his daughter is mistreated. If her father supports her husband in a dispute, she has little hope for relief. Fathers and sons can be the closest allies, with similar gender expectations, as they work at the same tasks and live together.

Uncles and Aunts; Nieces and Nephews   The relationships expected between siblings and children of a set of parents vary widely from casual companionship to formal authority. Various English dictionaries use terms such as "friendly," "kindly," and "caring" along with "uncle-like" in their definitions of avuncular, and this gives evidence that English speakers perceive the role of uncle as positive. An uncle, or an aunt, has no formal duties toward the younger generation but is expected to be warm and supportive toward them. The nieces and nephews, likewise, have no specific obligations other than a positive emotional response to their elders. In many societies, these same relations are specified more formally. For example, in many languages the term for "mother's sister" may be the same as for "mother" or may be "little mother," and the term for "father's brother" could be the same or similar to "father." In these societies, father's brothers and mother's sisters are treated as second mothers or fathers and are expected to be very close to the children.

In matrilineal societies, of course, the role of mother's brother is clearly drawn. Mother's brother, as a child's closest senior lineal kinsman, takes on many of the roles that a father would in a society in which he was the closest adult kinsman. In patrilineal societies, the role of father's sister is rarely so strongly defined, although she is the child's closest senior lineal kinswoman. She may have special roles at the birth of a new niece or nephew or in training her nieces to be successful women of her clan. There does not seem to be a patrilineal puzzle in competing roles of mother and father's sister to parallel the apparent conflict between father and mother's brother reported in some matrilineal societies. It remains for future studies of gender in those cultures to determine whether the conflict is absent or simply previously unrecognized. In the past, conflicts between women were often seen as idiosyncratic rather than built into the societal structure.

Siblings

In Western society the relationships between siblings is expected to be informal, warm, and lasting, but they do not have the same structural intensity as the relationships between spouses or between parents and children. In many other societies, however, the relationship between siblings can be as strong or stronger than these other connections.

Same-sex siblings—brother–brother, sister–sister—are commonly reared together and have friendly relations throughout their lives. Depending on the kinship structure of their society, of course, they might live together as adults or be separated at marriage. In a uxorilocal family sisters live together throughout their lives and frequently work cooperatively. Children are reared together and chores are shared. Likewise, in a virilocal or avunculocal setting, brothers form lifelong work teams and support one another. Of course, age differences and positions of authority also affect these roles, and, as noted, brothers may be called on to compete to become their father's heir.

Siblings of different genders have relationships that are more complex. However, in either a matrilineal or a patrilineal system, they have connections that spouses cannot have because they are the male and female members of their clan or lineage. It is extraordinarily rare for a perason to give up membership in a clan at marriage. Even in systems that emphasize one gender over the other, siblings of the subordinate category remain clansmen and clanswomen. Their lives are clan lives. If they live them well, it reflects well on the clan, but, if they live them badly, or are abused, this diminishes the clan. Even in a patrilineal, virilocal society, then, the lives and the behavior of married sisters are important to the status of their brothers. A brother is expected, in most cases, to defend his sister if she is ill-treated in her husband's home. Likewise, when she visits her natal home, she returns with the status of a member of the community and should be treated with respect. This is more important, of course, in high-status families where there is much to lose than in lower status families.

In matrilineal societies, the connection between brother and sister is expected to be strong and enduring. In the particular role of mother's brother, he is required to take an active part in the rearing of his nieces, and more importantly, nephews. Among the Navajo, for example, such a man lived for extended periods in the hogan complexes of his mother and sisters. He was as much a resident there as he was in the hogan complex of his wife and children. When there were clan events or clan issues to be resolved, brothers and sisters were essential partners in these enterprises. In an avunculocal situation, like that of the Tlingit, this was more complex. Because women, even as children, never lived in their own clan house, there was no issue of returning there. As widows, they temporarily lived in their clan house because they always maintained a right to do so, but long-term widowhood was not common. Tlingit women had important economic roles in their society and were important in the raising of goods for potlatches. These activities were done as clanswomen, and their connections to their brothers and uncles were essential. Any abuse by non-clansmen or women, including those they married, was an immediate slight on the status of their clan and was dealt with by the clan. In fact, the ties between a brother and sister were expected to be stronger and longer lasting than those between a husband and wife. In times of disharmony between clans, and where raids were possible, the women and children of the household left and sought shelter in their own clan houses. The reason given for this was that these people were potential spies for the opposition. While they were expected to respect and have emotional attachments to their husbands and fathers, they were primarily expected to be loyal to their own clan. This was not seen as a weakness of women, who betrayed their own husbands, but as the strength of women, who placed the well-being of their own clan over all other desires. The brother–sister connection was stronger than the husband–wife connection because it was built into the structure of the society. An even stronger case of this is found among the Nayar of India, who are discussed later in this chapter.

If the matrilineal puzzle is seen as the conflict between two dyads rather than two specific roles, it can raise much broader issues than those found only in a matrilineal society. The classic matrilineal puzzle sees a conflict between husband and mother's brother over authority in the family. In fact, there is a competition between the obligations of the husband–wife relationship and those of the sister–brother relationship. As noted, the juggling of these two role classes between men and women are dealt with in a wide variety of societies to greater or lesser degree.

WIVES AND HUSBANDS: THE IDEOLOGIES OF MARRIAGE

The roles of husband and wife make up the core partnership in Western society according to contemporary ideals. It is with marriage that a new family begins, and ideally, although not statistically, this marriage lasts as long as both live. It is a relationship that is sexually exclusive, economically unified, and emotionally fulfilling. In fact, few societies define marriage in this way, and even those that do find the ideal difficult to fulfill. Anthropologists define marriage in a very general manner in order to fit the realities of most societies, but no one definition includes all the forms of spousal relationships that are found in the world. In general terms, *marriage* is a publicly recognized, sexual partnership between two people, usually male and female, that allows for the creation of socially legitimate children. As general as this is, there are cases that do not fit. Additionally, there are many cases in which a person may be involved in more than one such partnership at a time. Needless to say, the husband–wife, male–female relationships vary widely in definition. While it is impossible to cover all the variations, some of the types are common enough or significant enough to warrant review. In this chapter, discussions of the nature of monogamy and polygamy are followed by specific cases of marriage that involve "visiting husbands" and "female husbands." Questions of gender in the definition of marriage are inherent in each.

Monogamy

Monogamy is generally defined as the marriage between one man and one woman. It is the most common form of marriage in the world, and it is the only culturally and legally acceptable form in the Western world. Contemporary Americans see this form of marriage as a partnership with an ideal of equality between the spouses. While sexual exclusivity is the ideal within marriages, both partners may have had sexual partnerships before their marriage and may have other lovers and spouses after their first marriage. Americans in previous generations viewed marriage somewhat differently. The husband was the head of the family with the wife taking a subordinate, but supportive, role. The roles of father and mother were as central to the marriage as those of husband and wife are now. Additionally, this union was expected to last until the death of one of the spouses. Indeed, strong social penalties were afforded to those who divorced. Because women were expected to be virgins at marriage and sexually faithful to their husbands, few "respectable" women would have more than one sex partner in their lives. Men were expected, and allowed, to be more sexually active both before and within marriage, but their sexual partners were relegated to socially inferior status. It is clear that marriage forms change over time in societies and the meaning of monogamy at one time may be different than at another. Also monogamy refers only to socially sanctioned long-term unions; it can exist side by side with less binding sexual relationships.

Some cultures mandate that an individual marries once and that marriage involves only one other person. Even with this ideal, some few individuals in these societies will never marry, and others might marry twice. The ability to remarry after the death of a spouse, although commonly associated with restrictions on the range of possible second partners, is very widespread. In some extreme cases, such as the historical practice of suttee in India or the death practices of the highest ranked among a Native American group (the Natchez) at the time of contact with the French in America, the death of one spouse meant the death of the other. In India, the widow died on the funeral pyre of her husband; among the Natchez, the low-status widow or widower was killed before the funeral and buried with the spouse. In others societies, especially where marriage is considered a religious bond, divorce is deemed impossible. Ireland, for example, legalized divorce as recently as 1995. Before that, spouses in an unhappy marriage could live apart but could not marry other people as long as their spouses lived.

The form of monogamy practiced in the United States today is referred to as *serial monogamy*, meaning that a person can only have a single marriage partner at any time. During a lifetime, an individual, without breaking any social rules, can have multiple husbands or wives. Many societies that practice monogamy as the ideal form of marriage follow this pattern and allow divorce and remarriage after the divorce from or death of a spouse. In some, the pattern is embedded into the marriage practices. Among the Tlingit, for example, an old custom was for a young man or woman to marry a much older person. In this first marriage, the young spouse helped the older spouse with the chores that had become difficult with age, while the older spouse brought lessons of wisdom and training to the younger. After a time, it was expected that the older spouse would die and the younger one would be free to remarry, with the restriction that the next spouse must belong to the same clan unit as the first. At this time, a person closer to his or her age was a likely choice, and the relationship between these spouses would be different than in their earlier marriages. As old widows or widowers, the cycle was completed when they married young people. While the specifics of this may be drawn from one society, in fact, many cultures have similar expectations of age differences between husbands and wives that lead to a high probability of early widowhood.

At first glance, monogamy might seem a form of marriage that works toward gender equity: one man and one woman as a partnership. In fact, however, the form does not determine either a type of equality or inequality. It does suggest an intense relationship between partners that is not mediated by the help or interference of other individuals who have claims on either spouse. The responsibilities that are vested in the specific roles rest totally on each spouse's shoulders. The flexibility of societies in imprinting gender expectations on marriage is extraordinary regardless of the number of spouses involved.

Polygamy

Polygamy, marriage to more than one spouse at a time, in practice is not as different from Western customs as popular culture would have it. A polygamous system allows more than one culturally acceptable, sexual partnership, while Western customs now expect, if not wholeheartedly approve of, multiple partnerships over time or, discreetly, at the same time. The image of polygamy in media tends to place an image of overt, and somewhat lewd, sexuality on the men involved in these marriages and an image of debased servitude on the women. In fact, polygamy has virtually nothing to do with libidinous brutes setting up sexual playgrounds. As with everything else human, the reality is far more textured.

Scholars define two main types of polygamy. The first, *polygyny,* is what most people think of when they hear the term polygamy. Polygyny, literally "many women," is a system in which a man can have more than one wife at the same time. The second, *polyandry,* "many men," is a system in which a woman can have more than one husband at the same time. The first is far more common than the second form, but polyandry appears in several parts of the world. In either form of polygamy, unless there is an unusual distribution of men and women, only a limited number of people will be able to live the ideal, and most people will probably marry monogamously or not at all.

Polygyny When a man is married to more than one wife, the structure of his household takes on added dimensions. In some cultures, the husband sets up separate houses or even compounds for each wife. In that way, they each have their own place to maintain and a separation from the other women. If these houses are in different towns, the husband is expected to move among them and support each family equitably. In cases where the wives live together within a large household, he may maintain his own house in the compound and his wives may take turns visiting him. In these multiwife households, it is typical for the first wife to take a managerial role among the other women. Farm work, marketing, child care, and other chores are often shared in such households. It is not unusual to find both antagonisms and cooperation among women in polygynous households.

The primary problem that most Westerners see in these families is that of sexual jealousy. A woman is expected to be jealous when sharing her husband with other women, and, certainly, such jealousy is found in many such families. Of course, sexual relations are often not limited to marriage, and sexual jealousies can appear in many forms of marriage. In polygynous families, competition for resources and positions for the wives and their children is also common. The life of the mother whose son

A family portrait: An African polygynous family.

replaces his father is apt to be more appealing than that of the mother of his half-brother who does not. Families in which the wives are resentful and working against one another are chaotic and dysfunctional. Most polygynous societies have methods for making these families work.

A common and simple solution is *sororal polygyny*. All this means is that the husband marries women who are sisters to one another. If the wives are actual, or clan, sisters, they are likely to have good relationships before marriage that will continue. Their alliances to one another may supercede those to their husband. The literature is replete with descriptions of husbands in such marriages complaining about losing control of their household because their cooperating wives outmanuever them. It is common to read that a wife encourages her husband to marry her sister. In patrilineal households, sisters—and unrelated but friendly co-wives— can represent a supportive faction in an otherwise alien community.

A second solution is to set up rules for equal treatment. In Islam, where men are traditionally allowed to have up to four wives, the moral rules are well known. A man may have only as many wives and children as he can afford to support comfortably, and he must ensure that each wife is treated equally. His first wife, with whom he has lived for many years, and his most recent bride, who is amusing and young, must be treated as equals. This not only protects his household, but it is morally right. When a man follows these rules, there is no reason for an equally moral wife to be jealous.

A third solution lies more in the hands of the wives than the husband. In many households, women use the strength of their numbers and unique skills to improve their own lives. Every wife does not have to cook every night. Every wife does not have to be in the compound at all times to cater to her husband's needs. Every wife does not have to watch her children at all times. In other words, a division of labor among wives can free them to do what they enjoy most and excel at these pursuits. Ethnographies contain examples of wives asking their husbands to marry a particular girl in order to improve the household. In cases where women have their own money or wealth, as in the trading cultures of Africa, the wife might even pay for an additional bride of her choice. Cooperation between wives in the trading cultures meant that a trader woman could leave for distant markets, leaving her husband and children in good hands. The wife, or wives, left behind then expected a portion of her profit for the extra work they did. If there were only one wife, she would have been tied to her family obligations and would be unable to earn money.

News reports in August 2000 suggested another unusual solution. Asiyah Andrabi, an Islamic advocate for women's rights and Islamic hegemony in the Kashmir, a region under dispute by India and Pakistan, was quoted as advocating the responsibility of men, including her own husband, to take more wives. The war over the disputed region had had many casualties and this had left many women widowed. The remaining men should take care of them and their children by marrying them and giving them homes. Andrabi pictured polygyny in her violent homeland as a feminist solution to a wrenching problem for women.

Polyandry   At face value, polyandry is simply the same form as polygyny but with the genders reversed. In popular perception and local practice, however, there are many more differences. Casual observers tend to assume that polyandry does not exist. Indeed, to a Westerner, the idea that men would cooperatively share a wife seems absurd. According to this logic, women could be forced into sharing a husband, but men would never allow the opposite to occur. Men are too proud and would be too jealous. Even some of the scholarly work is underlined with these assumptions.[2] While it is true that it is much rarer than polygyny, polyandry does exist as the preferred marriage pattern in a variety of cultures in Africa, Australia, and, most broadly, in Asia. Much of the academic literature on this form of marriage has centered on the question, Why? Why did it develop, and what role does it play in the societies in which it occurs? These are questions less frequently asked of monogamy or polygyny, although they are valid and should be asked of the other configurations as well.

---

[2]See Ramesh Chandra's 1997 response to Levine and Silk and Trevithick for examples.

A wedding portrait: A wife and her husbands in the Himalayas.

A particularly interesting issue that is raised about polyandry involves reproduction. It seems reasonable that, as a rule, polyandrous households will have fewer children than polygynous households. All other things being equal, a woman will have the same number of children whether she has one sexual partner, two, or three. In a hypothetical polyandrous family with one wife and three husbands, the woman will have four children. That means that her husbands will have had, at least in the marriage, an average of one and one-third child each. In the hypothetical polygynous family in the next village that has one husband and three wives, each woman will have four children; thus, the husband will have twelve children in the marriage. The women all have four children, but the men average from less than two to twelve. This has led anthropologists to hypothesize that one of the purposes of adapting polyandry may be to control population size in societies with limited resources. In fact, many polyandrous societies are found in such environments. Others have asserted that in the end, the well-being of the children who are produced and taken care of in such families is much better than those reared in polygynous or monogamous homes. The support of multiple fathers for a small number of children increases the likelihood of their physical and economic well-being. Presumably, but this is rarely discussed, it does the same for the wife/mother of the family.

The most extensively studied polyandrous societies are in Asia, especially, but not exclusively, in the region of the Himalayas. Anthropologist Nancy E. Levine (Levine and Silk 1997) has long studied one of these, the Nyinba of Nepal. The Nyinba are of Tibetan ethnicity and practiced a form of polyandry called fraternal polyandry. Here a woman married a set of brothers. The economy of these people, unlike some other groups, was a prosperous combination of agriculture, herding, and trade, and the ideal for polyandry was having three husbands, one of whom specialized in each pursuit. Marriages were begun when an oldest brother reached adolescence and a slightly younger bride was chosen. She married him and his younger brothers. As they matured, the younger brothers became full partners in the marriage, although in a large family the youngest was considerably younger than his wife was. Also, one man in the "older brother" role had authority over his younger siblings, which translated into some differences of power and access in the household. Unlike in most other polyandrous households, where the children are all considered full siblings and all the husbands their fathers, here the paternity of a child was "revealed" by the mother. Full siblings were closer to one another and their fathers than they were with their half-siblings and "uncles." All of these factors could bring tension into the household, and some men left these marriages. Overall, however, the system appeared to fill the needs of many of the participants, and most of the marriages persisted.

Other Variations of Marriage

While most of the forms of marriage in the world can be roughly fit into the categories that anthropologists have created, these categories do not perfectly describe the specific realities of any one society. Additionally, there are several forms of marriage that defy general categorization at all. Two types that offer different conceptualizations of marriage and gender have been loosely referred to as "visiting spouses" and "female husbands."

Visiting Spouses   Is marriage universal? That question often is raised about midway through a student's first introductory anthropology course. The answer, like the answer to so many similar questions is this: It depends on your definition of marriage. The crucial example that is commonly cited is that of the Nayar of Central Kerala, India. Anthropologist Kathleen Gough (1961) described a marriage system among the precolonial Nayar that challenged virtually all definitions of marriage except that of the Nayars themselves. Briefly, before girls reached puberty, they were ritually married to men of the proper caste and status who were selected for them by lineage. The couples went through a communal religious service during which the groom gave the bride a gold token. The couples were secluded together for three days, and they were allowed to have sexual relations if the girl was old enough. After the festivities ended, the men left and the couples were not required to interact again. The wife continued to live with her matrilineal kin, including her brothers, but now was an adult and was allowed to have legitimate children. She began to take lovers who visited with her at this household. Her brothers, who resided near her, provided the support that husbands might be expected to be responsible for elsewhere. They, at the same time, were the husbands and lovers of women who live elsewhere. The legal father of the woman's children was the man she "married" in the formal ceremony, while the biological father of each was, more likely, one of her visiting lovers. The formal marriage had been arranged by the matrikin of both individuals, but the individuals themselves selected their lovers. Brothers and mother's brothers were the most permanent and immediate male partners in women's lives, and they had no sexual contact.

The more typical forms of marriage in the world assumed a husband would be his wife's ceremonial partner, lover, father of her children, and economic partner. Defining either the ceremonial husband or the lovers as the real husband in this case still left two other categories of men as partners in the women's lives. Women maintained households for themselves and their children while men "visited" them. A woman had relationships with a variety of men and the freedom to instigate new ones. Likewise, a man had a variety of women in his life. He had responsibility and connection with children as their social father, biological father, and mother's brother. Both men and women had a web of relationships that bound them to others. The common responsibilities that people have for children and others were fulfilled here, but not in the common way. The answer to the question, Is marriage universal? hinges on the case of the Nayar. Does marriage mean that a woman is bound to one or, in the case of polyandry, a small number of men in an alliance that legitimizes her children, allows her legitimate sexual experience, gives her economic support, creates a residence that includes the husband(s), and offers her new responsibilities toward these men? If so, did the Nayar have marriage? Who was the husband? If not, what are the patterns of marriage that may form in a world that defines gender in so many different ways?

In other areas of the world, it is the women who visit their husbands. Anthropologist Gracia Clark (1994) wrote of duolocality among the matrilineal Asante of Ghana. Here, as in some other West African societies, women and men retained their own residences in their childhood homes after marriage. A woman had distinct responsibilities toward her husband, including cleaning, cooking, and sleeping with him, but she could meet her obligations by visiting her husband at night and returning to her own home during the day. Her children or hired individuals took on some of the house chores for her. She maintained her own fields and took active part in trade. When she needed help with her farm, she most often sought it from her brothers or hired someone to do the work. As a woman aged, her wealth and responsibility to her maternal group grew. During this time she "retired" from the marriage by putting less energy into her subordinate role to her husband and more into her superior role in her own household group. Her husband could take younger wives at this time and accept the formal continuance of their marriage or the couple would divorce. In either case, the basic needs of each person continued to be met in their natal household. There is no dispute over the identity of marriage in the case of the Asante. What is in question here, and in other societies in which duolocality is practiced, is the connection between marriage and home.

Female Husbands   Most marriages, as anthropologists have traditionally defined them, involve men and women in relationships that allow the production of legal offspring. Certainly every marriage does not produce a child, but reproduction is one of the major rationales, if not *the* major rationale, that societies assert for marriage. Same-sex marriages, which are the subject of public debate in the United States, are said by some opponents to be "unnatural." Because kinship is cultural, rather than natural, in all forms, this argument might be considered a restatement of the possibility of reproduction being necessary for valid marriages. Of course, few would argue that individuals who are physically unable to reproduce even after having heterosexual relations should be disbarred from marriage. Marriage can exist without offspring or with offspring adopted from other parents.

In some societies, the difference between sex and gender is clear enough to be separated in the concept of marriage itself. The classic examples of this are in the category "female husband" in many African societies.[3] In these societies the role of "husband" is gendered as male, but the sex of the individual playing this role is more flexible. Denise O'Brien offered a clear definition in her 1977 article: "a woman who takes on the legal and social roles of husband and father by marrying another woman according to the approved rules and ceremonies of her society." (p. 109) There are a number of social reasons that women have entered into such marriages in African societies, but all appear to increase the status, and often, power of the female husbands.

A woman who takes a wife in a socially sanctioned marriage receives almost the same benefits as does a man who takes a wife. The main difference is sex. It appears that female husbands and their wives are not expected to become lovers, so this is not usually defined as a lesbian relationship.[4] Otherwise, the female husband functions similarly to a male husband. In other words, the female husband pays bridewealth where appropriate, receives the domestic services expected, and generally becomes the father of her wife's children.

---

[3]Beth Greene (1998) calculates there were about 40 such societies.
[4]See R. Jean Cadigan (1998: 90).

O'Brien defined two types of female husbands, surrogate and autonomous. (1977: 112–113) In *surrogate* situations, the woman becomes a substitute for a man and provides for the production of heirs. In a patrilineal family without male children, a daughter may take a wife and *become* the father who produces children for the patrilineage. She might also marry a wife in the name of a fictive male relative, and the children of that woman would be considered the children of the fictive husband. Her wife could give birth to her grandchildren in this fashion. In *autonomous* marriages, the female husband acts as her own agent. She uses her money to provide bridewealth for her wife and to secure rights to children for herself. There are several reasons she might do this. First, she may not have children as a wife and can now secure them as a husband. Second, she may need the services of a wife to help her in economic enterprises. A wife can expand the outreach of her trade networks or increase her land use. Third, a wife can be a political asset. In several societies that practice female husband marriage, women can be political leaders but their role as wife can be problematic. If a wife is subordinate to her husband, how can she be superior in public standing? The more powerful role in these societies is husband, and a female political leader is stronger as a husband than as a wife. In some societies, female leaders cannot marry men and remain leaders. The Lovedu Queen, a divine monarch, took wives but could not have husbands. Female husbands do not become men, but they are not defined by the role of wife. This distinction leads directly to a challenge of the idea of female subordination in these societies. It is not women, per se, who are socially limited, but wives. The definition of subordination, as far as it exists, is embedded in kinship.

SUMMARY

Kinship is the primary way that societies define people and their relationships. For most types of societies, it is the principal structure of the society itself. Even in states in which territorial and governmental principles take center stage, kinship defines personal relationships to a large degree. Real people do not live in the social structure or at the state level; these people live in their households and relate to others in personal ways. Where they live and with whom is more important to them than the definition of their citizenship. The actual relationship of a husband and wife is often more important than the laws that govern such relationships. People play roles of father, mother's brother, wife, and granddaughter, which have meaning to them. Most of these roles, in most societies, are gendered. Most fathers are male. Most wives are female. Because kinship is a cultural construction, however, some fathers can be female. Kinship situates us and sets gendered categories. It often allows enough flexibility to confound those categories. We cannot understand gender in a society without understanding its kinship system, but such understanding must go beyond simple categories.

Readings

Cadigan, R. Jean. "Woman-to-Woman Marriage: Practices and Benefits in Sub-Saharan Africa." *Journal of Comparative Family Studies* 29, no. 1 (Spring 1998), pp. 89–98.

Chandra, Ramesh. "Reply to Nancy E. Levine and Joan B. Silk, 'Why Polyandry Fails.'" *Current Anthropology* 38 (1997), pp. 389–390.

Clark, Gracia. *Onions Are My Husband: Survival and Accumulation by West African Market Women.* Chicago: University of Chicago Press, 1994.

Collier, Jane Fishburne, and Sylvia Junko Yanagisako. "Introduction." In *Gender and Kinship: Essays Toward a Unified Analysis,* eds. Jane Fishburne Collier and Sylvia Junko Yanagisako. Stanford, CA: Stanford University Press, 1987, pp. 1–13.

Douglas, Mary. "Is Matriliny Doomed in Africa?" In *Man in Africa,* eds. Mary Douglas and Phyllis M. Kaberry. Garden City, NY: Anchor Books, 1971, pp. 123–37.

Freed, Ruth S., and Stanley A. Freed. *Rites of Passage in Shanti Nagar,* Vol. 56: part 3. Anthropological Papers of the American Museum of Natural History, New York, 1980.

Gough, Kathleen. "Nayar: Central Kerala." In *Matrilineal Kinship,* eds. David M. Schneider and Kathleen Gough. Berkeley, CA: University of California Press, 1961, pp. 298–384.

Greene, Beth. "The Institution of Woman-Marriage in Africa: A Cross-Cultural Analysis." *Ethnology* 37, no. 4 (1998), pp. 395–412.

Klein, Laura. *Tlingit Women and Town Politics* (dissertation). Ann Arbor, MI: University Microfilms, 1975.

Levine, Nancy E., and Joan B. Silk. "Why Polyandry Fails." *Current Anthropology* 38 (1997), pp. 375–99.

Morgan, Lewis H. *Ancient Society or Researches in the Lines of Human Progress from Savagery, Through Barbarism to Civilization.* New York: Henry Holt and Company, 1877.

O'Brien, Denise. "Female Husbands in Southern Bantu Societies." In *Sexual Stratification: A Cross-Cultural View,* ed. Alice Schlegel. New York: Columbia University Press, 1977, pp. 109–26.

Richards, A. I. "Some Types of Family Structure Amongst the Central Bantu." In *African Systems of Kinship and Marriage,* eds. A. R. Radcliffe-Brown and Daryll Forde. London: Oxford University Press, 1950, pp. 207–51.

Slade, Doren. *Making the World Safe for Existence: Celebration of the Saints among the Sierra Nahuat of Chignautla, Mexico.* Ann Arbor, MI: University of Michigan Press, 1992.

Stone, Linda. *Kinship and Gender: An Introduction.* Boulder, CO: Westview Press, 1997.

Trevithick, Alan. "On a Panhuman Preference for Monandry: Is Polyandry an Example?" *Journal of Comparative Family Studies* 28 (1997), pp. 154–82.

CHAPTER EIGHT

Power and Powerlessness: Gender and Political Control

Is power always gender defined?
If some women have formal authority, do all women benefit?
Are there universal definitions of gender equality?

The issue of power is central to the most enduring questions that people ask about gender. Questions involving exploitation, inequality, and poverty to those involving mothers-in-law, goddesses, and queens are essentially questions of power, authority, and political control. This is not to say that all such questions are political, but they all have a significant political component.

Because different people, and even different fields of study, use terms that denote political concepts in contrary ways, we must begin this discussion by defining some basic terms, as anthropologists tend to use them. The word *political* simply refers to the use of power and authority. The overriding concept is that of power. Most anthropologists use *power* to mean that one party has the ability to force another party to do something. If a robber points a gun at you and demands your wallet, he or she has power over you at that point in time. A person with power can force another to do something he or she does not want to do. Authority is different. A person with *authority* has the socially recognized right to ask you to do something, and you are socially obliged to do it. A police officer who orders you do move your car from a loading zone has the authority to do so. Likewise, Queen Elizabeth II of Great Britain has the authority to open Parliament.

These two concepts, power and authority, do intermingle. Robbers may have the power to take your wallet, but they do not have the authority to do so. The Queen of England may have the authority to open the legislature, but she does not have the power to refuse to do it. The police officer has both the authority and power to make you move your car. If you do not, he or she could have it removed and write you a ticket. When power and authority reside together, the position of the person wielding them is quite secure. Every few years, newspapers run stories about political coups where legitimate, if perhaps not always admirable, governments are violently overthrown and replaced by the leaders of the rebellion. Those new leaders have demonstrated their power and, more than likely, will soon establish their authority. Rewriting constitutions to justify and give authority to the new government are quite common.

Related to power and authority are the less potent ideas of influence and prestige. To have *influence* is to have the ability to sway the opinions of someone else. If the person, or people, who are influenced are those who hold power and/or authority themselves, then the person with influence may be able to use that power/authority for his or her own ends. The classic American concept of the "Little Lady Behind the Throne" has long been put forward as a defense against the idea that lack of women political office holders demonstrates the lack of power for women in the United States. Men may hold the offices, the argument goes, but their wives influence what they do in that office. In other words, women have power through their influence over men. Clearly this is true only with an assumption that is indefensible: that men are weak and will do what they are told regardless of their own opinions. In fact, the person in the position of power or authority has the final word, and the influence of someone else is filtered through his or her perspective. Influence is not inconsequential. Being able to be part of a debate over an important issue is far better than being ignored, but, in either case, the final decision is made elsewhere.

Prestige is related to these ideas but is not really a political term. A person with *prestige* has social standing in the community. In a class society, people with prestige are those at the top of the social hierarchy. Others are expected to look up to prestigious people and admire them. However, unless they also have authority, there is no mandate to follow their orders or their teachings. This concept is linked to another popular image, that of the Victorian "Woman on the Pedestal." Women, in earlier days, as the story goes, were idolized and protected by men. They were figuratively placed on pedestals to be observed and adored. They did not have to trouble themselves with the sordid world of power because others took on this burden to protect them. Putting aside the historical fact that this simply was not true, the image is the exact opposite of power. These people, who are pictured as having tremendous prestige, at the same time had no power, authority, or influence. They gave up over control over their own lives to fulfill this status and certainly had no control over others. Now in reality, Victorian women were a far more diverse group of human beings than popular culture presents, and many had power and authority over those of lower station and influence over specific men. People with prestige, especially if they have access to wealth and connections, may well also have political clout, but prestige alone does not guarantee social or personal control over important events.

The popular movements that awakened the scholarly interest in women's issues in the United States and elsewhere were political. The call for votes for women in the early women's movement of the twentieth century and the call for equal political and economic rights in the latter half of the century both focused on the disempowerment of women, when compared with men. Feminists demanded equal rights for men and women. It should be little surprise, then, that academic feminists had much the same focus. The first generation of contemporary anthropological feminist scholars in the 1970s began work on the issue of women and power. One of the first and most powerful questions of this generation was this: Why are women universally subordinated to men?

UNIVERSAL SUBORDINATION OF WOMEN?

When gender studies began to gain acceptance in anthropology in the 1970s, the scholars of the time reviewed the ethnographies they knew. They recognized that women were largely missing from these ethnographies, that the interests that authors pursued were largely contemporary American (and male) interests, and that leadership in the societies studied were regularly described to be in the hands of men. The first two concerns were met with a concerted effort to change the methodology of anthropology to ensure that women and women's issues became part of any competent ethnography in the future. The third brought a different, and with the wisdom of hindsight, rather puzzling reaction. Rather than questioning the reality of this all male leadership concept, they asked why all cultures seemed to mandate that men are the societal leaders.

In the landmark book, *Woman, Culture and Society*, published in 1974, editors Michelle Rosaldo and Louise Lamphere asserted in the introduction, "Everywhere we find that women are excluded from certain crucial economic or political activities, that their roles as wives and mothers are associated with fewer powers and prerogatives than are the roles of men. It seems fair to say then, that all contemporary societies are to some extent male-dominated, and although the degree and expression of female subordination vary greatly, sexual asymmetry is presently a universal fact of human social life." (p. 3) All the contributors rejected the idea that there was any major physical or intellectual weakness in women that conferred any innate inequality between men and women. It is in this book that Rosaldo put forward the public-domestic dichotomy as an explanation for this asymmetry. (1974: 17–42) Sherry Ortner, who used a structural model to search for the core of gender inequality, took a different approach. Here she hypothesized a universal association of women to nature as opposed to the association of men to culture. Further, every culture devalues nature and thus, devalues women. The argument is far more elegant than that description suggests, but the fundamentals are correct. Because women, through childbirth, child rearing, menstruation, and personality, were perceived as closer to nature than men were, women as a category were judged inferior to the category of men. Other articles point to the attachment of women to children, and child rearing, as key to creating psychological and cultural differences that led to inequality. Ultimately none of these theories proved to be the final solution, and many of the authors went on to revise their ideas with the increase in primary research that followed the book. Also, even if the subordination of women is not universal, the reality is that societies more frequently than not do grant privilege to men in roles of power and authority. Why are women so often limited in these public roles?

What Happened to Equality?

One answer to this question came from the Marxist scholars. Friedrich Engels posited a precapitalistic society in which equality, including gender equality, was the norm. Feminist anthropologists of the 1970s and 1980s, who were influenced by Marxist scholarship, argued that the appearance of inequality found in the literature was largely based on the colonialist wave that forcefully transformed egalitarian societies. They denied that inequality was a human gender universal but argued that it was the contemporary Western system that worked against such equality. Inspired by the work on the Naskapi of Canada by Eleanor Leacock, many feminist anthropologists looked to ethnohistory for these precolonial societies. In *Women and Colonization*, edited by Mona Etienne and Leacock in 1980, examples from 11 of the 12 societies studied (from the Aztec of Mexico to the Baule of the Ivory Coast to the Tongans of the Pacific) showed evidence of the power of women in those societies in earlier times—power that was lost through the colonial experience.

Measuring Equality and Inequality

Any study of relative power between men and women must first come to terms with its scales for determining power. It might be noted that the argument in anthropology is not whether matriarchies existed. The concept of the turn of the twentieth century that asserted rule by women as an early stage of human evolution has not been seriously revived. The range of the debate is between patriarchy and equality. Most anthropologists today appear to agree that absolute patriarchy, where men as a class rule over women as a class, is rare and, perhaps nonexistent, if it is defined strictly. Some women have power over some men in virtually all societies, and women have power over some aspects of culture in virtually all societies. This may be due to the fact that highly ranked women can order their servants or that women have a voice in the rearing of children or the creation of valuable resources. Neither might be considered by that society or by theorists as societal power, however. The definitions of power, authority, and the like become essential to the state of the argument.

Additionally, the definition of *equality* itself appears very elusive. What constitutes full equality? Obviously equality and identity are not the same thing. Things can be different *and* equal. A U.S. nickel and five pennies have equal spending power but they are different in size and material. A U.S. adult man and woman may cast votes in an election that are counted in the same way, but the man and woman can be very different individuals. Can experiences be separate and equal? Most Americans would say no. This is based on the Supreme Court ruling against racially segregated schools that concluded that the very nature of separation made such schools unequal. If, in a specific society, women were expected to function in a domestic realm while men were expected to function in a public realm, would this necessarily be inequality? Can men and women be perceived as different and still be treated as social equals? The problem is that the concept of equality is such an absolute term that, without a generally accepted scale of attributes and a method for determining the measurement of those attributed, it is virtually impossible to prove. Trying to create such a measurement scale that would work cross-culturally seems almost impossible. More important, it may not be worth the trouble. If a society could be labeled as having 100 percent gender equality while another would be labeled as having only 93 percent true equality, what would we really know? The questions that could be answered in this way seem naïve in a modern context.

One suggestion came from Eleanor Leacock (Leacock 1980), who rejected the term *gender equality,* although it was important to her theoretical stance, and suggested that *personal autonomy* instead, was a preferable concept. Turning the focus from a universal scale to the reality of an individual, this concept became easier to examine. Her question became this: Does an individual have control over the important aspects of his or her life? (pp. 25–42) In other words, is the individual subjugated or subordinated to others? While this concept does not demand a universal scale, it is still problematic. All people have limits on their personal options by the nature of society. Complete autonomy is not possible, and limits on it are again difficult to measure. It is a very useful concept in evaluating the lives of individuals in a system but, like equality, becomes a difficult concept to use in a cross-cultural comparison.

A third concept that has been used to promote the understanding of individual cultures or societies, if not cross-cultural comparison, is that of *complementarity.* This concept comes close to the idea of separate but equal. If men are responsible for one important aspect of society and women are responsible for another and if both are viewed as necessary for the successful lives of the society and its members, is this a form of equality? Many anthropologists, including Lillian A. Ackerman (1995) who studied the Colville, a Native American people of Washington State, say it is and that meaningful measurement is possible. For the Colville people, who have an ideology of gender equality, men's and women's roles are distinctively different. Examining the roles of men and women in the economic, domestic, political, and religious spheres in the culture at the time of early contact with Europeans, Ackerman finds that men and women have the same access to many important roles in each category and different but important jobs in each as well. In no category are women, or men, superior. With this she counters Louise Lamphere's 1977 contention that complementarity is not equality. Ackerman further supports this contention by demonstrating that in contemporary life, Colville women and men have identical access to important roles in each of the spheres.

A Different Question

Understanding the nature of power in the hands of men or women ultimately may not be promoted by focusing on the measuring of categories or in the comparison of the amount of power women may have compared with men. It is the complexity of the question that is most apparent today, and it is not one that is open to simple statements or conclusions. The measuring of any concept against a single standard limits questions and, consequently, answers. Equality may be a feminist goal, but determining how well any society fits this goal may ultimately not be a sound anthropological approach. Perhaps a broader set of questions that ask where, when, and why positions of power are gender designated in different societies may produce more interesting results. A review of different ways in which gender intersects with power, authority, prestige, and influence should illustrate the scope of the issue.

AUTHORITY AND POLITICAL OFFICE

When considering the issue of power for women, Americans tend to look first at the public offices in their society and ask how many women have held high political office. Because there have yet to be any women in the highest office, that of President of the United States, and few in the Senate or Supreme Court, this analysis tends to be rather bleak. However, while the relative number of U.S. female senators and representatives has grown slowly, the number of women in state offices has increased more significantly. Many people have suggested that this demonstrates that the lack of women in high office is a factor of time. Women raised with expectations of equality have not yet matured into high office. The female governors and heads of legislatures should move up into important elected federal offices shortly. However, few have, and the short lists of potential presidential and vice presidential candidates for the future still contain few feminine names.

When Americans look at women leaders in other countries, they find a confusing reality. Some of the states that have had female heads of state (England, Israel, Canada, and the Scandinavian countries) have a history of Western-style feminist movements and progress in women's rights. Although the feminist movements in these countries do not seem to be especially stronger or longer lived than in the United States, the political results for women seem far more advanced. More peculiarly, other states (including India, Sri Lanka, Indonesia, and Mongolia), where women's overall status appears, from a distance at least, to be far more oppressed than that of the average middle-class American woman, have, or have had, female heads of state as well.

In all these cases, both obvious and unexpected, the women who held these offices exerted true societal power. They led the creation of national policies and led their countries, in several cases, through major military conflicts. Some, such as Indira Ghandi, Golda Meir, and Gro Bruntland, were significant leaders in the world community as well. Such leaders demonstrated that individual elite women could become powerful in their countries. It is important to ask if they promoted the welfare of nonelite women and issues of importance to them. Did they affect everyday life?

Societal Powers

States have historically placed societal power in permanent offices, such as monarch or Prime Minister, which are held by designated individuals. In some societies wealth, itself, confers significant power and authority. Gender is often a key factor in these designations. The place of gender in systems of power based on monarchies, heads of state, and wealth indicates that different criteria for power can be used in different arenas.

Monarchies   From the beginning of the state system up until about two centuries ago, state-level governments around the world were monarchies. Many such states still exist in the modern world, and the designation of elected leaders is a relatively recent change. In a monarchy the ruling head of state is a specific member of a royal family who had legal right to the position. Different societies varied in their mandates about which family member should succeed to office on the death of the current monarch, but most commonly that successor was a brother or son.

Direct descent, birth order, and gender were usually key factors used for choosing a legitimate new monarch. Even in societies where bilateral descent is the rule for common people and domestic relations, the rules for succession to office are often unilineal. In ordinary cases, the paternal line that leads from father to son takes priority. This rule, however, includes the sons and brothers of the current ruler as well as his father's brothers and their sons. Consequently, an additional rule would involve the closeness of the claimant to the predecessor. Cousins give place to sons and brothers by this requirement. Many monarchies are much more structured than this. These states define the rule of inheritance by order of birth. The final common rule often mandates that only males may inherit or that males within a category take priority over females. The practical result of these rules is to limit the number of legitimate claimants to an office and lessen the likelihood of dispute within the royal family. As noted in the Swazi case in Chapter 5, the rules of selection for royal succession can be flexible enough to provide for myriad eligible candidates. This can lead to intrigue and division within the family during the life of the current monarch and violent battles after his death.

Ruling Queens in Kingdoms: Cases *England* The kingdom best known to Americans is that of Great Britain. Modern royals are often in the news, and segments of English history are part of American history as well. The rules for the accession to the British throne are relatively straightforward and consistent through the years. The eldest male son of a monarch is the presumed heir. If there are no sons, the eldest daughter will take the throne. Thus, it is only in cases in which a king or queen only has daughters, or when the closest lineal relative has no brothers, that a female will become the ruling monarch. Even given these restrictions, England has had several queens including Elizabeth I, Victoria, and Elizabeth II who are part of popular history. These women reigned under different governmental forms and were very different in personality. A brief review of their reigns illustrates their differences, demonstrates the diversity in this role, and raises questions about the role of female leadership for the general status of women.

Elizabeth I ruled England for 45 years, from 1558 to 1603. She was the middle child of Henry VIII and the second daughter. Her younger half-brother, Edward VI, reigned at the death of their father but died young. Her older half-sister, Mary I, took the throne at the death of Edward VI in 1553 until her death in 1558. Neither left children. While there was a keen preference for a king, happenstance left only female claimants to the throne. Mary, Queen of Scots, and Lady Jane Gray were two royal women with significant claims to the throne of England, and, under Elizabeth's reign, both died for forcing those claims.

Historian Wallace MacCaffrey wrote that the English during this period saw a female monarch as unnatural. The obvious solution lay in marriage so that "On his shoulders would fall the burden which only a male could carry. He would, in fact and in right, be king." (1993: 14) This was the path taken by Elizabeth's sister Mary, who married Phillip, the King of Spain, but this earned her tremendous unpopularity in England because this union suggested that England was being given to foreigners to rule. Elizabeth never married, although she used the promise of marriage as a diplomatic ploy. Unmarried, and the monarch, no one had claim to superiority in power over her. During her long reign, she established the power of England in Europe, supported the exploration of New World lands, resolved religious conflicts, reestablished the Church of England as the permanent state church, and negotiated wars and peace with European states. Historian John Guy concluded that "Perhaps better than any other European ruler, Elizabeth mastered the political game." (1988: 252)

Elizabeth I wielded tremendous power in England and internationally, but did this change the lot of less privileged women in Europe? The answer to this is basically, no. English women during Elizabethan times had few legal rights. As daughters, they were the controlled by their fathers and as wives, by their husbands. Even wealthy women generally had their inheritance folded into dowries at marriage. Women had little public say in political matters and little protection outside of their male relatives. Elizabeth appointed no female advisors nor did she encourage women in politics. While undoubtedly some of the noble women in her service had her ear, none were appointed to positions of power in the political realm. Elizabeth I demonstrated that a woman could be a monarch as strong as any man but not that women socially should be equal to men.

Queen Victoria, who like Elizabeth lent her name to an era, had a long and significant reign. Victoria ascended to the throne in 1837 at the death of her uncle, William IV. By that time, the powers of the monarch were strongly reduced from the Elizabethan era. Parliament had become the real power in the empire, but the Queen still remained a significant personage. Unlike Elizabeth I, however, she was not a politician and would have rejected such a demeaning notion. Also, unlike Elizabeth, she married and made her role as wife and mother a central part of her public identity. In fact when her husband, Prince Albert, died, she retired from public life for 10 years. Her nine children married royals throughout Europe, and she became a grandmother with a fair degree of influence over the next generation of European royalty.

While Victoria had extraordinary influence and significant power, the Victorian era became known, perhaps erroneously, as one of the most restrictive for English women. Women as wives and daughters remained under the control of their male relatives, and few controlled any wealth or power. Politically they could not vote, nor could they hold political office. Job opportunities were limited, and middle- and upper-class women in public positions were dishonored. The ideal of the woman as the perfect homemaker and selfless nurturer of her children was at its height, and Victoria supported this ideal with public persona and pronouncement. One of the ironies of this period is that internationally in its colonial enterprises, British colonizers mandated the subordination of women in political settings—all in the name of their female queen. Victoria proved that a woman could be a strong reigning monarch but only by emphasizing the womanly traits of scientific motherhood and nurturing.

The current Queen of England, Elizabeth II, became monarch on the death of her father, George VI, in 1952. She had one younger sister and no brothers. Her father came to the throne with the abdication of his brother, Edward VIII. By the mid-twentieth century, the British monarch had become a symbol of her country rather than a political leader. While she retained the right to open Parliament each year, she had no real power because no one would allow her to actually dissolve Parliament. England is a parliamentary democracy with elected political leaders taking precedence over the monarchy and House of Lords. In the late part of the century, another woman, Margaret Thatcher, as Prime Minister, had significantly more political power, although protocol compelled a public performance of subordination to her monarch.

While this queen is far less powerful than her predecessors, she is not a powerless woman. Her great fortune and access to important people throughout the world afford her considerable personal power. Also, British women of all classes have much more access to power than their sisters under previous queens. While Thatcher may be the best example of this, other women hold public office and significant positions in economic settings. Personally they hold individual rights separate from their husbands and can vote and own property. While the monarchy has lost considerable stature and power in the modern world, as it represents modern England, with all its problems, the standard of living for women has transformed dramatically. The queen is weaker, but the woman is stronger.

Queens in Africa   While it is extremely rare to find a society in which the gender designated for the ruling monarch is female, such cases do occur. One such case, described in a classic article by Annie M. D. Lebeuf in 1971, is that of the Lovedu queens of the nineteenth and early twentieth centuries. The Lovedu kingdom was composed of semiautonomous districts headed by men or women that were bound together in their allegiance to a central monarchy. The Lovedu had a small kingdom economically dependent on agriculture and domesticated animals. Kinship descent was patrilineal with a virilocal residence pattern. The queens of this period, Mujaji I, II, and III, were descendants of the last king of the Lovedu.

The queen was the head of the judicial system for the entire kingdom, and, in this role, she appointed women assistants called "mothers of the kingdom." (Lebeuf 1971: 99) She built alliances with lower chiefs and chiefs from other areas through kinship and reciprocal marriages. The queen, herself, had no official husband but married multiple women who were provided by chiefly families. Through these wives, she had control over "their" children, who could claim rights to the throne. By marrying her children and her wives to others, she further expanded her political ties. These ties to the queen raised the status of the families of the wives.

The most important role of the queen was ritual. She acted as the rainmaker for her kingdom. Through complex supernatural rituals she was expected to bring the rains that her economy depended on and to bring droughts to her enemies. This sacred position dictated strict behavior rules and defined her to her followers as more than a mere human. One rule limited her reign and life: She was not allowed to rule for more than four initiation ceremonies. At the end of this time, a ritual suicide was mandated. Because the initiations occurred every 10 years, this limit might be more apparent than real.

The Lovedu case is very different than most. First, of course, the ruling position is mandated to be held by a woman. However, she not only ruled as a woman but had women as district leaders and assistants. She also was supernaturally empowered to hold her position and had to demonstrate her success in rituals. In other ways, her use of marriage exchanges, her marriage to other women, and her high position in a royal family appear in some other African societies as well, where a woman is not a sole monarch but where chosen women of the royal family have positions of power with men.

There are numerous examples of royal families in Africa in which the royal women held positions of power second only to that of the king himself. In others, the senior woman and senior man held equal and complementary powers. The society of the Swazi, where the king and his mother were supreme rulers, was described in Chapter 5, and Lebeuf gives a number of similar accounts from throughout sub-Saharan Africa. In these societies, the mother, sister, or primary wife of the king have specific societal powers. Among the Asante of Ghana, the senior woman of the king's matrilineal line, often his mother, was similar to the Swazi queen in many ways. She had her own estate and courts and had authority over issues of marriage, children, women's rituals, and royal rituals. She was the chief genealogist with influence over the line of royal descent and headed the kingdom when the king was away at war. As Lebeuf notes, "Throughout her life she remains the only person in the kingdom who may give him advice, guide him, and criticize him to his face, even in public." (Lebeuf 1971: 101)

Probably among the most well-known African kingdoms was the system in place at the time of colonization of the Buganda of current-day Uganda. The heads of the kingdom were the Kabakas. The Kabakas were the heads of a complex bureaucracy that included levels of administration and control with district chiefs and subchiefs. Women, in general, had few rights and were subservient to their husbands and economically dependent on them. High-ranking women, however, shared in their husbands' status and could use their authority over lower ranking men and women. According to A. I. Richards (1964), royal women, "princesses" as they were sometimes referred to, however, received male titles and could act publicly as equals to the men of the same rank. ⤷ male titles? Or power titles?

Princesses, unlike common women, were allowed to own their own lands, take lovers at will, move freely, and use language otherwise reserved for men. Until well into the nineteenth century, princesses were not allowed to marry or have children. The king's official wife and his queen, who would be his half-sister, could not be his sexual partner, but "she sat with him on his enthronement day, shared office with him, and was viewed by some observers as his wife." (Musisi 1991: 782) The highest ranked women, those with titles, had estates throughout the kingdom and chiefs and tax collectors reported to them, including "the majority of Buganda chiefs, including the Prime Minister himself." (Musisi 1991: 780) The elite women had more power and public authority than most men in their society. They also had immediate control over the less highly ranked women living in their estates and in their extensive homes. They were not wives in the normal sense used in Bugandan society and, therefore, did not suffer from the subservience of typical Bugandan wives. The lot of most women was a highly restricted and controlled one. The elite lived very differently.

Outside of Africa It should be noted that the form of power held by elite women was not limited to African societies. Certainly the role of women chiefs and queens in the complex societies of the Pacific Islands, including the Hawaiians described in Chapter 5, show similarities in power relations to those described in Africa. Even in North America, there are echoes of these systems. The Natchez of the southern Mississippi valley may be one of the rare North American cases.

The Natchez were described originally in the records of the French religious and military officials who arrived with the first colonial invasion. This group was a surprise to the Europeans, who found a matrilineal kingdom/complex chiefdom with a unique class system. The top of the social pyramid was a class called the Suns. They were the absolute political and religious leaders of the society. The Great Sun was the highest ranked male and was coupled with the so-called White Woman, the "woman Chief," who was a clan sister. (Usner 1998:19) One White Woman was compared to her brother, the Great Sun, with admiration for her greater intellect. At the death of a White Woman the elaborate funeral followed the same pattern as that of the Great Sun.

To understand the Natchez, the social class systems needs to be further described. Below the Suns were noble classes, called the Nobles, and then the Honored People. At the bottom rung of the social ladder were the Commoners. What makes this system unusual is that the Suns were required to marry Commoners. In fact, the Nobles and Honored were also married to Commoners. The rank of the children depended on the gender of their noble parents. The child of a female Sun and male Commoner was a Sun, but the child of a male Sun and female Commoner was a Noble. In other words, the children of Noble women took their mother's rank, while the children of Noble fathers dropped one class in rank. Consequently, the next Suns, including the Great Sun and White Woman, were children of female Suns. The female Suns could choose their own husbands, and these men were required to serve their wives and remain faithful to them. The wives owed their husbands neither. Sun women demanded complete freedom in their lives and seem to have received it. Most drastically, the husband was sacrificed along with scores of other servants and faithful followers at her funeral in the same way that a Commoner wife would die with her Sun husband. (Fisher 1964: 57–58)

While much is unknown about the Natchez before the advent of the French, it is clear that it was a highly stratified society with a role for the highest ranked women that differed dramatically from their lower class sisters. Also, the lives and power of these women are similar to those of their brothers. In many societies around the world before the hegemony of the European model, class was a major determinant of gender differentiation. While this is true today in social matters, in this past it appears to have been true in political power as well.

Elected Heads of State   While it is clear from Chapter 6 that gender differences are strongly written into the power structures of the state system, it may be premature, and overly pessimistic, to conclude that all states are doomed to strict patriarchy. In recent times there are indications that women are entering into political leadership positions in a wide variety of countries, although the vast majority of states still are largely male dominated. In the last 25 years, one country, the Philippines, has named two female ruling presidents, Corazon Aquino and Gloria Arroyo, while Nicaragua (Violeta Chammoro), Iceland (Bigdis Finnbogadottir), Indonesia (Megawati Sukarnoputri), and Ireland (Mary Robinson) have selected one each. Likewise, in countries with prime ministers as head of state, a number—including Pakistan (Benazir Bhutto), Norway (Gro Harlem Brundtland), Canada (Kim Campbell), France (Edith Cresson), India (Indira Ghandi), Lithuania (Dazimiera Prumskiene), England (Margaret Thatcher), and Bangladesh (Khaleda Zia)—have elected women during these years. These women, and others, have been added to the short list of women who have been political leaders in modern states. While this list is relatively short, few would have predicted 50 years ago that so many women would head countries before the end of the twentieth century.

A number of questions are prompted by this list. Probably most surprising to many people is the presence of non-European countries on the list. When most Americans think of the status of women in Pakistan,

Gro Harlem Brundtland of Norway: Director-General of the World Health Organization (1998–2003).

India, the Philippines, and Bangladesh, they envision total male dominance, and yet, each of these countries has had strong female leaders before the United States. This questions both the status of women in the United States as well as the relationship between female political leadership and female status at lower levels. Can a male-dominated country allow for equal status at less powerful levels of society? Do female leaders encourage the participation of other women in the political system and protect the status of less powerful women? Clearly the answers to both questions are complex and deserve study. Investigation of different states will lead to different conclusions. Recent events and investigation in the Scandinavian states provide the most encouraging results.

Scandinavian Cases   While only two of the five Scandinavian countries (Iceland, Norway, Sweden, Denmark, and Finland) have had female heads of state, all have and have had women in significant numbers in important state offices. Just as important, federal laws in these states support gender equality at all levels of society. If gender equality can exist in the political systems of state societies, these countries offer one model of its development.

Since the end of World War II, women have entered the work force in Scandinavian countries in large numbers. They have also achieved educational levels equal to or beyond those of men. (Currently, they rank among the world's leaders in women's participation in the work force and educational attainment.) By the beginning of the 1970s, these increasingly public women began to contest the patriarchy of the traditional state policies on gender and issues that affected the lives of women. Women in Iceland led with a general strike in 1976. Later that year the Equal Rights Act became Icelandic law. In 1978 and 1979, the Equal Status Act and Equal Opportunities Act became law in Norway. Similar laws soon became common throughout the Scandinavian states. These laws not only mandated a goal of equal opportunity for citizens regardless of gender but also compelled agencies to work to increase the roles of women in positions of power and influence. These included, in some cases, quotas. In Norway the goal established was that no less than 40 percent of office holders at different levels of government should be of either gender. In other words, no less than 40 percent of the offices should be held by men and no less than 40 percent should be held by women. In fact, as Nina Raaum concluded, while the goal had not yet been reached for women in all types of positions, at the national level it was close at hand. (1995: 43) Clearly, local-level positions lagged behind but, here too, women began to take positions of mayors, and deputy mayors, which had been uncommon in earlier years. Most importantly, perhaps, in societies where multiple political parties negotiated and cooperated for power, women became heads of these parties in significant numbers.

With the increase in the numbers of women involved in politics, a similar emphasis on the social concerns that affected the lives of women has become central to political debates. Significantly, in a state with high female employment, issues of reproductive control and child care became major national issues. Abortion services and contraception are free in Scandanavia, and women have the sole right to determine their use. Parental leaves are supported; in Sweden a parent may take 64 weeks leave at 90 percent of their salary to care for a new baby. Laws in Sweden also extend beyond infancy, with out-of-home care guaranteed to children from 18 months to 10 years. Other Scandinavian countries have laws similarly easing the lives of children and their working parents. More recently, focus has extended to the similar concerns of health care and care of the elderly. In fact, the areas of health, social services, and education make up the "lion's share" of national budgets, and the importance of these issues stems from the push to equality. (Raaum 1995: 31–32)

Opponents, who argue that the Scandinavian model is not a positive model for the rest of the world to follow, differ in their criticisms. One argument says that the situation in Scandinavia is not as good as it seems to foreign feminists. First, it is true that the numbers of women in important political offices have not yet reached equality and that women as a whole earn less than men. This appears largely due to the concentration of women in helping professions. Women largely are employed in medical, educational, and social service professions, and many of these jobs are in the lower paid public sector. Men in private business are more likely to be highly paid than their spouses who are social workers or teachers. In public office this bias toward topical specialization continues. A study of the Norwegian Parliament in 1991 demonstrated that the primary interests of men and women in that body were very different: Women legislators named the environment, social welfare, disarmament, equality, and education, while men named economics, energy, transportation, and foreign affairs. (Solheim 2000: 32–33) Members of the other sex named none of these issues as their primary interest. Women and men may be becoming more equal, but there is a deep difference between the sexes.

Another argument begins where the first ends—with the observation that this form of equality is culturally embedded within Scandinavian culture and might not fit in other countries, including the United States. Political society in Scandinavia is deeply oriented toward social welfare. The governments are expected to take responsibility for community well-being. This strong ideology equates the health of the whole society with the health of all individuals within it. (Solheim 2000: 32–36) A parallel belief system is that men and women are different and naturally have different interests. This idea of complementarity is used in Scandinavia to support the need for equal male and female participation. Women as citizens will not have their needs served by male politicians alone, and the same would be true of men led by a government of women. Both of these cultural concepts are quite contrary to common American beliefs, of course. Americans tend to reject the social service focus of these governments as "state welfare" and support individualism within capitalism as the opposite of a "socialist state." Further, the common assertion among those supporting gender equality in the United States is that men and women are more the same than different. Both share concerns for the well-being of their state, families, and communities.

The Scandinavian model for gender equality may not be a universal solution. It does seem to be a solution for many of the problems that beset the citizens of the Scandinavian countries after World War II. Whatever the ideology or imperfections of the outcome, the amount of political activity of women and their substantial presence in primary political offices in these countries demonstrates an unexpected flexibility of the state system in the realm of gender equality.

Great Wealth as Societal Power

States, of course, by definition have centralized governments, and office holders in the central core are recognized as societal leaders. In less centralized systems, and even in states, others hold roles of power and authority that are socially powerful but, in some cases, less publicly recognized. Many societies do not have permanent offices or designations of authority but have recognized political leaders. The skills that the society defines for leadership in both the formal and informal roles can often be gendered.

It should be of little surprise that people with great wealth often have equal influence and power in their societies. Even in state societies, the role of wealthy families and corporations is often integrated into the power system. In some such states, run on the ideology of democracy, the concept that some people have more say than others, based on wealth, is seen as a corruption of the system. In other states, where power is expected to be concentrated in the hands of a class of wealthy elites, it seems only right. In either case, the issue of gender tends to be quite complex. In general, wealthy women have more access to power or influence in a society than poorer women and have more power over individuals of lesser wealth. The employment, and with it the standard of living, of men and women in countless societies depends on the favor of wealthier women. Even in cases like that of the Saudi Arabian elite, mentioned in Chapter 6, where women cannot control the wealth they may inherit, these wealthy women do have considerable power over the lives of their servants. Likewise, such women often have access to those in political offices that poorer individuals do not. At very least, they can attempt to influence the brothers, husbands, and fathers who hold important offices; at most, they hold these offices themselves. What is more variable than their relative power to those poorer or lower in class is their standing relative to men of their own status. To return to the Saudi Arabian case, it is clear that wealthy women have far less access to positions of power than their male counterparts. This is the case in many states in the world—wealthy women have more power than poorer men but less power than wealthy men.

There are situations in which the power of wealth is not gendered. The Tlingit provide a case for this. As noted in Chapter 5, before the advent of European control, the status of Tlingit individuals was largely based on their wealth and that of their families. (Klein 1975: 101–18) Luxury goods were collected through trade with other nations, and these goods were turned into social capital when distributed in potlatches. At these pot-latches, men and women alike could obtain new names to reflect their acceptance of higher ranks. The ranking of a Tlingit determined who could be a spouse, where he or she would live in a house, what clothes and emblems could be worn, and relative power over others.

At the highest level was a category of people called *aankaawoo*. (Klein 1995: 35–38) These "wealthy people," who included a small percentage of those who lived comfortably, demanded the respect of all Tlingits. They had the right to claim the property of those who ranked lower and to expect that such people follow their wishes. In fact, there was no inherent right for aankaawoos to order less highly ranked people to follow their commands, but it was considered foolish for a poor person to ignore the wisdom of their betters. Likewise, the aankaawoo had no right to kill or harm those of lesser rank, but the punishment for having done so was far less than it would be for one of lower rank. A person of high rank, how-ever, was expected to behave with dignity and restraint. A rash act against someone would lead others to question the worth of the aggressor. Direct punishment for a low-ranked person harming an aankaawoo would be extremely severe and, as noted in Chapter 5, could involve punishment for relatives innocent of the offense. The only power that low-ranked persons could invoke against aankaawoo would be to publicly humiliate them, and any use of this power was severely sanctioned. In these issues both men and women functioned in the same way at all levels. A man could humili-ate or be humiliated by a woman, as could a woman by a man.

A contemporary example of this was an issue in a community I had only recently come to observe. That town had just hosted Tlingit delegates from other towns in a public meeting and celebration. Toward the end of the celebration, a man from another town drank more than was wise and while in an intoxicated state, hugged a higher ranked woman and publicly treated her as a familiar. While there was nothing sexually explicit nor grossly inappropriate from a Western point of view, the woman felt herself highly abused and humiliated. For the next few weeks, she telephoned people throughout the area asserting her anger. In one such call, which I heard from her end of the phone, she asserted several times "I am aankaa-woo" and announced her name and standing in her clan. "He can't do this to an aankaawoo." While he profusely and publicly apologized, the harm had been done. The ultimate way she cleansed her name and reasserted her position was to host a potlatch that her clan supported. Her dignity was restored and the status of the offender was further lowered.

Wealth, properly established through its distribution, was the key to social standing, and both men and women had to follow the same rules.

The fact that women were trained to negotiate favorable economic deals in trade gave them a central role in economic transactions. In one example, described by a distraught missionary in Sitka, Alaska, at the end of the nineteenth century, the economic position of women at lower levels was clearly laid out. In a letter home, the missionary complained about a Tlingit couple who had been arrested for fighting on the street.[1] When they were arrested, the woman paid her bail and left her husband behind bars. The next day, according to this letter, his kin bailed him out. The missionary lamented that among Tlingit women it was the hand that held the purse strings rather than the hand that rocked the cradle that was valued. Money, and the status it conferred, were more important considerations for power than gender itself.

Power in Local Spheres

While state leaders have power over the lives of citizens of their countries and, frequently, people in other countries as well, the power of these leaders is focused on war, federal legislation and policy, and taxation. To a person in a war zone or facing criminal charges or high tax bills, the decisions of these national leaders are very important. In fact, however, these high-level decisions rarely have much power over the everyday lives of individuals. In the course of the day, few of us design our lives in reaction to the decisions of presidents or monarchs. It is local laws and, even more so, family decisions that affect what we do. So while no one would argue that the power to set tuition prices for state colleges was greater than the power to bomb another country, in fact, the more immediate power is very significant for the plans of many people. In other words, concentrating only on the "most powerful" ignores the reality of power we all experience.

As seen in Chapter 7, kinship defines the heads of families as the primary leaders for many people in the world. Even in countries with weak kinship organizations, such as the United States, the authority role of parents over children is powerful throughout life. Elsewhere, the family leaders can dictate marriage, residence, access to economic opportunities, and many smaller rights for their kinsmen and -women. This form of power and authority, although described under kinship, should be reaffirmed as politically significant.

Chapter 9 also addresses people with power and authority, but it focuses on religion and supernatural power. Individuals who are able to mediate or control access to supernatural power are, in fact, secularly powerful as well. A classic example of this is the Inuit. In this arctic hunting society, there are no secular leaders and kinship is highly flexible. Individualism is combined with an ethos of cooperation. The one role that stands out in this culture is that of the shaman, a person with supernatural and

[1]Printed in a mission journal. (Anonymous 1924: 257–59).

curing expertise. A male role, for the most part, the shaman was called on to cure illness and lessen misfortune. Through his close relationship to supernatural power, he was feared as much as he was needed. Some shamans had the reputation of demanding wives and material goods from families in payment for their services. Still others were said to threaten people with supernatural harm if they did not follow their orders. (Hall 1984: 344) In other words, through control of supernatural forces the shamans became the only Inuit with secular power. This and many other cases noted in Chapter 9 demonstrate the intimate interaction between the use of societal and supernatural powers. As you will see, this entry to power positions is often used by women, who otherwise might have no access to secular power.

The roles of local leaders and community councils are also important in most societies. Clan heads, subchiefs, and village leaders, of course, are significant authorities over limited groups of people. The case of the Iroquois presented in Chapter 4 show various power roles at the local levels that include those played by both men and women. For example, the role of the sachem, which is held by men, is modified by the role of matrons, who select them. Further, all issues are discussed first at village councils that are open to all people, and the results of these councils direct the larger meetings of sachem that follow. Likewise, the roles of clanswomen in kinship positions and their roles as treasurers of the villages are immediately powerful in everyday affairs.

Not all societies are as gender inclusive as the Iroquois nations in issues of public power. In some societies, women are not heard in open councils. The only route for women to get their opinions aired in such cases is through their influence on men who could speak in council. The old cliché that behind every great man stands a great woman glorifies this rather weak position. After all, the man cannot be forced to listen to a great idea, much less be forced to support it in a public forum. In some societies, however, this is the only option for women with hopes of changing public life.

INFLUENCE AND PRESTIGE

Influence is the weakest form of public power and the most difficult to observe. By definition, influence takes place behind the scenes, where people with no public authority but with social connections to those who do use these powerful allies to obtain their own ends. Similar to this is prestige. People with prestige are seen as models for desirable behavior and thoughts; consequently, their goals take on social importance beyond the power of the person alone. Many societies have positions of ceremonial importance with little power and others of little authority with behind-the-scenes influence. Even in societies that reject female power and authority, women often hold roles with influence and prestige. Women in these positions usually support the system that has granted them these privileges. While they enjoy the personal benefits of high status and the gratification of being able to influence those around them, they rarely move beyond this to a more socially powerful position. Every so often, however, women have seized the advantages of these positions and transformed them into power that they have used to change public policy.

Women at the Top

Women frequently stand at the side of men in the top political offices. As seen above, although some of these women are co-rulers, more often they are the wives or close relatives of these men and hold the same relative gender status to their men as do poorer women in the society. In other words, the wife of the king or prime minister is expected to behave as the perfect wife in public and private. She is the model of female deference.

Queen consorts and other royal ladies, first ladies, and wives of prime ministers have historically followed this pattern in Europe and the United States. They are expected to be the ideal wives and mothers of their countries. They support their husbands and bring prestige to their country through public appearances. Their views on issues of public policy are shared with their husbands in private and may actually sway them, especially in areas in the domain of women. If husbands do not agree, wives have no legitimate outlets for their advocacy. Women who publicly act in ways their men disapprove of or who publicly advocate ideas the men do not support were historically removed from the public arena. Because this is far more difficult today than in the past, the "proper" political wife can now be far more critical of modern male leaders. Such public misbehavior still brings shame to the country and questions the ability of the husbands, who are seen as unable to control their wives.

European Royalty   The marriages of Prince Charles and Prince Andrew of Great Britain to young, aristocratic Englishwomen brought an air of modernity to a somewhat old-fashioned royal house that was becoming perceived as irrelevant. Press headlines in England in the 1980s and 1990s that lamented the exuberant behavior of the wives of the royal princes appeared to Americans to be overblown. To Americans these were attractive and fun-loving girls having a good time. To many British, certainly led by the tabloid press, they were misbehaving in their roles as models of ideal behavior and representing their country in a negative light. Although they played their roles as mothers and sponsors of charities, as royal women were expected to do, their influence in society was being used in a manner disapproved of by the royal family. They were too independent. Their marriages created their influence and prestige, but even their very public divorces did not extinguish those elements. As Princess Diana became a well-loved, but tragic, figure, her influence with the English people became a problem to the royal family, who had little control over her.

Her influence over her husband and the royal household in policy matters was clearly insignificant. Her public stature, however, allowed her to become an important advocate for controversial issues including advocacy for HIV patients and banning of land mines.

U.S. First Ladies   The role of First Lady of the United States has taken on official status during the twentieth century. The wives of presidents have their own offices and staffs and are expected to take part in government events. Their role is to support the efforts of the president and act as the hostess for state functions. Since Martha Washington, the wives have represented the country in social events that their husbands could not attend. While the role is important and socially significant, it holds no policymaking function. In fact, it is common for first ladies to be publicly chastised by the press when they appear to promote their own political agendas too strongly or too successfully. Even the appearance of having significant influence over their husband's policy decisions is challenged because "they are not elected," strangely ignoring the fact that most presidential advisors are appointed or unofficial. Recent first ladies—including Rosalyn Carter, who was reported to sit in on Cabinet meetings, Betty Ford, who supported the Equal Rights Amendment, Nancy Reagan, who was referred to as an associate president in the press, and Hillary Clinton, who headed an unsuccessful health care policy initiative—were all called to task for their efforts. First ladies in the last half of the twentieth century often had educations that rivaled their husbands and fostered expectations that they would be independent thinkers. This conflict of the concept of the traditional woman with that of the modern woman has made the recent roles of first lady quite diverse. Most recent first ladies have attempted a role that mixes the tactics of the most famous of their twentieth-century predecessors, Jacqueline Kennedy and Eleanor Roosevelt.

Jacqueline Kennedy became one of the most esteemed first ladies in modern history. While a well-educated, independent woman, she defined the role of first lady as a nonpolicy office with social and family responsibilities. Early in his presidential term, President John F. Kennedy and his wife, Jacqueline, visited Europe. American news reports of this state visit highlighted the glamour and elegance of the first lady, her ease in high society, and her ability to speak French fluently. President Kennedy introduced himself in one speech as the man who brought Mrs. Kennedy to Europe to great applause. Mrs. Kennedy was an international success and a symbol that the United States could compete in style with the elite of Europe. In the White House, her focus was on her children and on projecting an elite level of taste at state affairs. Her renovation of the White House, which she introduced to the American public in a national television documentary, and her promotion of classical musicians and other artists at state dinners followed this path. She was highly regarded in a country that generally disapproved of high society. Her accomplishment as an educated and quite independent woman was celebrated only in praise for her appearance, success as a hostess, and public role as wife and mother. She was not a political activist and did not use the office to promote her own political agenda. Political advances for women during the short Kennedy presidency were not significant, and it seems likely that Mrs. Kennedy had little influence on any major political policy.

Eleanor Roosevelt, as described by historian Betty Boyd Caroli, was also a properly educated, socially elite woman, but she was neither attractive nor elegant. (1987: 192–200) As first lady for 12 years, she became a significant political person. For this, she was revered by many and loathed by many others. Mrs. Roosevelt was a politically active individual throughout her life. In the While House she wielded considerable influence over her husband on the progress of the New Deal. Additionally, she was active in getting supporters, especially women, appointed to critical positions throughout the Democratic party and the government. Through magazine and newspaper articles, radio talks, and lectures, she also publicly expressed her political positions on a wide variety of issues. She was a strong supporter of women's rights, civil rights, and the rights of the poor. She traveled widely in the United States and abroad, reporting back to her husband who was not able to travel as easily. It was her descriptions of what she saw that helped inform his discussions. Mrs. Roosevelt publicly insisted that she was only a wife whose role was to help her husband, but it was clear that her influence was far more than that expected of a first lady. Further, it was clear that she was a power in her own right. While she rejected running for public office after her husband's death in 1945, she spent the remainder of her life as a public figure and was a significant figure in the drafting of the United Nation's Universal Declaration of Human Rights, which stands as the international understanding on human rights to this day. Eleanor Roosevelt was a wife and mother in her White House years, yet, that is not her public legacy. She was one of the most powerful women of her time. The role of first lady was not, in itself, powerful, but it opened doors and gave her tools to build a power base that she was eager to use.

SUMMARY

The complexity of power relationships and gender understandings goes far beyond the names of people in office or the nature of a government. Some women have, and continue to have, positions of power, authority, and influence, while many, or most, do not. The gender of the person in a particular office may not be directly linked to the situation of the rest of the women in that society. Likewise, in a class-based society, a person's class status may prove far more powerful than his or her gender. The case of Scandinavia should prove that modern state systems can make determined efforts to equalize the power, authority, and influence of both men and women. It also suggests that the effort must fit the ideology and practical realities of that specific case. Finally, because local politics, and family politics, are the most important to daily existence, it is vital to ask the small questions about individual autonomy.

Readings

Ackerman, Lillian A. "Complementary but Equal: Gender Status in the Plateau." In *Women and Power in Native North America*, eds. Laura F. Klein and Lillian A. Ackerman. Norman, OK: University of Oklahoma Press, 1995, pp. 75–100.

Anonymous. "Stories from a Real Home." *Women and Missions*. Philadelphia: Presbyterian Church, 1924, pp. 257–59.

Caroli, Betty Boyd. *First Ladies*. New York: Oxford University Press, 1987.

Engels, Friedrich. *The Origin of the Family, Private Property and the State*. New York: International Publishers, 1975.

Etienne, Mona, and Eleanor Leacock, eds. *Women and Colonization: Anthropological Perspectives*. New York: Praeger Publishers, 1980.

Fisher, J. L. "Solutions for the Natchez Paradox." *Ethnology* 3, no. 1 (1964), pp. 53–65.

Guy, John. *Tudor England*. Oxford: Oxford University Press, 1988.

Hall, Edwin S. "Interior North Alaska Eskimo." In *Handbook of North American Indians*, gen. ed. William C. Sturtevant; Vol. 5, *Arctic*, ed. David Damas. Washington: Smithsonian Institution, 1984, pp. 320–37.

Klein, Laura. "Contending with Colonization: Tlingit Men and Women in Change." In *Women and Colonization: Anthropological Perspectives*, eds. Mona Etienne, and Eleanor Leacock. New York: Praeger Publishers, 1980, pp. 88–108.

———. "Mother as Clanswoman: Rank and Gender in Tlingit Society." In *Women and Power in Native North America*, eds. Laura F. Klein and Lillian A. Ackerman. Norman, OK: University of Oklahoma Press, 1995, pp. 28–45.

———. *Tlingit Women and Town Politics* (dissertation). Ann Arbor, MI: University Microfilms, 1975.

Lamphere, Louise. "Review: Anthropology." *Signs* 2, no. 3 (1977), pp. 612–27.

Leacock, Eleanor. "Montaigne's Women and the Jesuit Program for Colonization." In *Women and Colonization: Anthropological Perspectives*, eds. Mona Etienne and Eleanor Leacock. New York: Praeger Publishers, 1980, pp. 25–42.

Lebeuf, Annie M. D. "The Role of Women in the Political Organization of African Societies." In *Women of Tropical Africa*, ed. Denise Paulme, trans. H. M. Wright. Berkeley, CA: University of California Press, 1971, pp. 93–119.

MacCaffrey, Wallace T. *Elizabeth I*. London: Edward Arnold, 1993.

McMurtry, Jo. *Understanding Shakespeare's England*. Hamden, CT: Archon Books, 1989.

Musisi, Nakanyike B. "Women, 'Elite Polygyny,' and Buganda State Formation." *Signs* 16 (1991), pp. 757–86.

Ortner, Sherry B. "Is Female to Male as Nature Is to Culture?" In *Woman, Culture and Society*, eds. Michelle Zimbalist Rosaldo and Louise Lamphere. Stanford, CA: Stanford University Press, 1974, pp. 67–88.

Raaum, Nina Cecilie. "The Political Representation of Women: A Bird's Eye View." In *Women in Nordic Politics: Closing the Gap,* eds. Lauri Karvonen and Per Selle. Aldershot: Dartmouth, 1995, pp. 25–56.

Richards, A. I. "Authority Patterns in Traditional Buganda." In *The King's Men: Leadership and Status in Buganda on the Eve of Independence,* ed. L. A. Fallers. London: Oxford University Press, 1964, pp. 256–65.

Rosaldo, Michelle Zimbalist. "Woman, Culture, and Society: A Theoretical Overview." In *Woman, Culture and Society,* ed. M. Z. Rosaldo and Louise Lamphere. Stanford, CA: Stanford University Press, 1974, pp. 17–42.

Rosaldo, Michelle Zimbalist, and Louise Lamphere, eds. *Woman, Culture and Society.* Stanford, CA: Stanford University Press, 1974.

Solheim, Bruce O. *On Top of the World: Women's Political Leadership in Scandinavia and Beyond.* Westport, CT: Greenwood Press, 2000.

Usner, Daniel H., Jr. *American Indians in the Lower Mississippi Valley: Social and Economic Histories.* Lincoln, NE: University of Nebraska Press, 1998.

CHAPTER NINE

A Cosmological Plan?
Gender and the Supernatural

Can religions empower or disempower women?
Does the gender of the deity or religious leader affect secular gender
* relationships?*
Have the missions of Islam and Christianity throughout the world
* affected the status of women?*

Virtually all societies have a concept or concepts of the universe beyond their immediate knowledge. Those concepts that include supernatural beings or powers are generally called *religion*. Feminist scholars have long looked to this area of cultural understanding to better define both societal conceptualizations of gender and the depth of rules that regulate gender relations in practical settings. Some have found that religious belief systems have severely restricted the possibilities of women in societies, while others have found that religious systems have offered women roles with power and expression they could not have otherwise. In other words, religion is a very powerful force in most cultures, and it colors gender categories in sometimes surprising ways.

PERSPECTIVES ON THE SUPERNATURAL

As noted, feminists can hold very different views about the nature of religion. One early perception that still lives in some circles is that religion originally was based on a mother goddess as creator. Through time, in these theories, religion has become corrupted and manipulated to reject the feminine in cosmology and society. Most modern religions, according to this perspective, are seen as inauthentic. "Real religions" celebrate the female and worship goddesses. Other feminists reject the historical assertion of original female-based cosmologies but focus on the centrality of male authority in most of the great world religions. These scholars focus on the implicit patriarchy they seen in the image of the supernatural as well as the moral rules for behavior they generate. Such religions, they assert, are among the most important adversaries of the goal of a world with gender equality. A third view, less vocal but strong in anthropology, holds that religions can open doors for women and allow them significant powers, especially in societies that do not have other open avenues for women. Focusing on religions that emphasize personal relationships between individual humans and specific supernatural forces or beings, these scholars argue that religion can be subversive, acting as a force for gender equality even in the face of societies that reject such ideas.

FEMALE DEITIES AND MATRIARCHIES REVISITED

The issue of mother goddesses and matriarchies was discussed within the chapters of Section II, but they deserve another visit at this time. From these earlier discussions, it is obvious that there are many feminist scholars who believe that there literally was a time when humans worshipped female deities, who inherently supported the values of female fertility and power. Some go as far as asserting an actual historical event when men, with superior physical strength, overpowered the women and replaced the original relations with one that asserted male power and authority. Matriarchy and the goddess religion go hand in hand, just as do patriarchy and later religions. As Chapter 2 demonstrates, this is now clearly a minority opinion in most mainstream feminist scholarship. As Paula Webster noted in an important 1974 article, much of the discussion about original matriarchies was really a way for feminists to "imagine a society that is not patriarchal, one in which women might for the first time have power over their lives." (p. 155) In the past 30 years scholars have looked at societies with new eyes, and it has become clear that there are, and have been, other roads traveled by much of the world's societies that are neither classically patriarchal nor matriarchal in any sense imagined for these terms.

Beyond thinking about a unity of mother goddesses and matriarchies, scholars have generally given less thought to the search for autocratic goddesses and female societal leadership. Even so, the idea that religions that worship powerful female deities should also have a strong secular parallel is still seen in popular literature. Those religions with a perception of male and female deities who interact on equal footing should, at least, be models for the people who worship them. In fact, however, it appears that sacred and secular unanimity is more apparent than real.

One of the world's largest religions, Hinduism, has a pantheon of deities personified as both male and female. Among the goddesses, or aspects of the female goddess, are individuals such as Kali, who is pictured as a terrifying, blood-drinking figure who wears severed heads and limbs, and Durga, a calm warrior goddess. In these forms the violence and abandon that make up part of the female personality are highlighted. In other forms, such as Sarasvati or Sati, the goddess appears in a beautiful, more restrained persona as a devoted wife and mother. (Flood 1996: 177–78) All the images include complex aspects that make the devoted deities appear less benevolent and the violent ones less evil. The male deities are likewise flexible and show diverse aspects of masculinity. Shiva, Kali's husband, appears as both highly sexual and highly ascetic. He, like Krishna and Vishnu, have both "male" and "female" characteristics, and some mythic stories have them transforming from one sex to another. Religious scholar Rita Gross argues against the androcentric tendency for Western scholars to focus on gender as the major distinguishing factor. (1998: 325) Nevertheless, she notes that Hinduism is "the major theistic alternative to monotheism among world religions [and it] views goddesses as normal and important to religious life." (p. 321) She concludes that "the primary deities are a Preserver, who also destroys and a Destroyer who also preserves, sometimes seen as a couple, sometimes as a male, and sometimes as a female. However, in all cases, the primary division is not also gender lines." (p. 326) As noted in the final chapter, the Indian third gender, Hijras, base their sexual form in the context of Hindu religion. (Nanda 1999)

Given such a variety of gender aspects in the deities, a similar gender pattern might be expected in daily life. Of course, this is not the case. Few would look at the status of Hindu women and celebrate their freedom from gender restrictions. One of the most sensationalized traditions in the world is that of the suttee, or sati, where a widow placed herself on the funeral pyre of her deceased husband and was burned along with his body. Although this practice has been illegal since 1829, one case of an eighteen-year-old woman, Roop Kanwar, in 1987 was widely celebrated in India as proof of the continuance of the practice of traditional honor among Indian women. Contemporary academic theories on the nature of suttee range from those that focus on it as the ultimate patriarchal control to those who see it as an opportunity for women to assert their empowerment through self-sacrifice in an otherwise powerless world. (Sugirharajah 2001; Young 1994) Some scholars of Indian society argue that the belief in the power and potential violence and free sexuality in women that reflect the traits of the goddesses are, in part at least, what necessitates the strict regulations of their behavior. It is because they have the natural propensity for wild behavior that society must control them. According to this cultural logic, a strong goddess translates into a constrained female role.

MONOTHEISTIC RELIGIONS AND PATRIARCHIES

Christianity and Islam are the first and second world religions in terms of the number of people in the world who practice them. Additionally, they are the fastest growing religions. Consequently, they each have enormous authority reaching far beyond their historic areas of influence. World politics has also been intertwined with religious affiliation in many cases, and the philosophies of the religions have become the rationales of state governments. It is also important to note, however, that the variations between specific traditions, for example, Catholic and Baptist, Sunni and Shi'ite, in each religion can be significant.

While religious women have been leaders in the promotion of modern feminism and though many contemporary churches, synagogues, and Muslim states have accepted female leadership, most feminists assert that the policies, and politics, of major world religions have historically been patriarchal. Jews, Muslims, and Christians can all point to significant female heroes from their most sacred scriptures, but few would argue that these heroines reflect the reality of the lives of female adherents during historic times. Each era, culture, and state accepted, and accept, unique understandings of the complex documents of their chosen religions. Despite this, in most cases, the religious leaders of the organizational hierarchy asserted a priority for men, whom they supported with religious lessons and strong role models. The lives of the women in the texts are interpreted to support the ideal roles that the culture of the time held for women. The predominant visions of Mary, Fatima, and Ruth, to name a few, emphasized the parts of their stories that involved duty and support for the important men they served. Many were told that for a woman to be holy, she should aspire to imitate the sacrifice and suffering of a mother like Mary, of a daughter like Fatima, or a daughter-in-law like Ruth. Even Esther, who is recorded as saving her people from destruction, is presented as an obedient niece who followed her uncle's lead and, thereby, he saved his people. Also, women, until recently, were not educated enough to read the texts and had no access to the information they needed to challenge the teachings as traditional religious leaders presented them.

Gender in Christian History

Within Christianity, many people have found an inherent value in equality and the concept that gender is unimportant in the larger scheme of things, while others, in different times and places, have found a deep patriarchal bias. (Ruether 1999: 214) As Mary T. Malone, a scholar of religion, reviewed: "The history of Christianity shows great ambivalence toward women. On the one hand, women have been included, called, graced, inspired and canonized by Christianity throughout the centuries. On the other . . . women have not always felt appreciated within the Christian tradition and indeed have often felt excluded and oppressed by church leaders. It is this ambivalence toward women that characterizes the whole of Christian history." (2001: 17)

As scholar Barbara MacHaffie observed, "The past movement of women toward equality and full participation has not been one of constant progress. Rather, equality and full participation have been approximated at various times throughout Christian history only to be followed by periods of repression and retrenchment." (1986: 153) Christianity, as it first developed in Europe, was under the strong hierarchical authority of the Roman Catholic Church. Since about the year 400, concepts about the innate nature of women and the theologically predetermined gender of the priesthood, determined that the leaders of the Roman church were men and that women were deemed ineligible for most powerful formal sacred roles. (Cardman 1999: 149) Women's roles as wife and mother in the domestic domain were glorified as religiously predestined. Women in religious communities were limited to cloistered existences of prayer. Beginning in the twelfth century, more religious women became involved in community charity work, but this was curtailed by a religious ruling, a papal bull in 1298 that mandated the cloistering of women's groups. While some women's groups found ways to continue their public charitable works, the church reconfirmed the rules for cloistering in 1566. (Mooney 1999: 175) With the Protestant Reformation, many women left the cloistered communities, which were not supported in the new churches.

The "golden age" of women's religious communities in Catholicism was in the nineteenth century, when religious women outnumbered men. (Mooney 1999: 176) The Second Vatican Council in the second half of the twentieth century encouraged many orders to open themselves even more to the concerns of their communities. Many sisters found themselves living and working among lay women and men in the service of their religious and secular communities. For a number of reasons, however, the religious communities in the West experienced a sharp loss of membership, with a 50 percent decline in Catholic sisters in the United States between 1965 and 1995. (Mooney 1999: 177) At the same time, women's religious orders have grown in other areas of the world, and religious sisters have become increasingly important social and religious activists.

The domestic arena is another location for a good Christian woman. Marriage is a sacrament in the Catholic faith and a "religious vocation" as defined by Martin Luther. (Cardman 1999: 151) A woman was expected to be obedient and faithful to her husband and nurturing to her children. Subordination to husbands and fathers was expected without question. Divorce was against the laws of man and God. Later in history when divorce was reluctantly accepted within Protestant churches, a divorce, even from an abusive husband, brought disgrace and often economic ruin to the wife. Because European princes all followed Christian teachings, the laws of the states followed the social proscriptions of the churches. A husband's rights over his wife were nearly absolute; he was the legal head of the family who could sell his wife's property or arrange his children's marriages without her agreement. A rebellious woman crossed not only the conventions of her society but the teachings of her religion as well. Over time, of course, the role of the state and the role of the church split in Europe. State leaders made laws that allowed behaviors that violated church teachings. The religious laws did not radically change, but the possibilities to break them did.

While the secular part of women's lives may have been highly constrained by these rules, women's religious lives were celebrated in domestic ways. Prayers, food preparation for festivals, home altars, and other domestic activities held important religious meanings. Devotions to specific saints or Mary helped women empower their religious convictions as well. The image of the wife/power has been, in itself, glorified in Christianity. As religion scholar Deborah Ann Bailey explained about Protestantism in the nineteenth century: "Men presided over the daily family worship service, but women were perceived as the moral center and example of Christian living in the home." (1999: 153) As the example of Colombian Pentecostals illustrates later in this chapter, in some circumstances this ideal can go far beyond image to empower women's lives.

Contemporary Christianity, in its many varieties, is far different from the church of the past. While some churches still limit the positions of power to celibate heterosexual men and others to monogamously married men, others have opened these roles to women and gay men. Christianity, even if limited only to churches in Europe or the United States, offers a broad spectrum of gender inclusion and exclusion that makes solid generalizations impossible. In many liberal Protestant churches, women are ministers and leaders of their communities. The first ordination of a woman was in 1853, and today many churches have large numbers of female ministers. Even in some churches that do not accept women into the clergy, charismatic experiences that women, like men, have are deeply respected and valued.

The role of women as independent actors has generally not replaced the ideal of monogamy and motherhood, but single and divorced women are full members of their churches. However, not all churches have embraced the social changes of the larger society. Many more conservative churches have chosen to reemphasize the "traditional" family as central to their message and encourage authoritarian, but just, husbands and subordinate, but dedicated, wives. In fact, many churches are now teaching that the moral decay they see in society is caused in large part by the breakdown of the patriarchal family and that men must step up to their leadership roles in the family. Women are not the primary voices in Christianity today, but the voices of Christian women are heard more than ever before. Women can read the scripture themselves and rediscover role models for more powerful lives. Many feminists argue that the teachings of Christianity are so deeply male oriented that true gender equality may not be possible within the faith. Some have left the church for female-based religion like that of Wicca discussed a bit later. However, others continue to believe that the basic teachings of Jesus are gender equal and that in time the churches will return to what they see as the original faith. As Christian feminist scholar Patricia Killen writes: "I have come to believe that women of faith have found this liberating truth by drawing on two resources as they journeyed in faith: their Christian heritage and their own lived experience of God." (1997: 3)

Gender in Islam

Islam, like Christianity, is a major world religion that has spread through-out much of the globe. Consequently, given the broad sweep of cultures that have adopted the faith, there is now a great variation in the teachings and practices from country to country. The practices in Turkey, for exam-ple, especially as they affect gender, are worlds apart from those once mandated by the Tailban-led government in Afghanistan. Westerners have long looked on Islam as an exotic, and foreign, faith. The fact is that Islam, Judaism, and Christianity share a common heritage, and many agreements over the fundamentals of gender relations are often ignored.

Like these other faiths, Islam places the family as the central institu-tion for the defense of moral behavior. The appropriate roles of wives and husbands, parents and children are clearly described as part of the defini-tion of being a faithful member of the religion. Wives are to be faithful, obedient, and dedicated to their families. Husbands are to be the economic providers and authorities within their families. Women are expected to be modest and obedient and bring no shame to their kin. They are also responsible for the smooth running of the household and the basic needs of small children. This description, of course, fits the ideals that teachers from Islam, Judaism, and Christianity have demanded for centuries. Dur-ing the last century, the roles of women in many Christian countries have expanded widely, allowing them legal rights and social positions previ-ously limited to men. In Muslim countries, changes have also occurred; in some Muslim states, however, the seclusion of women in the private domain has kept them closer to the traditional ideals.

While many scholars (including Hassan 2001; Sonn 1999; Mernissi 1991; and Saliba 2000) have pointed to the Qur'an, the holiest text, as advocating the equality of men and women in the eyes of God, it is clear that traditional practice in Muslim societies defined women as inferior to men. Sonn, for example, argues that "Although women and men are not equal in social status in the Qur'an, women are on a spiritual and moral par with men." (1999: 490) The Qur'an, she points out, was a strong cri-tique of the pre-Islam traditions that granted women few rights or little respect. The hadith literature (oral traditions with scriptural commentary) are holy writings that are second to the Qur'an. It was in these that the idea of the moral inferiority of women compared with men appeared, and these influenced law and tradition. (Sonn 1999: 491–92)

With these new understandings, women were relegated to legal and social wards of their fathers and husbands and had virtually no rights other than those granted to them by these men. In society, women lived in the household, while men lived in the world. Even in the household, the rooms were divided into male and female domains. On a daily basis then, tradition held that men and women lived dramatically separate lives. Men were allowed more than one wife, but they were required to treat them all as equals. Divorce was largely the choice of the man and was often a disaster for the woman. In divorce she lost both her home and her children, who remained with their father. A woman's security came from fulfilling her female role in a manner that made her an exemplary wife and daughter. She could then hope to live her life with a generous husband, and if he failed to live up to his role, to be welcomed by a supportive father or brother. The option of living independent of a man was not open to respectable women.

Women had religious responsibilities similar to those of men, but their lifestyles meant that they were often fulfilled differently. The five pillars or duties of the faithful were required of both men and women. These called for profession of faith, a pilgrimage to Mecca, charity, fasting during Ramadan, and regular prayers. Household duties, limited access to public areas, and lack of personal funds often meant that women were dependent on men in order to fulfill these requirements. Domestic and local religious activities with other women allowed many to independently honor their religion while working communally on socially worthy endeavors. (Beck 1999: 494–96)

The twentieth century brought changes to many different areas of the Muslim world. Modernization with new technologies and opportunities brought new forms of wealth. During the twentieth century, Muslim women in most countries have received increased, though sometimes limited, legal rights and more access to the public world. Many can now receive secular, as well as religious, education and hold jobs outside of the home. In some cases (but not all), the jobs that are available to women are limited. Women can be schoolteachers, nurses, and doctors, for example, and can then teach and heal other women. This allows both the practitioners and their clients to remain modest and gender appropriate in a respectable woman's world while giving and receiving modern services. The professional woman, in such cases, can support the traditional roles while working at a level with her peers around the world. Such work, and certainly the less educated positions that women fill, can still be seen in a negative light. It can taint the honor of the husbands of such women with the suggestion that they are unable to fulfill their roles as providers. Further, because men are not encouraged to perform domestic tasks around the home, working women are suspected of injuring their husbands and children by neglecting household duties. Wealthy households, such as those described in the Saudi Arabian case in Chapter 6, have servants to do the chores, but the wife remains the manager of the home. In some Muslim countries, including Saudi Arabia, women are not allowed to drive a car, and they remain dependent on men for transportation outside of the home. In other areas public transportation is available to women, but they are often disrespected on buses and similar mass transport systems.

While modernization has been largely welcomed, its counterpart, Westernization, often has not. The cultural hegemony of the United States and Europe is viewed in many countries as a threat to Islamic religious and social values. Western popular culture is seen as decadent and political organizations as dangerous. Especially since the beginning of the Palestinian-Israeli conflicts, an Islamic political ideology has grown in many different countries. In some, such as Egypt and Turkey, it is viewed as a threat to the governing elite while in others, such as Iran after the Shah and Afghanistan during the Taliban government, it was the governing theme. Many Islamists are far more moderate than others but firmly believe that the Western ideal of individualism leads to a lack of responsibility that endangers the Muslim ideal of family and community obligation. Many Islamic women who look to improving the roles of women in their own communities look for role models in their own traditions and reject the images of Westernization. Western women appear self-indulgent and, strategically, any alliance with Western feminists throws suspicion on their own motives. Muslim scholar Riffat Hassan observes: "While the West constantly bemoans what it refers to as the 'rise of Islamic fundamentalism,' it does not extend significant recognition or support to progressive Muslims who are far more representative of 'mainstream' modern Islam than either the conservative Muslims on the right or the 'secular' Muslims on the left." (2001: 69)

The strongest representation of this clash between Western and Islamic ideals appears in women's clothing, and this makes the issue far more volatile than it might seriously be. In all but the most Westernized Muslim countries, women are required or encouraged to wear modest clothing with head coverings outside of their homes. Many traditions dictate some degree of veils or face covering, and, in the most Islamist countries, women are draped with cloth from head to foot. To Westerners, the image of a women in a veil, who is covered with loose flowing dark fabric to the ground, is one that personifies inequality and unreasonable servitude.[1] Many Western feminists have campaigned for the end of the veil and the "liberation" of women who wear it. Many Muslim women, as well, have rejected this form of clothing and can be seen publicly in the West, and in many Muslim countries, in the latest Western high fashions. At the beginning of the twenty-first century, however, Western feminists were startled by a trend by Muslim women, who had previously worn Western clothing, to adopt Islamic dress in public. The veil has been forced on some women by law in some newly Islamist states, but many others have made the choice to dress in a Muslim, rather than Western, way in public. (Brink 1997)

Arab feminist and scholar Lam Abu-Odeh, who herself wears Western dress, asserts that to some Arab women, the veil and its accompanying dress can be "empowering and seductive." (1992: 1527) Young women in dresses that would be fashionable to their peers in New York or Paris are open to accusations of sexual impropriety and unwanted sexual attention by men on the street. Further, they are often blamed for men's conduct in

---

[1]It should be noted that in dress as much as in dogma there is great variation between ideals in Islamic cultures. The full draping that leaves only the eyes uncovered is far rarer than the ensemble that includes a full dark coat with a headscarf. The woman in the more unusual dress unfortunately has become the stereotype for all Islamic women.

Islamic women in modest dress go
about their daily lives.

their presence. In Islamic dress, the women become invisible on the street
and are safe to go on about their business without fear. If a stranger
attempts to treat them inappropriately, he is severely sanctioned by others.
To explain their preferences to the disapproving Westerners, these women
compare their sense of public safety and freedom to the dangers of the
city streets for women in the West. They do not fear rape, public ridicule,
or embarrassment when they are modestly dressed, while Western women
face these fears daily. Western women resent being treated as sex objects,
and these Islamic women believe that, with proper care, they can avoid
being treated in this manner.

Today Muslim women can be found as political leaders, as prominent
academics, as successful businesswomen, and in many other public roles.
These are the exceptions, of course. Most women, of any faith, live at a far
more modest level of society. Islam, at its most Islamist extreme, like that
established in Afghanistan during the Taliban period, can leave women
without legal rights and under the threat of death for breaking any of the
myriad of strict patriarchal rules. Women in less extreme states have more
protection and less danger if they live normal respectable lives. Men, in

general, have more power and access to public opportunities, while women's life choices are far more limited. Many women do live contented lives in the domestic works of their families and women friends. A woman's world is not inherently an unhappy one. In the most liberal Muslim states, and in non-Muslim states with Muslim minorities, the laws and public arenas for women can approximate those of men. Here too, however, many choose to live their lives within their families. The faith and tradition of Islam can be very strong, and women's choices may be very complex.

POLYTHEISTIC RELIGIONS

As seen in the many examples of bands, tribes, and stratified societies discussed in Chapters 3, 4, and 5, the place of high gods, whether male or female, has often meant less than the position of less powerful spirits in the everyday lives of individual people. Omnipotent supernatural beings, if they are present at all, are often quite remote from human affairs. Their existence in some societies may well explain the nature of the universe or the moral precepts on which human societies should be based, but the deities themselves may be perceived as having little or no interest in living people. When the focus moves from omnipotent deities to less powerful supernatural spirits, the picture of the relationship of people to the supernatural appears quite different. When individuals join into partnerships with unique supernatural beings, the worth of the person is compounded with that of the spirit. In other words, the fact that the supreme deity is female may have far less to do with the quality of life of a living woman than the nature of the guardian spirit who protects her. In societies where all people have equal access to spiritual help (like the Sambia, Iroquois, Navajo, or Tlingit previously described), the personal power of the individual cannot be completely dismissed. In others (like the Yanomamö), where only males have access to these spirits, the power of masculinity can be supernaturally inflated in a way femininity is not. However, very frequently, gender is not an issue.

While the details of spirit beliefs vary widely from culture to culture as the cases described demonstrate, it is possible to describe a general pattern commonly found in traditional Native North America religions and similar to that found elsewhere. When young people were coming into adulthood, they were encouraged to seek guardian spirits to support them throughout their lives. To come into contact with the spirits, the young people went into the wilderness to fast and meditate. In these rough conditions, and with no external interruptions, they prayed and waited for their spirits to come and adopt them. With luck, after a few days of deprivation, they had visions of the spirit that would introduce their guardians and instruct them on the desired progress of their lives. With this new spiritual power, the individuals could move to adulthood with a deeper connection to the supernatural world. Because only rarely were these spirits personified as human or humanoid, they were seldom personified as gendered in a human fashion. The supernaturals, in these cases, then did not support any specific ideology of gender inequality. In fact, what they supported, more than anything else, was the individuality of people in society. Each person was attached to his or her own unique part of the supernatural pantheon.

WOMEN AS RELIGIOUS PRACTITIONERS

While the major world religions, including, most notably, Islam and Christianity as just discussed, have historically limited the kind and importance of positions in the religion that are open to women, other routes to supernatural powers have not. In fact, the lack of access to the world religions by women has increased the importance of belief systems such as those of the Wicca and Zar, described in this section, to many believers. While neither is exclusively a woman's religion, both have a majority of female followers and leaders. The most widespread type of non-Western religious practitioner, however, is the shaman or healer. Generally working independently, shamans form the base on which more complex ritual practices, perhaps including those of Wicca and Zar, have developed.

Shamans

When Americans think of religious practice in non-Western cultures, they often imagine "witch doctors" and "medicine men" wearing macabre masks while wildly dancing around a fire. In fact, the most common type of non-Western religious practitioner, the shaman, is often involved with witches and medicine in dramatic settings, but the reality is far more profound than the comic opera version so often portrayed. The term *shaman* came from Siberia, but it is currently used for a type of religious practitioner who uses supernatural elements for the health or well-being of clients. Spirit possession is a hallmark of the shaman. Several cases in bands, tribes, and stratified societies have been described in earlier chapters. Two more examples now demonstrate the different forms that shamanism can take in dramatically different societies. A preferred gender of the shaman role is defined in each society. In one of these cases, that of the Tlingit, both men and women became shamans, and in the other, that of Korean shamans, women are preferred.

Tlingit Indian Doctors   The *Ikt*, or "Indian doctor," was the only role in precolonial Tlingit society that was inherently powerful. The doctor, who could be either male or female, got his or her power from commanding personal spirits. When individuals wanted to take on this role, they enticed multiple spirits by going on spirit quests or seeking spirits in sacred areas. Different spirits might have different powers that could compound the skills of the doctor. The doctor also needed to apprentice with a practicing doctor in order to learn the secular skills involving medicines and physical techniques that would be needed to cure patients. After he or she completed training, the doctor was called in for health problems or concerns about general well-being.

The doctor cured serious illness in patients by combating the witch who brought illness. The witch was an individual, male or female, who used potions or spells for evil purposes. Personal dislike, frequently based on jealously, was often found to be the motive for sending illness. The doctors were called when illness occurred, and they would first find the source of the trouble. The doctor went into a trance and allowed the spirits to roam into the supernatural world to discover the cause. There the spirits fought the evil that plagued the patient and attempted to overcome them. If the illness was the result of evil magic, the doctor named the witch, and the community responded. A severe case meant the death of the witch.

Successful doctors held socially significant powers in this culture. First, the doctors had the ability to make accusations of witchcraft. Not only was this an issue in curing, it had serious repercussions in the all-important status system. Having a witch in a family or clan was bound to lower the status of the whole group. The doctor, then, could threaten the way of life of important people. Second, the doctor could become quite wealthy through his or her curing, and wealth, of course, conferred social influence. A successful doctor was paid according to the value of the cure. This meant that a doctor who cured a high-status person was paid more than a similar cure for a lesser person. A doctor was a professional who was well paid. Finally, the doctor's ability to invoke supernatural spirits gave them spiritual power. Powerful doctors were said to have the ability to predict the future and, even, foresee their own deaths. After death, their spirits remained close to their bodies, and the region of their burial became a supernaturally powerful area.

The role of ikt was an individual accomplishment. The men and women who took on the position did so for personal reasons. Some felt called by their spirits, while others desired the power that the role of doctor could bring. Not all doctors were successful, and, if they failed to heal, they were not further employed. Many others had more limited knowledge of healing techniques and fewer, or less powerful, spiritual helpers. These men and women were called on by relatives and neighbors to cure the more minor concerns in which witches were less likely to be involved. In daily routine, this fit well with the woman's domestic role of caring for family and friends. At this level, doctors were admired for their community service and a bit feared for their heightened supernatural knowledge.

Mansins in Korea   Korean shamans, called *mansins*, are women who have been possessed by powerful deities. As anthropologist Laurel Kendall summarized: "By virtue of the powerful gods who possess her, she can summon up divination visions and probe the source of a client's misfortunes, exorcise the sick and the chronically unlucky, remove ill humors from those who have difficulty finding mates, and coax a reluctant birth spirit into a infertile womb." (1989: 138) Ceremonies can be quite elaborate, with mansins donning colorful costumes and publicly dancing and seeing visions.

In a society where respectable women are expected to focus on their homes and families and be quiet and respectful in public, the mansin role can free its players from such social restrictions. In another sense the mansin role fits with women's more normal concerns. Women in their households are responsible for household ancestor shrines and for calming jealous or angry ancestral spirits. If these spirits are not tamed, the domestic tranquility of the household is threatened. Women, therefore, are the clients of mansins, who call on them to solve their problems. Women who become mansins are said to be chosen by the gods themselves. The gods bother the future mansins with sickness, supernatural visitations, and bad luck, and if these women choose to ignore this summons, they can become crazy and die. Mansins, then, cannot be blamed for taking on this abnormal role or for the behavior it entails. It is the choice of the gods, and people are helpless to combat it. That it offers them opportunities to broaden their worlds beyond the norm for women is seen as an unexpected consequence of an unsought divine intervention.

A patient who complains of illness or ill fortune comes to the mansin to seek help. The mansin uses divination to determine the cause of the complaint and recommends rituals for solving the problem. These can range from formal and expensive public rituals to simple offerings or procedures. A successful mansin can become famous when her satisfied clients recommend her to others. This shaman role in Korea is considered a profession and, thus, mansins are paid for their services. A successful mansin can make a comfortable living from her work. Moreover, the profession is viewed as a socially beneficial one. The mansins do a public service with their work. They are valued because they cure the ill and return a home to peace.

Witchcraft: The American Wicca

Not all women religious practitioners are found in non-Western settings. One reaction to the historical exclusion of women from leadership positions has been the attraction of many women to other practices, including witchcraft. Witchcraft, meaning the ability of individuals to manipulate the supernatural for desired ends, has existed throughout the world and is practiced by both men and women. The witchcraft label has been used by Europeans and Americans to include satanism, neo-paganism, and heresy. The witchcraft that women have gravitated to has been largely in the realm of the nature-worshipping religions, which have often been labeled as heresy by Christian churches.

Witchcraft has a long and peculiar history in the Western world. It is estimated that during the fourteenth to seventeenth centuries in Europe, hundreds of thousands of people were executed for being witches. It has been calculated that about 80 percent of these victims were women. Some of those women accused of witchcraft were traditional healers, others were pagans, still others were unruly, and almost all were peasants. In a classic feminist work, Barbara Ehrenreich and Deidre English depicted this era of witchhunts as a "ruling class campaign of terror directed against the female peasant population." (1973: 5) The document that defined the rules for the official witch-hunts was a late-thirteenth-century book, the *Malleus Malefi-carium*. The Malleus set down the means of torture and execution that should follow the discovery of a witch. According to this book, women were more likely than men to become witches. They were also likely to become the sexual consorts of Satan, who organized and used their magical potions to cause chaos. This blatant anti-woman bias in the Malleus and the entire witchhunt era is clear. As this book warned: "When a woman thinks alone, she thinks evil" (quoted in Ehrenreich and English 1973: 8). Clearly the woman who shows independence from a man is, by definition, a witch. That this war against witches was, in part, a war against women appears clear in hindsight. What remains unknown is how many of the women accused and killed were, in fact, pagan worshippers or local healers. Certainly some of these witches were women who preferred other forms of worship to the patriarchal Christianity of their day.

Since the 1960s, a new form of witchcraft began to spread in the United States. Many people who were attracted to Wicca, this new religion, rejected the Christianity they knew as still patriarchal. Wicca, or neo-paganism, is based on an adoration of nature and a goddess, sometimes personified as Mother Nature. Members of Wicca covens see themselves as modern descendents of nature worshippers, who predated Christianity in Europe. Often, Americans confuse witchcraft with Satanism, which is another religion that celebrates the Christian devil. Wicca, to the contrary, celebrates nature and the female principle in the world.

Believers in Wicca join into covens that are facilitated by priests or priestesses or both. Some covens are limited to women worshippers, and their leaders are priestesses. Mixed-gendered covens often have priests as well. According to Helen Berger, feminism and ecological awareness are the central concepts. (1998: 214) The goddess who appears as the central deity is worshipped in three female aspects: maiden, mother, and crone. Worship of her, and the ideals of femininity and nature she projects, are the central doctrines of this faith. Community rituals that include song, dance, and magic celebrate a concept of the religion that purposefully excludes patriarchal ideas. Contemporary Wiccans are attracted to the religion by its inclusiveness and interest in ecology.

Women's Religious Organizations: The Zar

The Zar cult is the name given to a type of religious movement found in many areas of Africa and the Middle East, from Egypt to the Sudan to Kuwait. Islam is the major faith in most of these cultures, but it is found in Christian-dominated areas as well. In either case, it is an alternate, and generally socially depreciated, religion. Like many religions around the world, Zar cults focus on spirits that are able to possess specific individuals. People so possessed fall ill and seek ritual specialists, who can return them to health. After being cured, those possessed by Zar spirits enter a social community that includes others, who also have these spirits. The fact that makes these cults of special interest in gender studies is that gender inequality appears to be a central problem that is "solved" by these cults. Zar cults provide secular as well as religious benefits for women in these largely patriarchal societies.

Zar spirits are foreign or alien personalities who possess women and some nonprivileged men. The spirits can be inherited, caught from others who are possessed, or acquired without explanation. When a woman becomes physically or emotionally sick, she calls in cult leaders, who are possessed by Zar spirits, to discover if she too may be troubled by these spirits. If, in fact, possession is the problem, the family sponsors a cure that will placate the angry spirits. Once possessed, however, the victim is possessed forever. In the future, she needs to be careful to prevent angering her spirits to avoid repeated illness. Lifelong nurturing of the spirit is required for maintenance of a normal life. As Susan Kenyon described, in the Sudan a woman can often explain away socially unacceptable behavior like cigarette smoking by blaming it on the spirits. (1995: 115–17) She becomes part of a large and public community led by the women who cured her. Her support for the Zar cult and her sisters in the community means that she is expected to help them out in the future by giving funds to pay for large ceremonies and lending personal support. In fact, it is said that her spirits are generous in the ceremonies, but the funds must come from her male relatives, who control all the monies. Thus, she is isolated from blame by the spirits and her men are compelled to sacrifice—not by the whims of a woman, but by the supernatural.

The Zar cult has been most intensely studied in various communities in the Sudan. There the roles of women are strongly constricted. Men are the owners of property, the sole economic providers for the family, and the final authorities in the home. Women are secluded in the private domain, while men travel and work wherever they please. Women are totally dependent on men. In this Muslim nation, religious leadership and worship is similarly part of the male realm. Muslim healers are male as well. Women are defined as inferior and their lives are secondary.

Possession by Zar spirits opens the lives of women. The exotic nature of the spirits themselves connects the women to the public in a way they otherwise would never know. The diseases that often initiate the awareness of possession are often related to problems with reproduction. A woman's reproductive success is as important to her husband as to herself. When she needs a cure, even one that is expensive, her husband needs to cater to her needs, and this is a relatively unique occurrence. As I. M. Lewis, who has studied Zar cults in Sudan, concluded, "Whatever the conscious motivations of those concerned, episodes of spirit illness and their treatment thus constitute an important weapon in the armory with which women (and sometimes also men of inferior status) exert leverage on their male superiors." (1991: 2) Also, a woman's association with nonrelatives in the Zar cult is an otherwise unlikely opportunity that opens her previously restricted field of relationships. Lewis continues: "This brings us to what modern Sudanese feminists are apt to see as the ultimate cause of Zar: conservative male-constituted society. Especially because it is so expensive and encourages 'superstition' and rebellious female sentiments, Zar may thus be readily branded by male-dominated officialdom as a 'harmful custom.' But for many women it remains an available and viable means of coping with life within the existing social parameters of a highly 'traditional' Muslim society." (1991: 5) Janice Boddy, another anthropologist who worked in the Sudan and studied Zar there, suggested that scholars should focus on the positive aspects of these cults. She saw possessed women as "working in the spiritual realm on behalf of themselves, their families, households, or communities, channeling spirits' assistance or heading off their wrath, protecting future generations, even protesting injustice." (1994: 416) In either perspective, Zar offers women an access to power and public influence that they could get nowhere else.

MISSIONS OF CHANGE

Most of the areas of the world today are heavily influenced by a handful of major religions. Christianity and Islam, as noted, have adherents in virtually all countries around the world and are still expanding at significant rates. The remarkable spread of these religions has been the result of a long, purposeful effort by missionaries from each faith. Many missionaries, both male and female, have sacrificed their familiar lives in order to bring the lessons of their faith to people very different from themselves. While feminists are just now studying the story of these individuals,[2] the effects of their missions on the people they worked with have long been issues for study. Such studies have often described a process of culture loss that went along with the change in religious beliefs that proved damaging to the people of the missionized culture. Others showed both benefits and loses.

---

[2]Many women missionaries were able to build lives of power and authority for themselves that they would not have otherwise known.

Until recently, however, few have looked at the role of the changes that came with modernization on the gender systems of the societies involved. Virtually all early missionaries taught that conversion could only be complete when the trappings of civilization went with it. This meant that family, occupation, household, political systems, and other domestic issues were almost as important as concepts of faith in the training of new adherents to the faith. Because both Christianity and Islam sprang from patriarchal authority structures, the social rules they taught were also largely patriarchal. Because Christian and Muslim missions, at least until recently, taught the importance of a subservient position for women in society. That missionaries have been deleterious to the status of women in society has now become somewhat of a normal assumption in modern feminist studies. However, as with most things, such simple conclusions are rarely absolute. In fact, as in the case of Pentecostal missions in Colombia, conversion has been seen as actually improving women's lives.

Gifts from the Mission: Steel Axes

One of the most famous early articles familiar to many students in anthropology dealt with the effect of mission policies on nonreligious culture change. Anthropologist Lauriston Sharp described how one specific mission gift, the steel axe, interrupted the balance of the Yir Yoront of Australia, a still largely isolated society. (1952: 17–22) In fact, the article postulates that the actions of the mission unintentionally threw the society into chaos.

The Yir Yoront were hunters, gatherers, and fishers with a patrilineal clan system. All members of the society used the primary tool, a stone axe. Women, however, used these axes in most of their daily activities—gathering, house building, and food preparation. Beyond the practical uses for stone axes, these tools were also social and symbolic keystones in Yir Yoront culture. At this level, the axes were central to men's positions and activities. Only men could own stone axes. They made the axes themselves, but they needed to trade with partners in other groups to obtain appropriate stone. This linked them into a far-ranging trading network. Also, one clan used the stone axe as a major totem figure in their sacred ceremonies. Most important to the issue of gender, the relationship between women and their significant men was tempered through the axes. While men owned the axes, women needed to use them regularly. To perform their daily tasks, women were required to "borrow" and return the axes from and to their husbands, or, if unmarried, fathers or brothers. This interaction reinforced, on a daily basis, a woman's dependency on her male relatives. Further, it supported a social ideology that asserted that women were subordinate while men were dominant.

In 1915 an Anglican mission was established; it was a three-day journey from the territory of the Yir Yoront. While they did not settle among the Yir Yoront, members of this group did travel to the mission and interacted with Australians in the mission area. When the missionaries began to distribute steel axes to local people, they rapidly became available to the Yir Yoront. Missionaries believed that steel axes would ease the workload of the Australians and leave them more leisure time to devote to progressive enterprises. Consequently, the missionaries gave them to men, women, and young people alike. Anyone who came to mission ceremonies or worked for the missions received steel axes. In fact, it was the male elders who were least likely to interact with missionaries on a friendly footing and thus were least likely to get the new axes.

With the wide availability of steel axes, many of the traditional anchors of Yir Yoront culture lost their grip. Trade relations, clan totems, and, of course, gender relationships were fundamentally changed. Women, who no longer had to find men to loan them implements to do their work, found new independence. They no longer had to display their acquiescence to an ideology of male superiority. Soon the roles that had hinged on male dominance lost their importance, and confusion over social relations became the norm. The missions brought the Yir Yoront into a state of dependency. The trade routes to other Australians were replaced with a relationship to the mission. The missionaries saw this new dependence on the missions in a positive light because it allowed them an opportunity to influence the "civilizing" of these people. They encouraged a new form of formal leadership at the same time the general concept of general male leadership waned. Certainly the goal of the mission was not to lessen the importance of the husband in a family and to destabilize marriages, but that is what happened. The missions directly affected the positions of women and men in Yir Yoront culture, but it was an unanticipated outcome to a simple, apparently pragmatic promotion.

Jesuits in Canada

In the 1600s the Montagnais-Naskapi, now Innu, of eastern Canada were, as described in Chapter 3, a hunting group. They hunted moose and caribou as well as smaller mammals, birds, and fish. Like other hunting groups, they moved frequently, followed their game, and maintained a cooperative, generally egalitarian society. They had neither chiefs nor formal councils. Individualism allied with cooperation was the hallmark of Innu life before contact.

Jesuit priests led by Paul Le Jeune brought the Catholic faith to the Innu in 1632. Their mission was to convert and bring civilization to the people they regarded as pagans. The society they met fell far from their ideal. The priests found polygamy, shamanism, sexual freedom, and anarchy. These were all traits that the fathers saw as antithetical to the acceptance of Christianity. Anthropologist Eleanor Leacock examined the Jesuit Relations, in which the fathers recorded their observations of their success in converting the Innu people and bringing the sexes into a more acceptable accord. The priests reported that women had societal power and little fear of their husbands or fathers. In fact, they lived at ease as equals with the men of their culture. This was interpreted in a totally negative light. The priests pitied the women because, in their minds, they were worked too hard, were sexually exploited, were unprotected by men, and were forced into inappropriate marriages. This analysis, of course, reflected the ideals of the European church of the time. A more modern interpretation of the same aspects of women's lives would emphasize that women were part of the economic life of the society, they lived lives of sexual freedom, and they could choose marriages different than the lifelong monogamous unions the church mandated. Father Le Jeune described four goals in the civilizing of Montagnais-Naskapi: settling into permanent villages headed by chiefs, the inclusion of punishment as a social sanction, the education of children in a European manner, and adoption of the European family structure. "Male authority, female fidelity, and the elimination of the right to divorce" were specifically targeted objectives. (Leacock 1980: 27–28)

Leacock first worked among the Innu in the north during the 1950s. The society she found there was far different than that of their ancestors before the missions came to the area. What she did find, however, was a group of people who still treasured cooperation and tolerance. Children were never physically punished, and men and women remained at ease with one another. On the other hand, these were now people living in nuclear family units with wage labor increasingly important. Also, virilo-cal residence had taken precedent over uxorilocal, male chiefs led bands, and shamans were then exclusively men. As Leacock noted, "the status of women, although still relatively high, had clearly changed." (1980: 41) The success of the mission was broader than that of faith and ritual, but their goals were only partially fulfilled.

Presbyterians and the Tlingit

The story of Presbyterian missions among the Tlingit of southeastern Alaska, who were introduced in Chapter 5, is similar in many ways to the case of the Jesuits. Because this mission existed more than a century later and in a Protestant, rather than Catholic, context, these cases demonstrate the stay-ing power of the idea that proper gender patterns and Christianity must go hand in hand. One added factor in this case is the prominence of women missionaries in the actions of the missions. In fact, as one contemporary reporter put it, "Timid women do not make good missionaries in Alaska." (Wright 1883: 260) The irony of this, of course, is that one of their con-scious goals was to weaken the positions of Tlingit women in that society.

The Alaska mission began in the late 1870s when Sheldon Jackson and Amanda McFarland came to the town of Wrangell to establish a mission station. Jackson went south to raise money, and McFarland organized the mission. The societal strengths of Tlingit women, which included their importance in trade, status determination, subsistence work, and commu-nity decisions, when combined with their kin positions in the matrilineal system was defined as "degradation" by Jackson. (1880: 115–18) These women could divorce and remarry, they could argue publicly with husbands, and they could be leaders as shamans in the "pagan" religion. McFarland perceived a change in the position of women as the key to the success of her mission. She petitioned repeatedly until she was given the right to open a school, her "home" for young women. McFarland's school—first in Wrangell and then moved after a fire to the site of the newer young men's school in Sitka—had a tight curriculum that emphasized sewing, cleaning, cooking, and other domestic skills as well as religion. The students consisted of the daughters of families who saw a Western education as beneficial to their daughters and the girls that McFarland and other missionaries "saved" from lives of sin. Oftentimes, this meant girls who had been promised in marriage to spouses the missionaries found unacceptable because of age or ethnicity. Over the years, many girls "escaped" from the school. Those who prospered in the school and reached graduation were expected to marry boys from the mission school, set up nuclear family homes, and act as models for others. The problem they found was that the graduates who returned to their family villages settled into the more traditional houses and marriages too easily. To combat this, cottages were built on the school grounds, and selected married graduates used these. After decades of mission teaching, including intensive boarding school instruction, the missionaries only trusted those who remained on their lands to carry on their concept of good behavior.

This does not mean that the missions were unsuccessful at all levels. Certainly the Presbyterian faith spread quickly throughout the population and remains significant today. Community houses gave way to nuclear houses during the twentieth century, and Western style kinship forms increased in importance. Polygamy, arranged marriages, and traditional shamanism have faded from daily life. Today it is common for people to have traditional matrilineal names and statuses that are used in potlatches and clan business and Western names that descend from father to child that are used in broader American contexts. Most significant are the public and traditional positions of Tlingit women that appear to be as powerful as they were in precontact times. Women as political and economic leaders are just as common in village, Tlingit, and state contexts as men in these roles. Women, like men, work, determine marriages and divorces, and take part in traditional and Christian religious ceremonies. The Presbyterian missionaries did not lessen the importance of Tlingit women, although this was a goal. Ironically, the roles that strong women missionaries played in the history of the missions did nothing to model the submissive women as the only good Christian.

Pentecostals in Colombia

Examples like those of the Tlingit and Innu missions (and other similar cases) have created an assumption that Christian missions led inevitably to a more patriarchal system. The ideal of the nuclear family with a supportive wife and mother and a wage-earning, concerned husband and father appear integral to the core of Christian moral values. While change to this system was often a central mission goal, it was not true that actions to reach this goal always lowered the status of women in society. Anthropologist Elizabeth Brusco, in her book *The Reformation of Machismo* (1995), recorded a case of Christian missionary activity in contemporary Colombia in which the acceptance of these Christian teachings resulted in the improvement in the lives of women in the community. What makes this case even more of a challenge to popular assumptions is the fact that these Colombian missionaries were Pentecostal Christians, a category often associated with the preaching of the subordination of women.

Evangelical missionaries came to Colombia in 1956 with the goal of bringing their understanding of Christianity to an overwhelmingly Catholic country. Not only were the people of Colombia members of the Catholic church, but the state, itself, had official ties with the Vatican, which left public education and public ceremonies including marriage and death rites in the hands of the Catholic church. The Pentecostals came to convert other Christians in a social context that gave the older church a superior social and political position.

The mission lessons about the proper roles for women in Pentecostal families appear familiar. The pious woman was expected to be a helpmate to her husband and a mentor to her children. She maintained a nurturing, rather than ruling, role in her family. She and her husband were partners in the family, and the family was defined as the heart of society. Women's roles in public life, other than the church, were less important, and men were expected to hold other significant, public secular roles. Women in Catholic families were also largely defined as belonging in the domestic domain, with the public domain, in both church and secular matters, defined as male. The separation of women in the domestic domain and men in the public domain became even more distinct in recent history with increasing urbanization leaving more families dependent on wage labor, rather than agriculture. The more significant difference in Catholic and Pentecostal gender roles was the ideal role of the man, rather than the woman.

In Colombia men were expected to live a life of machismo. This involved living their lives in public with other men. As Brusco notes this behavior is more "anti-domestic" than merely public. (1995: 80) Drinking, smoking, gambling, and extramarital sexual exploits were laudable behaviors. Men made the money, and they spent much of it on themselves and their public persona. While clearly this was not part of the teaching of the Catholic church, such behavior did not estrange a man from that church. It was, however, in complete opposition to meaningful membership in the Evangelical churches. To quote Brusco, "The machismo roles and the male role defined by evangelicalism are almost diametrical opposites. Aggression, violence, pride, self-indulgence, and an individualistic orientation in the public sphere are replaced by peace seeking, humility, self-restraint, and a collective orientation and identity with the church and home."

(1995: 137) The focus of the Pentecostal man on his home and church had significant benefits to his wife and children. His total income was shared in the household, while previously 20 to 40 percent of it went to alcohol. He spent time with his family, and he was faithful to his wife. Family violence and neglect no longer demonstrated the superiority of the man but, quite the opposite, revealed his decadence.

The lives of Colombian Evangelical women were elevated when they and their husbands joined the new church. They were still largely situated in the domestic domain, but this domain was no longer devalued. It was now raised to the highest importance. Women and men were both active in the leadership roles in the church, opening specific public roles to women. While there were clear benefits to male converts as well, women were especially advantaged in a family's conversion to Evangelical churches. As Brusco asserted, "Colombian Pentecostalism can be seen as a form of female collective action." (1995: 13)

Islam in Nigeria

If the Christian missions played their roles in the changing gender concepts of missionized people, it should be of little wonder that the Muslim missions did the same. Islam had been one of the most successful religions during the colonial period in gaining converts in Asia and Africa. The willingness to accept multiple marriages, divorce, and other widespread customs, which Christianity rejected, made conversion to Islam an easier transformation in many places. The ideology of strict gender separation that many Muslim missionaries brought to their converts had effects on cultures that have lasted to this day. An example of such a result can be found among the Hausa of northern Nigeria, who have been studied by anthropologist Barbara Callaway. (Callaway and Creevey 1994) Islam came early to northern Nigeria and was well established by the fifteenth century. Modern forms of Islam, however, date to an early nineteenth century jihad that "purified" the existing religious practices and dogma and established contemporary custom. (1994: 4) The erosion of a woman's place in public affairs began at the beginning of Islam but was completed by the nineteenth century.

Pre-Muslim Hausa society was a complex, bureaucratic organization with significant differences among classes. The aristocratic class allowed both men and women to exert power and authority. Royal women held gender-specific public offices and shared power in other realms. The mothers, sisters, and wives of the rulers held especially important roles, perhaps dating back to a matrilineal system that predated the patrilineal system then in place. Common women enjoyed less power than their high-status counterparts, but they also held roles of significance in local economic and political affairs. Men, at this level, had more authority than their female counterparts, but the gap between them was not large.

Women, until the nineteenth century jihad, were active leaders in another religious practice, bori. Bori, which was similar to Zar, focused on spirit possession and curing. Royal women among the Hausa acted as leaders of bori in the early days. In fact, Callaway and Creevey noted that "Bori was, in effect, a state religion led by women of the ruling class." (1994: 12) During the early days of Islam, both religions existed side by side—with women predominating in one and men in the other. After the jihad, however, Muslim leaders outlawed bori and advocated the education of women in proper Muslim belief and practice. Bori, although forbidden and socially demeaned, long remained important in the lives of many Hausa, especially women.

Traditional Hausa culture showed a male bias but allowed women prominent roles in both the public and private arenas. After the nineteenth century, however, this dramatically changed. Women in modern Muslim Hausa society were relegated to their homes. In fact, Hausa women were expected to live in complete seclusion. After their marriages, which were ideally at a young age, they were physically separated from any men other than their relatives. They had no public power because, in fact, they were expected to have no public presence at all. Their lives focused on the betterment of their families, and their social relationships were limited to women friends and family members. Brothers, fathers, and husbands were the few men they met with any frequency.

The roles of mothers and daughters intermeshed in important ways. Anthropologist Enid Schildkrout (1981) observed that a Hausa woman depended on children, especially daughters, to help them earn money and that a woman without a child often brought an unmarried relative into her household for this purpose. Daughters learned their domestic roles in their childhood homes, but, at the same time, they acted as contacts with the outside world for their mothers. Unmarried girls were allowed to travel out of the home and so could bring messages to other households and go into the market. They sold the produce of their mothers and bought the material goods they wanted. They also had to learn to take care of children and household chores because, as Callaway and Creevey noted: "From a time a girl marries until after menopause, she has virtually no freedom of movement or association." (1994: 34) At the age of 10 or 12, a girl married and went to her husband's compound, where her seclusion began.

Hausa women were not totally dependent people, however, and their roles continued to change with national and international circumstances. Because men were expected to be the providers to their households, the money that women earned in their trading enterprises belonged to them. In the last two decades, the economy of Nigeria has changed, and women's incomes have become important to the maintenance of many households. The preparation and sale of foods has become a common economic venture. Other domestic skills and products have been turned into money-making enterprises as well. While the money still belongs to the women, they can choose to use it in their homes, and husbands, while humbled, need this income. The mandate for seclusion has meant that few Hausa women have entered into public wage labor. Only elite women, who have the education for professional positions with women clients, have entered this domain in any numbers. As they enter the twenty-first century, the Hausa are still among the most segregated women in the world, and this segregation is a result of their acceptance of the teachings of Muslim missions over the centuries. Their interpretation of Muslim teachings, like those in other parts of the world, relies on local cultural history as well as religious teachings.

SUMMARY

Religion provides the central ideology of most societies. People throughout the world draw comfort and clarity from their religious beliefs. A religion can also define the nature and value of gender positions. The effects of missions on the social lives of the missionized, as well as their religious lives, demonstrate this. Further, religions offer support for the social construction of gender. In other words, if women are restricted from culturally significant roles in a society, teachings of the religion that support gender equality will not be emphasized. This is how the god, or gods, want it to be. Women, like men, define and adjust to their roles using a cosmological understanding of the world. Similarly, a society that is more egalitarian focuses on religious teachings that support gender equity.

It is also apparent that the readings of religious teachings change with the times. The lessons of proper Christian and Muslim life taught by early missionaries might appear antique to current members of the faith. Even in universal religions like these, which depend on written texts that have been read for many centuries, core understandings have changed with new religious scholars' interpretations of the true meanings of the sacred writings.

Readings

Abu-Odeh, Lama. "Post-Colonial Feminism and the Veil: Considering the Differences." *New England Law Review* 26, no. 4 (1992), pp. 1527–39.

Bailey, Deborah Ann. "Christianity: Religious Rites and Practices." In *Encyclopedia of Women and World Religion*, ed. Serinity Young. New York: Macmillan, 1999, pp. 152–55.

Beck, Lois. "Islam: Religious Rites and Practice." In *Encyclopedia of Women and World Religion*, ed. Serinity Young. New York: Macmillan, 1999, pp. 494–96.

Berger, Helen A. "The Earth Is Sacred: Ecological Concerns in American Wicca." In *Religion in a Changing World*, ed. Madeleine Cousineau. Westport, CT: Praeger, 1998.

Boddy, Janice. "Spirit Possession Revisited: Beyond Instrumentality." *Annual Review of Anthropology* 23 (1994): pp. 407–34.

Brink, Judy. "Lost Rituals: Sunni Muslim Women in Rural Egypt." In *Mixed Blessings: Gender and Religious Fundamentalism Cross Culturally,* eds. Judy Brink and Joan Mencher. New York: Routledge, 1997, pp. 199–208.

Brusco, Elizabeth. *The Reformation of Machismo: Evangelical Conversion and Gender in Colombia.* Austin, TX: University of Texas Press, 1995.

Callaway, Barbara, and Lucy Creevey. *The Heritage of Islam: Women, Religion, and Politics in West Africa.* London: Lynne Rienner Publishers, 1994.

Cardman, Francine. "Christianity: Historical Overview from 300 to 1800." In *Encyclopedia of Women and World Religion,* ed. Serinity Young. New York: Macmillan, 1999, pp. 140–52.

Ehrenreich, Barbara, and Deirdre English. *Witches, Midwives, and Nurses: A History of Women Healers.* Old Westbury, NY: The Feminist Press, 1973.

Flood, Gavin. *An Introduction to Hinduism.* Cambridge: Cambridge University Press, 1996.

Gross, Rita M. "Toward a New Model of the Hindu Pantheon: A Report on Twenty-some Years of Feminist Reflection." *Religion* 28 (1998), pp. 319–27.

Harland, Lindsey, and Paul B. Courtright. "Introduction: On Hindu Marriage and Its Margins." In *From the Margins of Hindu Marriage: Essays on Gender, Religion, and Culture,* eds. Lindsey Harlan and Paul B. Courtright. New York: Oxford University Press, 1995, pp. 3–18.

Hassan, Riffat. "Challenging the Stereotype of Fundamentalism: An Islamic Feminist Perspective." *The Muslim World* 91 (2001), pp. 55–69.

Jackson, Sheldon. *Alaska and Missions on the North Pacific Coast.* New York: Dodd Mead & Co., 1880.

Kendall, Laurel. "Old Ghosts and Ungrateful Children: A Korean Shaman's Story." In *Women as Healers: Cross-Cultural Perspectives,* ed. Carole Shepherd McClain. New Brunswick, NJ: Rutgers University Press, 1989, pp. 138–56.

Kenyon, Susan M. "Zar as Modernization in Contemporary Sudan." *Anthropological Quarterly* 68, no. 2 (1995), pp. 107–20.

Killen, Patricia O'Connell. *Finding Our Voices: Women, Wisdom, and Faith.* New York: Crossroad Publishing Company, 1997.

Leacock, Eleanor. "Montagnais Women and the Jesuit Program for Colonization." In *Women and Colonization: Anthropological Perspectives,* eds. Mona Etienne and Eleanor Leacock. New York: Praeger, 1980, pp. 25–42.

Lewis, I. M. "Introduction: Zar in Context: The Past, the Present and Future of an African Healing Cult." In *Women's Medicine: The Zar-Bori Cult in Africa and Beyond,* eds. I. M. Lewis, Ahmed Al-Safi, and Sayyid Hurreiz. Edinburgh: Edinburgh University Press, 1991.

MacHaffie, Barbara J. *Her Story: Women in Christian Tradition.* Philadelphia: Fortress Press, 1986.

Malone, Mary T. *Women and Christianity,* Vol. I. Maryknoll, NY: Orbis Books, 2001.

Mernissi, Fatima. *The Veil and the Male Elite: A Feminist Interpretation of Women's Rights in Islam,* trans. Mary Jo Lakeland. Reading, MA: Addison-Wesley, 1991.

Mooney, Catherine M. "Christianity: Apostolic Religious Orders and Communities." In *Encyclopedia of Women and World Religion,* ed. Serinity Young. New York: Macmillan, 1999, pp. 174–77.

Nanda, Serena. *Neither Man nor Woman: The Hijras of India,* 2nd ed. Belmont, CA: Wadsworth, 1999.

Ruether, Rosemary Radford. "Feminism in World Christianity." In *Feminism and World Religions,* eds. Arvind Sharma and Katherine K. Young. Albany, NY: State University of New York Press, 1999, pp. 214–47.

Saliba, Therese. "Arab Feminism at the Millennium." *Signs* 25 (2000), pp. 1087–92.

Schildkrout, Enid. "Young Traders of Northern Nigeria." *Natural History*, no. 6 (1981), pp. 44–53.

Sharp, Lauriston. "Steel Axes for Stone-Age Australians." *Human Organization* 11, no. 2 (1952), pp. 17–22.

Sonn, Tamara. "Islam: An Overview." In *Encyclopedia of Women and World Religion,* ed. Serinity Young. New York: Macmillan, 1999, pp. 488–94.

Sugirharajah, Sharada. "Courtly Text and Courting Sati." *Journal of Feminist Studies in Religion* 17, no. 1 (2001), pp. 5–31.

Webster, Paula. "Matriarchy: A Vision of Power." In *Women, Culture, and Society,* eds. Michelle Rosaldo Zimbalist and Louise Lamphere. Stanford, CA: Stanford University Press, 1974, pp. 141–56.

Wright, Julia. *Among the Alaskans*. Philadelphia: Presbyterian Board of Publications, 1883.

Young, Katherine K. "Women in Hinduism." In *Today's Woman in World Religions,* ed. Arvind Sharma. Albany, NY: State University of New York Press, 1994, pp. 77–136.

CHAPTER TEN

Colonialism and Development: Gendered Realities

How has social "progress" affected gender?
Do development programs favor men over women? How do they treat men and
What is the definition of gender differences in globalization? women differently?

This book has reviewed gender in different cultures with an emphasis on the broad variety of sex roles in the world today and in the past. However, as many have noted, the world is getting smaller. In reality this means that virtually all parts of the world are in immediate contact with all others. Moreover, some societies have more power and influence than do others in these interactions. The northern, so-called developed countries have economic, military, and technology resources that others do not, and they have used them to formulate a world system that is compatible with their needs. What happens in London affects people in Swaziland and India. Many movies filmed in Hollywood are seen in Tokyo, Cairo, and Rio de Janeiro. The fiction that there are separate cultures and separate states is today a fundamental fiction. This does not mean that cultural variations in gender and other issues do not still exist, but that all cultures are influenced by others as well. This is not new, but the degree of this commonality is new.

When anthropologists of the first half of the twentieth century began to study other cultures, they often traveled weeks or even months to reach their field sites. Contact with their families and colleagues was via mail, which often took at least as long as their original travel time. Today, of course, anthropologists reach their field sites within days and often reach home via e-mail and telephones. Additionally, when they return home they find that they can stay in contact with friends and informants from the field by the same means. Often people they know from the communities they have studied show up in the anthropologists' home communities as welcomed visitors and as migrants looking for short-term or permanent employment. The concept of the global community has become a reality.

Ours remains a culturally diverse community—but not a culturally isolated world. The polygynous family in London, the veiled girl in Paris, and the mother from Somalia looking for safe genital surgery for her daughter in Seattle have all become challenges for localities that have not previously dealt with these issues on their own soil. Likewise, the mission preaching against polygamy in sub-Saharan Africa, the international aid predicated on a ban on specific birth control methods in India, and the military aid that includes female jet pilots in Saudi Arabia present gender challenges in those regions. The world, as always, is highly variable, but now, it is also highly integrated.

This chapter reviews issues of colonialism, transnationalism, and development with a focus on the effect these rapid change agents have had on gender categories and roles around the world. As colonialism changed to economic colonialism, powerful governments directed the development of nonindustrialized states. While the stated goal was the improvement of the standard of living of the world's peoples, very often the lives of women were not considered. As the editors for a special issue of the journal *Signs* wrote: "If globalization exemplifies capitalism's worst tendencies of expansion and domination, we need to know whether and why globalization can also provide opportunities for certain groups of women to leave the worst excesses of patriarchal domination behind." (Basu et al. 2001: 943).

COLONIALISM AND GENDERED REALITIES

American and European students learn the history of the colonial enterprise in a very different way than students in most parts of the world. High school and elementary texts tell stories of the adventure of European explorers and the intrigue of competition over foreign lands. The stories of Indian, Chinese, and Arab explorers never appear. Further, the idea that these "new lands" were actually owned and home to millions of people is ignored. In American history one aspect of the colonial enterprise, the "discovery" and "settlement" of the New World, is the origin story of the country. As anthropologists, our perspective is quite different. We know that the so-called discovery of the Americas, Africa, Australia, and the rest of the non-European world came millennia before the Europeans arrived. We also know that the European, and other colonial, projects were ones in which the newcomers dispossessed the local people of control over their lands, and to some extent, their lives. As feminist anthropologists, we also have learned that this colonial enterprise affected the status of women around the world, both directly and indirectly, in a manner that few texts relate.

On Progress

Until recently the concept of progress was unquestioned in American culture. As times changed, things became better. New technology is better than old technology, and human cultures change with technological achievement. Following this line of thinking, colonialism brought new technology and new ideas to socially "backward" countries. It opened the modern world to local people and, therefore, liberated them from cultures that still allowed traditions such as polygamy and paganism, and primitive economics that Westerners found repugnant. As the previous chapters have shown, the marriage, economic, and religious systems that would be counted under these categories often were the backbone of the culture, and many supported gender systems that worked well for women.

In the flush of the energy of the feminist movement of the 1960s and 1970s, feminists compared their newly won access to schools, jobs, and public positions with the options open to their mothers, which confirmed the idea of progress. A century earlier, middle-class European and Euro-American women were tied to domestic chores with the goal of being the perfect modern wife. Modern women, then, seem to have come "a long way," and must be much further away from women in less progressive societies. What was missing from these reviews of progress was the understanding of the reality of other women's lives. Theories of progress in gender relationships under Western influence were based on Eurocentric images of the rest of the world as less highly evolved and suffering from the ills that earlier European cultures had overcome.

When the ethnographies of the 1970s and 1980s focused on women and as gender roles began to emerge, the image of the enslaved primitive woman began to fade. In fact, as the examples in the preceding chapters have shown, women in many precolonial cultures had access to power and authority that their contemporary European sisters could only approach in their dreams. Also these women had relationships with the men in their societies that did not neatly fit into the categories of Western gender concepts. Certainly this is not to say that these non-Western women all lived in equality with men or that they were the rulers of their societies, but the reality was far more complex than anyone had thought.

If this is true, then a reexamination of the effect of colonization on gender relations was long overdue. In 1980 a collection of articles entitled *Women and Colonization* was published and edited by Mona Etienne and Eleanor Leacock. It asserted that rather than improve the lives of women, colonialism generally lowered their status. Drawing on geographic examples from Tonga to the Ivory Coast and historical examples from the fifteenth century to the 1960s, recurrent themes emerged. Colonial powers brought their understanding of the proper social structure to succeed in the modern world. This meant that families should be nuclear families, men should own the property and provide for families, societal leadership should be clear and in the hands of men, and the economic base should be compatible with that of the Western world. All had significance for the status of women in most societies.

The example from that book of the Bari, a forest horticultural and foraging society in Colombia, illustrates this clearly. (Buenaventura-Posso and *were they?*

Brown 1980: 109–33) Before colonization the Bari were a "classless, non-stratified, and fully egalitarian" communal society in which men and women lived equal and compatible lives. (p. 118) After being declared "pacified" in 1964, their future was directed by the "Motilon Development Plan." In this plan, the Bari were encouraged to leave their communal family system for small nuclear family units in which the husbands were the economic and authoritarian cores. Given no traditional community leaders, male chiefs were appointed and young boys were sent for urban education to learn to be proper future leaders. Replacing traditional subsistence farming, fishing, and hunting was wage labor and trade in surplus crops. Men were deemed eligible for these new roles, and women became dependent on them. Women's work became service for male income earners. Also, the prominent role of women as healers was displaced with the advent of new Western medicines and healers. While neither Bari men nor women gave up on their traditional ways of life, the trend toward gender inequity was set in motion with little support for continued equality.

It is not necessary to believe that colonialism was inherently bad to accept that the goal of colonialism was to recreate the gender system most familiar to the colonists. The colonists pressed for this conclusion because they believed it to be best for people or that it was the easiest to work with, but in either case the model was a colonial pattern. During most of the years of intensive colonialism, the gender pattern of Europe and European colonists was patriarchal in flavor. Religion supported it, and the idea of male superiority was written deeply into the social rules. The newly met cultures were seen as exotic and primitive, and the different sex roles substantiated this view. When men were not leaders over women, this was a sign that men were weak. When men appeared to have advantages over women, this was a sign that they were cruel and women were abused. In all cases, the ethnocentrism of the colonists influenced their understanding of the colonized societies. The colonized were not helpless victims, though, and most were energetic in reacting to colonial mandates, so the outcome was rarely what the colonial powers envisioned. In any case, societies were changed and gender relations were redefined.

Regendering Governments

When Europeans first came into contact with societies in which women held important political positions, their reactions ranged from horror to ridicule. Even the British during the reign of Victoria preached against the powers of the queens in African societies. Because European social mores were held up as the model for civilized society and because European political systems were clearly patriarchal, other forms of political systems had to be reformed. This meant the loss of public power and authority for women in many societies around the world. The case of the Seneca nation of the Iroquois Confederacy and that of the Tonga of the Pacific demonstrate how devastating the effects of this policy were.

The Seneca Iroquois women as described in Chapter 4 are known in the feminist literature as among the most politically powerful. While hardly the matriarchy some claimed this society to be, it is clear that Iroquois women, like men, had a say in the running of their society. The votes of the matrons selected and deposed sachems. More importantly, their authority in the uxorilocal households and villages was unchallenged as was their control over the lands they cultivated. Anthropologist Joy Bilharz (1995) studied changes that the women of the Seneca of the Allegheny and Cattaraugus reservations experienced after the colonial period.

The organization of the Seneca was troubling to the Quaker missionaries and the federal officials first assigned to the area. Civilization to them mandated nuclear family households headed by fathers who farmed and provided for their families. Handsome Lake, a mystical religious leader, and his half brother, Cornplanter, were influenced by the Quaker teachings. In 1801 their "social gospel" supported the Quaker ideal, and soon nuclear family houses replaced communal longhouses. Economic roles and kinship patterns changed, although the new religion included significant roles for women leaders. Half a century later, in 1848, when the Seneca Nation of Indians was established with a modern form of government, there was little room for women. An elected council and executive committee replaced traditional positions of chiefs. In this transformation, women were disenfranchised. The constitution for the new nation was based on the work of the tribe's attorney and, according to Bilharz, "replicated contemporary white customs, [where] women were disenfranchised: only men could vote, and only males could hold office." (1995: 109) For the next century Seneca women focused their energies on their homes and children.

The crisis of the mid-twentieth century was the building of the Kinzua Dam, which flooded a large part of the Allegheny reservation and forced relocation of a significant part of the population. In the failed fight to stop the building of the dam, women emerged as energetic managers and leaders. They also were active in organizing the relocation when the fight failed and the dam was built. During this period, women's lack of the vote became an issue, and some women challenged the authority of the president over them because they did not, and could not, vote for him. In 1964 Seneca women again were able to vote within their society. Since the move that followed the Kinzua Dam, women have become more and more politically active. Joy Bilharz reported, "It is clear that women have regained a position of, at least, equality." (1995: 112)

The Tongans The people of Tonga in the Pacific Ocean ended the nineteenth century as a kingdom with a chiefly elite, but this centralized political form was new. It was created in a futile attempt to avoid colonial takeover. Just before this, the chiefly ranks were the apex of power without a titular high chief or king. The role of gender in this system was very complex. Rank took precedence over gender as a determinant of social position, and both chiefly and nonchiefly women had some authority and personal

autonomy. Chiefly women, moreover, had considerable political and economic power. Chiefly women also produced *koloa*, socially and ritually
valuable products that supported roles of honor and rank. Chiefly people
were guardians of lands and labor supplies and, as such, could allocate
these resources. They were not, however, the owners of either land or people. Nonchiefly men and women, however, were dependent on the chiefly
Tongans, but here too, gender was not a significant factor in their status.

Anthropologist Christine Ward Gailey (1980), who studied the effect of
colonization on the status of these women, highlighted the major elements
of women's authority. Tongan kinship defied easy categorization. A clear
patrilateral bias for inheritance was modified by the importance of
mother's clan in many contexts. Seniority was a strong issue in power relationships. In terms of gender, the position of wife was subordinate to that
of husband, and a wife was expected to defer to her husband. However, sisters were superior to brothers and chiefly women were more highly ranked
than were their brothers. This meant that the most highly ranked individuals were women. The term *fahu*, or "above the law," defined a sister's rights
over her brother, his wives and children, and his descendants. These rights
included a call on their labor and the ability to arrange marriages and,
thus, create alliances. The brother–sister pair was a rank element in Tongan politics and economics as well as kinship. Senior chiefly women used
marriage arrangements and knowledge of genealogies to support or dis-
credit rising chiefs. These women, although categorized as inferior to their
husbands, acted independent both economically and politically from them
in a forum in which their husbands had no power.

Europeans first came to Tonga in the mid-seventeenth century, and
the British imposed a protectorate in 1900. Tonga only regained its independence in the 1960s. The missionaries who came to Tonga reacted
against the open sexuality of Tongan women, their autonomy from their
husbands, and their obvious political authority. The goal of creating obedient wives and authoritarian, economically responsible husbands, here,
as elsewhere, was a conscious goal, and the missionaries and supportive
British officials worked to bring that about.

Economic changes undermined the value of women's products, but
more important, in terms of political authority, were the laws that were
established. A critical law blatantly outlawed the fahu rights. This, of
course, made the political aspects of the sister role illegal. This meant a
loss of the power for the status of sister, which meant that the subordinat-
ing role of wife became the primary role for women. Dependency on husbands became the only option. Chiefly women lost the right to "create"
chiefs and to hold regent positions. While the chiefly women retained the
influence of elite women in a class society, they lost their legitimate roles
that had actual power and authority. Other laws affected land owned and
inheritable from elite father to son and created voting rights that were only
open to tax-paying males. As Gailey concluded: "After the British Protectorate of 1900, legislation relating to land tenure, voting, wage regulation,

and inheritance and kinship practices continued to limit access to resources, occupations, and traditional sources of both authority and personal autonomy for women, and especially for nonchiefly women." (1980: 315) Today, no one would mistake a chiefly woman for a meek nonperson. The force of their personalities, and informal fahu traditions, still make them people to reckon with; however, their formal political status has been radically reduced under British rule.

Economic Repercussions of Colonialism

Colonialism was as much an economic endeavor as it was a political enterprise. Today, as the political goals of colonialism have faded away, the economic dominance of the former colonial powers remains in place. Colonialism, with its emphasis on cash crops and wage labor, has had the same profound effect on the lives of women as did the emphasis on religion and politics. The new economies that followed colonialism have transformed women's lives.

Trade in Primary Commodities: Cash Cropping   Horticulture and agriculture have been the arenas of women in many parts of the world. Women fed their families from the fruits of their gardens and traded the surplus for other goods. In cases like the Iroquois and others, the high status of women was supported by their economic standing as farmers. With the beginnings of colonialism, this stronghold for women was often eroded because of the European idea that men should be the farmers.

Even while encouraging farming as a civilizing advance, the missionaries and secular colonists recognized only male farmers as legitimate. In reality, the fact that women worked at the hard labor that farming entails was used to support their conclusions that these people were uncivilized. Civilized women did not perform hard labor. Even in recent years, this gender bias is clear and detrimental to women. In many development projects, training and equipment are only made available to men. In a recent development project in Thailand aimed at improving rice production, only men were trained to use the new fertilizing techniques, power tillers, and planting techniques. Because women actually did much of the rice farming, the plants were planted, fertilized, and tilled improperly, causing the project to fail. (Thrupp and Estes 1995: 49) Other barriers to the expansion of women's farming in the modern world have included their inability to purchase new technology for use in subsistence gardens. Also, new technologies have not been designed with women or unique cultural contexts in mind. Maladaptive designs as simple as setting a pump handle for a well too high for women to easily reach have made the technology inappropriate for their use. Additionally, most agricultural experts and teachers employed to spread the new techniques have been men and, thus, speak to men.

Men have taken advantage of the new opportunities that have been made available to them, and this has sometimes meant that men have come to dominate some formerly female industries. One case from Nigeria presented by Thrupp and Estes can illustrate this. (1995: 49) Women in Nigeria long processed the cassava crop by hand. When mechanical graters were introduced to the area in the 1960s, women were unable to purchase these machines. Men, however, could and did buy the new technology, and they soon dominated the cassava industry and earned the profits. When farming became a cash-based industry dictated by the nature of the world market, the expectations of the industrialized world overwhelmed the traditional division of labor and mandated their vision of the male farmer.

Regardless of the ownership of cash cropping enterprises, there are critical aspects of cash cropping that have broader implications for women's lives. First, cash crops take fields that have been used for subsistence crops, which means that food for families is limited. In place of the food crops, money made from cash cropping is expected to allow the families to purchase food. Because the major world cash crops include sugar, coffee, cotton, tea, tobacco, and bananas, there is no option to eat the crops if the market price is not sufficient to buy enough food for family use. Farmers always have to be concerned about climatic conditions. Cash crop farmers also have to worry about the policies of government elites and the prices available on the international markets. The variables that lead to failure are increased. Additional worries include the new diseases and physical problems that follow irrigation and the use of new fertilizers. Cash cropping has been encouraged throughout the developing world, and it has created problems in every country. There are special problems for women, who have lost their economic positions, their family and economic security, and often their health.

Land Ownership The pressure for men to become the primary farmers increased with the bias to aid and teach men to take over this profession in colonial settings. This soon began to erode the priority of women in this economic arena. On top of this, access to land became an issue. One factor, of course, was the new competition between women and men for fertile land. Another factor involved the familiar issue of colonial laws. Ester Boserup, in her classic study, *Women's Role in Economic Development* (1970), described several examples of specific land tenure laws that were aimed at limiting female land rights. One case was the 1957 land reform law in what was then Rhodesia. This law allowed all men and women who were not married to own land. Because most women were married and farmed to support their families, this law increased the dependency of wives on their husbands. Further, because the land they farmed now belonged to their husbands, a divorce meant that they lost access to the lands they had worked for years. Similar laws in Mexico, southeastern Asia, and South Africa proved that the same situation existed for women there. In the South African law of 1898, each man could own one field.

This meant that co-wives had to share land, and, at the death of the husband, they were left landless.

More recent sources tell similar stories that indicate that these policies have had lasting effects. A 1994–1995 report concluded: "Throughout most of the developing world, women lack either ownership or effective control of land, water, and other resources." (Thrupp and Estes 1995: 51) Given the fact that women still depend on the results of their farming in many parts of the world, this only emphasizes the degree of their dependency. It appears that this trend is continuing. A recent study of African development supports the conclusion that, with increasing pressure on agricultural lands, women are still losing out. This study described the problems of governments that ignored matrilineal inheritance, passed discriminatory legislation, and planned irrigation projects and resettlement programs that reduced women's land holdings. (Whitehead and Bloom 1992: 41–56) Further, women's lack of political clout made them unable to turn these policies around.

Wage Labor   If women are removed from their traditional means of making a living, new means of survival have to be found. One means, of course, is dependency on male family members, and this has often been the reality—often happy, sometimes sad—of many women. Some women—divorced, deserted, orphaned, unmarried, or widowed—do not have this choice. Others select lives different than their lot. For well-educated, middle- or upper-class women, other choices are frequently available. Often their choices lower their standard of living, but middle-class women are generally able to maintain a respectable style of life. However, in the developing world, only a tiny percentage of the population live middle-class or elite lives. Far more troubling are the millions of women in the world who need to support themselves and their children and who have few desirable economic opportunities in the developing world system. Some of these women choose to migrate for employment and split their lives between different countries.

India   Contemporary India offers a picture of the opportunities for such women. First, in India, and probably in most of the developing world, women generally work in what is called the informal sector. This is work that is performed among people without organization or government involvement. These jobs often have poor pay and work conditions and no legal protection for the workers. Of the women workers in India in 1992, 94 percent were said to work in the informal sector. (Standing 1992: 59) While most women worked in agriculture, many worked in manufacturing. Most were in textile and food preparation operations. In recent years, the number of women employed in these traditional areas has fallen. Standing described the transformation of women's work in the jute industry. In 1921, 45,000 women worked in the factories; in 1972, only 7,000 did. The reasons for the loss of this employment are familiar. First, the most common work for women was hand sewing and material preparation, which have now been replaced by mechanical devices. Second, the increase in government-mandated benefits such as maternity benefits have caused owners to hire those who will not claim them. Finally, with male unemployment growing, owners, with the agreement of unions, argued that because men were responsible for families, they should get priority in employment. New urban assembly businesses have welcomed women to work in makeshift factories or in their homes but only for poorer wages and in more difficult working conditions. Women, who have few other alternatives, take the work. The only other real alternatives appear to be even worse. Working as domestic servants in the homes of the wealthy raised little money and provided an inopportune environment. Worse was the final wage opportunity, prostitution, which offered far less than domestic work and often meant an early death.

Opportunities for middle-class and wealthy women are far more comfortable and profitable. Educated women can now work in education, health care, and offices without shame. Wealthy women might shame some families by working for wages, but they are active in professions and volunteer work. Many have entered into political arenas in recent decades. Class, now that caste is illegal, is still the most important consideration in the life choices of men and women in India, as in most of the world.

Mexico   Americans often complain of the movement of manufacturing plants from the American communities that have hosted them for decades out of the country into areas of the world in which people will work more cheaply. High-paying union jobs are lost, and replacement jobs are often lower paying. The other side of this problem is located in the foreign communities to which they relocate. Multinational corporations, and most large businesses are multinational in the twenty-first century, seek out the most cost-effective business opportunities, wherever they may be. People in these new areas work for lower salaries, often in poorer working conditions, and often allow fewer environmental restrictions because the alternatives they face are worse. Many of these factories, like those in India, hire women at the lowest cost.

During the 1980s and 1990s, Americans became aware of the manufacturing districts that sprang up just south of the Mexican–U.S. border. Here the *maquiladoras,* mostly clothing or electrical equipment assembly plants, hired workers to labor doing piecework. This meant that workers did the same activity, either sewing a seam on a sleeve or connecting a specific wire to a specific piece of machinery, throughout the entire workday. Most often they were paid a base wage and then a small bounty for every piece over the minimum required. This work was boring, stressful, and often physically difficult. Failure to make quotas or absences due to illness often cost workers their jobs.

Women working on electronic components in a multinational assembly plant.

In 1978 anthropologist Maria Patricia Fernandez Kelly looked for employment and then worked in these factories to better learn what the experience meant for the women who worked there. (1997: 525–37) She discovered the difficulty of getting a decent job without connections in the industry. The piecework sewing job she did get was hard work and paid very little. In her work she earned 60¢ an hour for a 48-hour week with the promise of a small bonus if she reached a productive level of work. National social benefits raised the amount her employer paid her to $1.22 an hour. She was expected to sew 162 sleeves an hour, or one each 2.7 seconds, to meet her quota. The question, of course, is why women (and about 80 percent of the workers in these industries are women) chose to work like this. The answer is, again, the lack of better opportunities.

The women who worked in these industries came from poor families or had been deserted by their husbands. Many had children who depended on them for support. They had little education, and for most, their only hope for a comfortable future was that a man would marry and support them. Often they had migrated to this area to find work because even this level of employment was not available in their old villages. This left them without social support as well as economic support. Like the Indian women, domestic service and prostitution were alternatives, but here also, this could only make life worse.

Garifuna People have adapted to changing circumstances in many ways. One of the concerns expressed in the United States is that modernization is breaking up the family, and this is blamed for social wrongs from crime to forms of popular music. Sociologist, and later Senator, Daniel Patrick Moynihan highlighted the growing number of fatherless families as a cause for many of the problems in the United States as long ago as the 1960s. By fatherless, he meant a household without a live-in father who had authority over the family. Many feminists have also bewailed the mother-headed family. However, women in authority are not the problem. Poverty, lack of jobs, and numerous other factors have, in fact, made this structure most adaptive to many people, and this has been true, in some families, since before the Civil War. Feminist anthropologists have seen this female-headed, matrifocal family in many parts of the world and studied it as an adaptation to colonialism and development. Anthropologist Virginia Kerns (1997) studied just such a system among the Black Carib, now generally call the Garifuna, in Belize.

The Garifuna are an Afro-Caribbean people who settled in Belize about 200 years ago in coastal villages. Fishing and horticulture were the main subsistence activities, and many people were also involved in wage labor. Men were able to work in the forest industries and service jobs, which were low paying and often seasonal or part time. Women were restricted to even lower paying domestic jobs in non-Garifuna towns. Women, then, were dependent on others for support, but, because no one was totally economically secure, there was a web of kinship and other relations that provided a safety net for people in the village. The core of the Garifuna system was the link between mothers and children. In fact, the role of mother was the core identity for Garifuna women. The relationship between spouses was important because men were financially obliged for the support of their wives, legal or by custom, and children. The children, who lived with him, regardless of the identity of their fathers, were also his responsibility. Women were most reliant on their live-in husbands for the security of their families and worked to keep him in their home. Marriages, however, were brittle, and many women lived without the direct support of men. The most immediate assistance for these families came from the mother's mothers. Young, unmarried women who found work left their children with their mothers and went into towns to earn money for their families. When the mother was elderly, she expected her daughters to support her. Men were connected to this system as brothers, fathers, sons, and, of course, husbands. They, too, relied on their mothers and daughters but the tie was not as solid.

Because men traveled to work, there were typically more women than men in a community. The ideal of individual autonomy and self-reliance that was taught to girls and boys was paired with an admiration of people who were generous. No one was obliged to help anyone else, but women, especially, felt they had a duty to their community and kin. A woman with a reputation for generosity was held in high esteem in her village. Sexuality was considered a pleasure of life and a lifelong joy. The only serious restriction was on young women who were married or in a committed relationship. They had to behave with restraint so that their lovers would recognize any children they had as theirs. Because a father had obligations to his children, a wise woman left no doubt as to who was the genitor.

The permanent members of the village were the women who lived there as mothers and daughters. Men identified with their natal villages and had their core alliances there. The women in the village, then, formed a network of social relationships that protected villagers from the depths of poverty. Moreover, women, especially older women, were responsible for the rituals that cosmologically protected the village. Their relationships with the ancestors continued through generations, and these multi-generation lines defined home.

The Garifuna, then, represent one modern private–public adaptation to the problems of economic and political depravation so many people experience today. They have to live transnational lives to survive. The normal life for these people is situated in different settings. Men go into the non-Garifuna world to help preserve their families. Young women enter into this world for short periods for the same reason, but the wages and working conditions open to them make these stays temporary. Women, for most of their lives, remain in the home villages in a women's world. They carry on the daily chores of life and the important community ritual activities. "Domestic," here, went well beyond the household. It encompasses the entire home village. As they grow old, Garifuna men and women have a place where they belong. Those who work in other countries return home to spend their later years. The hard work and poverty of their lives is very real, but the support of the matrifocal structure of their society makes it possible for them to continue as a society.

Filipina Migrant Workers Women from the Philippines are found in the domestic labor force in industrialized societies throughout the world. Working as housekeeping staff, child and elder caretakers, and in some areas sex workers, these women live precarious lives depending on the integrity of employers and host governments. Their legal positions vary with states but they generally are restricted as noncitizens. In some states they can be openly abused with little consequence and are deported if they complain. As scholar Rhacel Salazar Parrenas noted: "They have come to constitute a diaspora—more precisely, a contemporary female labor diaspora." (2001b: 1129) The export of workers from the Philippines is encouraged by the government because such workers, male and female, send significant funds in hard currency back to their homeland. The country, however, is often unable to protect the rights and lives of these emigrants while they are in foreign states.

Filipina domestic workers tend to maintain close ties with their homeland. They have a Filipina identity and often look forward to returning home. They do have a status in their families that they may give up when they return. The role of money earner and independent agent that they have away from the family can ebb to a wifely dependence when they return. (Parrenas 2001b: 1141) Many women have left children behind, and this separation is very difficult. They are forbidden to bring their children to their new countries, and even where it is legal, there are other pressures against it. Mothers work hard and have little time of their own. Also there are often prejudices against new immigrants, and mothers prefer to shield their children from this. Finally, the money that allows their children to live comfortable, middle-class lives in the Philippines would only cover a working-class existence in more expensive countries. Mothers still worry about their children even as they earn money to send to the Philippines for their well-being. In another study, Parrenas looked at the emotional pain of such arrangements and concluded that "The pain of family separation creates various feelings, including helplessness, regret, and guilt for mothers and loneliness, vulnerability, and insecurity for children." (2001a: 361) The difficulties that Filipina transnational workers face are formidable, but millions have followed this road in order to create a more comfortable economic life for their families.

DEVELOPMENT: GENDERED ELEMENTS

Development is a term that can be used to describe projects that are based on very different goals and means. At its base, the concept of development entails improving the economies of poor areas so that individuals there can produce enough wealth to improve their standards of living. While this sounds altruistic and totally positive, it is not basically selfless. Industrialized countries benefit from better workers in developing areas and better markets for their products there. International governmental organizations, including the United Nations, recognize that benefits of improving economies often mean peace and fewer international problems, including epidemics and terrorism. The definition of what makes a suitable standard of living can produce different programs and goals. In most models of development, gender has not been considered at all until recently, and this has led to disasters for women and, consequently, their families. While there are many labels designated by advocates and opponents for the basic types of development theories, the terms *liberal economics, dependency,* and *participatory development,* as described by Kelleher and Klein (1999), might offer useful distinctions.

Liberal Economics   *Modernization Theory*

The term *liberal economics* represents the approach followed by industrialized countries of the world today. It is also the master approach of the World Bank and other important international financial and governmental organizations. Followers of this theoretical model believe that the way for the poor countries of the world to improve their lot is for them to follow the route taken by the industrialized countries in the past. Countries should focus on the products that give them a selective advantage in the world marketplace and allow free trade and the agency of supply and demand to power their economies. The products that most developing countries have that are needed in the world market tend to be primary commodities or cash crops. The success of this approach should result in higher incomes for citizens of the developing countries. With this surplus money, they could buy new consumer products, thereby creating new jobs. This interaction of increased wealth and new employment would trickle down to the lowest strata of society and eventually relieve their poverty.

Advantages to women in this strategy are actually difficult to find. Advocates assert that the general increasing economy would naturally benefit all, regardless of gender. It assumes that the lives and strategies of women are the same as men, and this, of course, is not necessarily the case. Moreover, this assumption tends to see the roles of men in the economically dominant category they hold in most industrialized countries as a universal norm. This misunderstanding of gender serves neither women nor men well. Further, there are few cases of development programs based on this approach that have benefited the women and men at the bottom of the social class structure. In fact, this form of development has often worsened the lives of women and children in the developing world. The dependency on cash crops that is often central to this approach is, as just noted, often erosive of the economic role of women and often destabilizes domestic situations. Wage labor is often an avenue for income for males who cannot maintain their standard of living by cash cropping. This male opportunity often restricts women in the household. In many situations, men are drawn into urban areas to earn a living, and they leave their wives behind to manage the household and perform the entire farm labor as well. This means that women and children are now burdened with their former work *and* the work that the men have left behind. The workload increases without an increase in the standard of living. Dangers of diseases, family breakups, and loss of family relationships are often a heavy cost of this modernization. The model of the developed country as an ideal is also a problem for women because the status of women has often been seen as dependent on men in the developed world.

In general the improvements in the standard of living that developing countries receive from such development approaches stay with the urban elites. A dual economy that involves a small, prosperous elite with the rest of the population remaining poor and suffering has become the norm for developing societies. The wealth of the elite has not "trickled down." Further, those social service programs that were enacted by the governments of developing countries to combat the worst of the problems of the poor have been called into question by developed countries and funding agencies. In a policy of the 1980s called structural adjustment, governments were instructed to eliminate such programs and to deflate the currencies of the countries. This was based on the huge debts that such countries were amassing in their efforts to build the infrastructure to develop within this perspective. Many were, and still are, using much of their government budgets to pay the interest on these debts. There was little left for social programs, and, under the edicts of structural adjustments, they needed to be eliminated. Not only did women and dependent children lose these services, they also lost their jobs in these agencies. Such action eliminated all help for the poor while devaluing the little money they had. Poverty became only deeper and more painful. Because the poorest of the world's poor continue to be women, this is very much a gender issue.

In the 1970s, 1980s, and 1990s, many scholars and development workers recognized the problems with these programs and began to intervene with proposals that were often couched in terms of "women in development" and "gender and development." They advocated that development projects needed to include women in them. New projects should include employment for women as well as men and involve women in positions of authority just as men. Many international feminist organizations were very vocal in this debate, and the United Nations and World Bank did change policies and guidelines with women in mind. Some in the developing world, however, felt that these new projects, and the Western feminists who championed them, themselves represented a foreign domination and did not understand the local realities of power and society. As Ester Njiro described for Kenya: "Many male-dominated African governments and NGOs have been reluctant to implement programs for women, even when these are essential for development. . . . The contempt was caused by the abrupt and aggressive lobbying by the North American feminists at high international offices. In many cases African heads of governments (men) did not understand the theories and practices behind the terminologies and acronyms of women's empowerment." (1999: 47) For Asian development prospects, Roces and Edwards argued, "Western feminism has also been viewed as disruptive and alien, challenging 'Asian values.' Asian women activists have been proactive in focusing the arguments away from the perceived disjunction or foreign source of Western liberal feminism by stressing the 'nationalist' aspect of such feminist principles in liberating women for 'development.'"(2000: 4)

Dependency Theory

Advocates of *dependency theory* look at the failures of liberal economics and assert that they are inevitable. (Kelleher and Klein 1999: 88–92) They affirm that in the long history of that approach, most of the world has been left in poverty. The developing countries cannot be expected to follow the paths the developed countries did because the nature of the world has changed. When the United States or France developed, there were no developed countries in the world with which to compete. The environment was different. Moreover, the developing countries today have been shaped by a colonial history that the United States and France never experienced. The countries that are now developed countries and were the colonial masters over the now developing countries created an infrastructure and commodity-based economy in their colonies that best served the dominant state. Roads and railroads led to areas of importance for colonial trade, and fields were planted with cash crops for colonial uses. When political colonialism ended by the mid-twentieth century, an economic dependency often referred to as *economic colonialism* remained. Developing countries provide low-valued cash crops while they need to purchase more expensive technology and consumer goods from the industrialized countries. This, of course, leads to an inequality of wealth that cannot be overcome by the liberal economic dynamics. The huge debts that lead to the imposition of structural adjustment are an inevitable outcome according to the logic of dependency theory.

The solution for these problems is found in the purposeful creation of a level economic playing field. Because the wealth of the developed countries was amassed through the use of the developing countries, the rich countries are obliged to restructure the world economy to accommodate their former colonies. Tariffs and quotas, seen as the enemies of free trade, need to be established to protect fledgling industries. Debts whose original amount has been repaid by interest payments many times over have to be forgiven. Encouragement for industrial growth rather than increase in primary commodity production needs to be international policy. If these objectives occur, then the industrialization of the developing world can actually be accomplished.

While advocates of dependency theory put the needs of the developing states first, they do not appreciably differ from liberal economics advocates when it comes to the welfare of individuals, in general, or women, in particular. There is an assumption that the wealth obtained by the elite of these governments will be shared with the poor, but there is no real mechanism to ensure this. Public funding of programs is advocated, and such funds may improve the lives of the nonelite masses, but this is a hope rather than a program. Like liberal economics, dependency theory does nothing to address the problems of the poor in poor countries. Women are expected to prosper when the jobs that the new industries create are taken by the husbands who will share their wages with their wives and families. This is still based on an assumption about a universal status for women that has little empirical support. This theory is based on the relationship between states rather than the actual status of people within those states.

Participatory Development

Participatory development, as it has been called, is a basic needs approach to development. (Kelleher and Klein 1999: 93–99) Individuals who advocate this approach have different goals than those who support liberal economics or dependency theory. Here the ultimate goal is the improvement of the quality of life of people throughout the world. The units of focus are people rather than states. Rather than industrialization, which has given little help to the poor, this approach advocates local answers to local problems. Different places have different problems and different cultural contexts. Solutions have to be crafted based on the specific situation. In other words, what works in one area may not be best for another. The ultimate questions must be how the standards of health, education, residence, and nutrition can be improved for people who need help. Technology, in this approach, needs to be appropriate to the task at hand. Expensive high technology that may solve a problem but be too expensive to use and too difficult to repair is rejected for simpler technology that works without those drawbacks. The concept of sustainability—that the project can be continued locally over the years—is very important to advocates of participatory development. The best project, in this theory, would be one that was conceived by local people who could lead it over the long term. Outsiders can be used for specific expertise, but the development is real only when it becomes a part of the community itself. Many such projects are labor intensive, giving local people employment, and are environmentally friendly.

Critics argue that this approach works only on small-scale projects and, thus, can have little effect on the huge problems of world development. A village or region may benefit, but, given the specificity of the project, it could not transfer the benefits to others. Advocates, of course, reject the efficacy of universal answers and contend that only local control can lead to the solution of local problems. Obviously, gender must be considered for these projects. It is a critical component in the puzzle of local problems. In fact, many participatory development programs have focused on women's activities because solution of their problems can be key in advancing the quality of life for men and children as well. Craft cooperatives and small-scale market enterprises that are run by women have become projects supported by development agencies, especially smaller nongovernmental organizations. These projects allow women to make money from their traditional skills while continuing their local domestic lives. Other projects that address health issues can often ease some of the fears of women over their own and their children's well-being. The level of health care often influences choices about child bearing. Even projects that focus on men's activities can benefit women by giving husbands, sons, and fathers local activities that will allow them to stay as part of the community. There are, of course, development projects that do not consider gender issues and can be harmful, but these are more and more unusual. A central operational goal is the understanding of the social context so that a project fits community needs—and a community includes both men and women. It is also possible to use a basic needs approach in larger cultural arenas. The case of the Kerala in India shows how one large project was created with the needs of men and women central to the structure of the project.

Grassroots Projects

Many of the development projects that have focused on women have been small, or at least, regional. Based on the participatory development model, they have substantially improved women's lives, but not transformed them. When women's lives improve, so do those of their children. Even small projects, then, can have important results. The spread of these projects in the past few decades has been rapid and widespread. Nongovernmental organizations (NGOs), including churches and women's groups, international governmental organizations (IGOs), including U.N. agencies and the World Bank, and governments sponsor programs such as these. Two small development projects described by Annabel Rodda in 1991 in *Women and the Environment* illustrate the types of projects that successfully include women. Another such project is described by Richard Franke and Barbara Chesrin (1994).

Kenya   The first project is a water program in Kenya. In 1980, 90 percent of rural Kenyans had no safe water supply. Women had to walk for miles to collect water, and this water was apt to make them ill. Efforts at building village water pumps had failed before, and such efforts had been expensive and disappointing. In 1983 a new effort was made, and it succeeded in providing safe water to many villages. This project was very different from those that came before.

The problems of the earlier projects were multiple. The earlier pumps were foreign and difficult to use and repair. It was decided that a locally manufactured pump would be developed, and this was finished in 1987. Support for the project was widespread. Kenyan NGOs as well as American, Swedish, and British NGOs joined with the World Bank, UNICEF, and the government of Kenya to offer money and expertise. The plan of organization was critical. The project had to be directed by local people in order to ensure sustainability. Women were trained in community development techniques as well as the skills needed to maintain a water supply. Villages elected water committees of men and women to oversee the project. The women who valued the pure water were put in charge of its continuation. With women in the project from the beginning and permanently installed in the maintenance, this project worked.

West Bengal   In one of the poorest areas of West Bengal, families had been driven away from their traditional forest-based economy after decades of deforestation. Families were disrupted, and violence was becoming common. Women were forced to travel for wage labor, and they had minimal shelter, poor wages, and no schooling for their children. They were sexually threatened and feared for their own health and that of their children. Women finally called for four reforms: access to forest resources, employment near their homes, land and houses for their families, and health and child care services.

With the help of the government, IGOs, and NGOs, the idea of the *samities*, or organizations of women, was put into practice. The demands of the desperate women were met. One group began to harvest forest plants and produce items for trade. Another was given seemingly used-up land. They planted trees for silkworm production and quickly developed a healthy, specialized forest. In seven years, the project involved 36 villages successfully. As Rodda concluded: "Bankura women are in control of their future. And they are not daunted by the fact that finally they will be wholly responsible for themselves." (1991: 41)

Kerala While large development programs generally focus on the public economy and, therefore, emphasize work performed by men, it has become clear that this approach often has negative consequences that work against sustainable development. Development projects that focus on women's issues in these societies help to reestablish women in the economy but are often aimed at problems that development has created. A more sophisticated method is found in development programs that recognize the problems of previous efforts in other development projects and design programs that address the issues of both men and women in society. The development project in Kerala, India, is one such example.

Kerala, as described by Franke and Chasin, is the southwest state of India and is, by any development standard, a very poor area. In 1991 the per-capita income was $298, one of the poorest averages in the world. (1994: ii, 10) The social quality of life indicators, however, place the state in a far better light than many wealthier areas and certainly the rest of India. The key to the development policies of Kerala is found in a radical land reform program that transferred the lands that poor farmers rented for rice production and domestic households from their previous owners to the poor tenants themselves. This created 1.5 million landowners who no longer feared being thrown off their lands. The wealthier owners were compensated with several years' rent, but they lost their ability to live off continuing rents. Many entered the professions, becoming teachers, doctors, and managers. For the agricultural poor, however, men and women gained land to use for market crops and to live on and raise subsistence crops.

Beyond the land reform, many social programs were set in place in Kerala. Food programs in schools and nurseries made certain that children and young mothers were fed. Low-cost shops made food more easily affordable for poor families. Public health programs focused on sanitation, safe water, vaccinations, and availability of clinics. Prenatal and postnatal care for mothers was dramatically increased. Public education was still another focus. Plans to help support the unemployed, underemployed, and elderly were also put in place.

The outcomes of these actions were, in many ways, extraordinary. Education reform in Kerala resulted in a 100 percent literacy rate. (Franke and Chasin 1994: iii) Even people who could not afford to purchase daily newspapers read freely available papers and were aware of national and international news. Educated women, moreover, were able to understand at least the basics of science and were able to control their fertility and take advantage of health programs for themselves and their children. Health care programs provided the people of Kerala with significant advances. The number of hospital beds rose to 192 per 100,000 in 1990 compared with 16 per 100,000 in the rest of India. Further, one-third of the mental health hospitals in the country were located in Kerala. Infant mortality dropped dramatically, and good children's health care was established as evidenced by a 100 percent vaccination rate for common childhood diseases (Franke and Chasin 1994: vi). Life expectancy rose well above the Indian average. While unemployment and underemployment continued to be high, government programs protected the extreme poor. During the 1980s, the pressure of the international rule of structural adjustment eroded these benefits, but elderly farm workers, both men and women, continued to have full coverage.

The poor clearly lived much better lives than their grandparents did before reforms. Women shared equally in these benefits. They were healthier and lived longer and could expect their children to live healthy, long lives. They increased their use of birth control devices, and the birth rate of Kerala dropped to a replacement level by 1992 (which meant that a typical couple would have no more than two children and that the population would remain stable). This is remarkable because, in other parts of India, the government had taken draconian measures to force sterilization and birth control use in order to bring the population crisis of the country under control. In Kerala, however, the stabilization of the population came from personal choices of women who had new hope for a stable future. As Franke and Chasin, who studied the events in Kerala, summarized: "Kerala's reforms are mutually reinforcing." (1994: vii)

In a country where dowry deaths and female infanticide were still major problems, Kerala stood out as a model for future reform. There was no indication of female infanticide in this state. Males and females were equally represented at all ages of life. While there was a preference for boys over girls, girls appeared to be equal to their brothers. Health care records showed both were taken to clinics and treated well. As brides, the women of Kerala were expected to be married with dowries, and the dowries were becoming larger and more male dominated. However, these brides were not murdered for their dowries as were so many in northern India. Also, in modern Kerala, women could, and did, decide not to marry at all, and they were able to live autonomous lives.

While the Kerala model, especially its land reforms, would not fit all societies, the lesson of concern for social and domestic needs of its people is powerful. The interaction of programs that address the basic needs of both men and women have solved problems that have been seen as intractable in other development projects. Population problems, murders of female babies and wives, caste and religious conflict, chronic health problems, and the unthinkable poverty that plague India were successfully addressed without major conflict or government mandate. This program suggests that real development that improves the lives of the members of society, regardless of gender, is possible. It also shows that the means for reaching these goals are neither secret nor extreme. Nor are they universal.

SUMMARY

Development, like its predecessor colonialism, has not solved the problems of world hunger and human inequality. In fact, both have had a hand in creating the modern versions of each. World poverty is staggering, and most people in poverty are women and children. Projects that can improve the lot of the poor will help women. However, in a lesson that has taken long to learn, these projects will not succeed if women are not involved in their development and management. While the governments of the world still argue about the best way to achieve industrial progress, other smaller agencies, both private and public, have been making human progress. Grassroots projects and radical regional reforms are looking at the specifics of the situations to a greater extent. This local consciousness, informed by a nonethnocentric view of the world, has helped to ease the burdens of distressed women and men.

In the midst of this great poverty, it is important to remember that there is real hope. We know now that gender is variable and flexible. The limitations we have placed on the options open to individuals because of our gender preconceptions are archaic and harmful. The answers to people's problems are endless, and, as long as people try to fit the answers to the actual questions, things can get better. We also know that poor women, like rich women and men, are actors in their own lives. They adapt and they prevail under almost all conditions. In the long run, the important answers will come from them.

Readings

Basu, Amrita; Inderpal Grewal; Caren Kaplan; and Liisa Malkki. "Editorial." *Signs* 26, no. 4 (2001), pp. 943–48.

Bilharz, Joy. "First Among Equals? The Changing Status of Seneca Women." In *Women and Power in Native North America*, eds. Laura F. Klein and Lillian A. Ackerman. Norman, OK: University of Oklahoma Press, 1995, pp. 101–12.

Boserup, Ester. *Women's Role in Economic Development*. New York: St. Martin's Press, 1970.

Buenaventura-Posso, Elisa, and Susan E. Brown. "Forced Transition from Egalitarianism to Male Dominance: The Bari of Colombia." In *Women and Colonization: Anthropological Perspectives*, eds. Mona Etienne and Eleanor Leacock. New York: Praeger, 1980, pp. 109–33.

Etienne, Mona, and Eleanor Leacock, eds. *Women and Colonization: Anthropological Perspectives*. New York: Praeger, 1980.

Franke, Richard W., and Barbara H. Chasin. *Kerala: Radical Reform as Development in an Indian State*, 2nd ed. Oakland, CA: The Institute for Food and Development Policy, 1994.

Gailey, Christine Ward. "Putting Down Sisters and Wives: Tongan Women and Colonization." In *Women and Colonization: Anthropological Perspectives*, eds. Mona Etienne and Eleanor Leacock. New York: Praeger, 1980, pp. 294–322.

Kelleher, Ann, and Laura Klein. *Global Perspectives.* New York: Prentice Hall, 1999.

Kelly, Maria Patricia Fernandez. *Maquiladoras: The View from the Inside.* In *Gender in Cross-Cultural Perspective,* 2nd ed., eds. Caroline B. Brettell and Carolyn F. Sargent. Upper Saddle River, NJ: Prentice Hall, 1997, pp. 525–37.

Kerns, Virginia. *Women and the Ancestors: Black Carib Kinship and Ritual,* 2nd ed. Urbana, IL: University of Illinois Press, 1997.

Njiro, Ester Igandu. "Women's Empowerment and the Anthropology of Participatory Development." In *The Feminization of Development Processes in Africa: Current and Future Perspectives,* eds. Valentine Udoh James and James S. Etim. Westport, CT: Praeger Publishers, 1999, pp. 31–50.

Parrenas, Rhacel Salazar. "Mothering from a Distance: Emotions, Gender, and Inter-generation Relations in Filipino Transnational Families." *Feminist Studies* 27, no. 2 (2001a): 361–90.

———. "Transgressing the Nation-State: The Partial Citizenship and 'Imagined (Global) Community' of Migrant Filipina Domestic Workers." *Signs* 26, no. 4 (2001b): 1129–54.

Roces, Mina, and Louise Edwards. "Contesting Gender Narratives, 1970–2000." In *Women in Asia: Tradition, Modernity and Globalization,* eds. Louise Edwards and Mina Roces. Ann Arbor, MI: University of Michigan Press, 2000, pp. 1–15.

Rodda, Annabel. *Women and the Environment.* London: Zed Books Ltd.

Standing, Hilary. "Employment." In *Gender and Development: A Practical Guide,* ed. Lise Ostergaard. London: Routledge, 1992, pp. 57–75.

Thrupp, Ann, and Deborah Estes. "Women and Sustainable Development." *World Resources 1994–95.*

Whitehead, Ann, and Helen Bloom. "Agriculture." In *Gender and Development: A Practical Guide,* ed. Lise Ostergaard. London: Routledge, 1992, pp. 41–56.

CHAPTER ELEVEN

An Afterword: Dealing with Gendered and Sexed Dualities

Are gender and sex the same concepts?
Are man and woman, female and male, the only realities?
How do cultures modify people's views of sex and gender?

When a child is born in an American hospital, he or she is packaged in a blue or pink blanket and categorized for the rest of his or her life with an endless series of rules based on the same logic that dictated the colors. When an individual who wore blue acts or looks like a person who wore pink is expected to act or look, there are apt to be serious social consequences because this challenges key assumptions of the system. At birth in American society, one of two boxes is checked on a baby's birth certificate. This check becomes a legal and social category. There is a deeply held belief in Western cultures that sex and gender are inherent and clear categories for humans and other complex animals. Not only are there two types of people—male or female, man or woman, boy or girl—but that distinction between people is firmly embedded in all aspects of society from religion to commerce to the arts.

Whenever an educated person approaches a new subject, the first step should be a review and questioning of what he or she already knows about that subject. Often much of what we think we know turns out to be untested "common knowledge" or even unsuspected prejudice. Science fiction fans talk about the need to suspend disbelief in order to enjoy their books and films. It seems that the same mindset is needed for entering a new area of academic study as well. Anthropologists, for example, purposely challenge their students to suspend their ethnocentrism when entering the study of a new culture. The belief that the ideals and beliefs of one's own culture are universally true is part of the enculturation system of all societies, but it blinds us to other truths. An informed inquiry has to begin with an investigation of prior assumptions.

This book challenges you to review your assumed "common knowledge" when considering sex and gender. Much of our knowledge on these concepts is deeply embedded in ethnocentric knowledge. This chapter attempts to challenge the most essential American assumptions of the makeup of human society. Most students enter college *knowing* that there are *two* sexes (male and female) and *two* genders (man and woman). More crucially, however, they *believe* that these dual categories are natural and, therefore, universal. Other cultures, and segments of our own, *know* that there are more than two sexes and two genders and *believe* that their definitions of the appearance and behavior of the individuals in these categories are obvious. This chapter attempts to deconstruct that certainty in order to open the way for a broader understanding of sex and gender throughout the world.

While most of this book examined varieties in gender, this final chapter takes a different direction and focuses on challenges to the duality of categories that divide people. While sex and gender, like the concept of culture itself, have different definitions in different disciplines, the definitions used here are straightforward and consistent with their uses in social science. Both sex and gender are categories that recognize differences in individuals based on their potential reproductive capabilities, but *sex* refers to biological differences between individuals while *gender* refers to cultural understandings of the nature of such differences. Gender, consequently, should be expected to be far more variable than sex between groups and over time. Genetic changes in humans are traced over hundreds of thousands or millions of years. Cultural changes, however, occur all the time. Most Americans would agree that the changes in gender concepts were immense during the twentieth century. The accepted relationships between men and women and the acceptable public roles of men and women in 2000 were radically different from those in 1900. Few would argue that the women and men of 2000 were dramatically different than their great grandparents in biology. It is in this manner that this book differentiates between sex and gender.

MALE AND FEMALE

As noted, Americans divide the people in their world into two sex categories: male and female. This is one of the core, unarguable "truths" of American culture. It is taught to children in kindergarten and to adolescents in science courses. This dichotomy is seen as absolute and defined by nature or God. Of course, people know there are individuals who do not easily fit into this system but, as the well-known truism goes, "The exception proves the rule." It is the people who fail to fit the pattern whose legitimacy is questioned rather than that of the pattern itself. For many Americans, there is something unsettling about "those people," and they are pitied at best and brutalized at worst.

It is the job of anthropology to understand limited cultural concepts but also to see the larger picture. If, as many cultures are said to do, a particular culture defines only two or three colors, this tells us something about the nature of that culture. It further can explain why other traditions exist within that culture. What it does not mean is that there are only two colors in the world. We understand that there is a spectrum of light that is integrated and defined differently. In some cultures, the differences in these perceptions are labeled into large categories; in others, like America, narrow categories like mauve and fuchsia emerge and are understood. Any discussion of cultural categories, be they color patterns or gender/sex patterns, then, should include a challenge to the categories themselves.

Sex and Genetics

Most American children learned about the genetic differences between males and females early in their first science classes. The lecture was similar to the simple genetics lesson that follows. Each person has 46 chromosomes, 23 pairs of chromosomes, in each cell nucleus in his or her body. The chromosome is the locus for the genes, which have matches on the paired chromosomes. One chromosome, and its set of genes, in each pair has been inherited from the mother and the other from the father. The genetic material of both men and women is inherited equally from both their mothers and fathers. Sexual differences, further, are specified on one specific sex chromosome, indicated as X or Y. In females both chromosomes in that pair are X (XX), while males have one X (from their mothers) and one Y (from their fathers) (XY). Because women can only contribute an X, it is the father's contribution that determines the sex status of the fetus. This pair of chromosomes determines the development of sexual characteristics. Millions of schoolchildren have left the classrooms, where they learned this lesson, assuming that they knew something very basic and intimate about themselves. Boys left knowing that they had XY configurations as this chromosomal pair while girls knew they were XX. The fact is that many were wrong. While the general lesson is sound, it denies the ambiguity of reality.

Challenging the Lesson   While the vast majority of people have either the XX or XY configuration they expect, some people have other configurations (for example, O, X, XXX, XYY, XXY). Individuals with sex chromosomes that include no Y chromosome appear physically to be female. The simplest configuration is multiple X chromosomes, and individuals with XXX (about 1 in 1,000 females) or XXXX (or even more), appear to be indistinguishable from XX women. The configuration that consists of only one X, sometimes seen as XO, is called Turner's syndrome, and it affects about 1 in 3,000 female births. People with this genetic makeup look like other women, except that they tend to be smaller than average, although still in the normal range, and some mental retardation may be present. The problematic consequence to some is a reduced reproductive capability. In fact, many women discover that they have this configuration when they go in for genetic consulting connected to infertility problems.

Men can also have a variety of sex chromosome patterns. The configuration XXY is often called Klinefelter's syndrome, and it affects about 1 in 700 male births. Men with this genetic makeup are largely indistinguishable from XY men. There is a tendency for these men to be taller than the norm and to have smaller than normal testes, but neither is exaggerated in most individuals. Like Turner's syndrome, however, there may be a reproductive problem that brings some individuals to seek fertility help, and sometimes, some degree of mental retardation may be present.

Reactions to the Challenges   The configurations described have caused little controversy because they are largely unknown to the general public. Americans know them at all only because of the increase in genetic knowledge and the improvement in genetic testing in recent years. Two other variations, however, reached the popular press with sensational stories and disturbing public policy plans. Reactions to each case asserted that individuals with configurations other than XX and XY were, in important ways, flawed.

XYY: More Male than Males   While the case of XYY males hit the press in the mid-1960s, it still speaks to the strong reactions the public can hold when sexual assumptions are challenged. (Jacobs et al. 1965) Unfortunately, the original argument is still heard. The original sociological study of inmates in a Scottish prison showed the percentage of inmates with an XYY chromosomal makeup to be higher than the expected rate for the general population. The analysis of these data suggested that the extra Y chromosome made these individuals superaggressive, and this tendency toward violence ultimately led to their imprisonment. This analysis seemed to fit into a long history of largely discredited theories of physical causation for antisocial behavior. Earlier theorists saw physical characteristics from bumps on the head to skin tone as evidence for criminality. This analysis saw it in the genes and the resultant hormones. When the analysis became public discourse, assumptions based on gender constructions became primary. Men are aggressive while women are submissive was the accepted assumption. Men are men because of the Y chromosome, so aggression must be located there. Men with two Y chromosomes are "supermales" and, thus, superaggressive. The flaws in this train of thought are obvious. Aggression is a complex reality, and both men and women demonstrate aggression. Specific displays of physical aggression may more often be seen in men than women in specific cultural settings, but the degree and form of aggression differ with each culture. The relative role of biology compared with the relative role of culture in these areas is still widely debated. A single locus for violence on the Y chromosome or elsewhere has not been isolated, and it appears highly unlikely that this complex behavior reality has a single locus.

The public reaction to the concept was rapid and ill considered. Calls for wide testing of people for this criminal genetic marker were soon heard. One school district suggested testing boys in the elementary grades for their potential for aggression. Caught early, the theory went, these pro-tocriminals could be controlled before they showed antisocial behavior. The general interest in social engineering based on flimsy scientific data proved strong. The popular ideas about male aggression and innately criminal people combined to give authority to a preliminary study.

The "supermale" study did not hold up to the scrutiny of further inves-tigation. (Barchas 1976: 326–27) First, the percentage of XYY males in the prison turned out to be in line with the norm in the general public, which had been underestimated. Second, it was found that most of the impris-oned XYY subjects were not incarcerated for violent crimes. In fact, the difference between XYY males and XY males appears to be very slight and essentially insignificant. XYY males, like XXY males, tend to be taller than the norm. While this has passed out of the canon of sociological literature, today there are still people who remember the early press stories and never heard the later disproof that saw far less press coverage.

XX(Y): Less Female than Females   The public reaction to this second case went longer and in some cases deeper. The case involved women who have a piece of Y chromosome attached to their X chromosomes. This type of attachment occurred in the separation of parental chromosomes during all divisions. In the past, there was no way of knowing that this Y piece existed in the makeup of any person. Recently, they have been seen in a very specific situation, in the testing of Olympic athletes.

Concerns were raised in the sports community in the 1950s and 1960s, when seemingly masculine women appeared in women's competition. Some believed that men were impersonating women and competing unfairly. In many cases, the use of various drugs and hormonal treatments to improve performance was responsible for this concern. The solution, according to the governing boards of athletic competitions, was to scientifi-cally define who was male and who female, although in reality it was only the women who had to prove their gender. The early testing involved physi-cal inspection of genitals of the female athletes. Athletes found this humili-ating and unfair. By the 1968 Olympics in Mexico City, a less physically humiliating, genetic test replaced the physical examinations. The problems of these tests became apparent; one such problem was that the definition of sex came down to XX or XY. Obviously, these were not the only patterns found through the testing.

Some women athletes, whose femininity had not been previously questioned, were disqualified[1] and abruptly informed that they were not really female. Obviously, they were not men in any normal use of the term. What was true for some was that a small piece of Y chromosome had adhered to one of their X chromosomes. This Y segment had not masculinized them physically, and their rearing as girls had feminized them socially, and yet, these women were faced with public accusations that they were pretending to be something they were not. The school-day lesson of XX, XY had become an absolute to the public: Everyone was male or female; if you have a Y, you are not female, therefore, these women were male. This would be just another lesson in the limitations of dogmatic thought, except for the harm that it did to actual people. These women, and clearly they had lived like other women in their societies, were debarred from pursuing the athletic careers they had prepared for most of their lives, they were publicly humiliated, and some reported abandonment by friends and lovers. An article in the *Journal of the American Medical Association* in 2000 concluded, "In reality, gender verification tests are difficult, expensive, and potentially inaccurate. Furthermore, these tests fail to exclude all potential imposters, are discriminatory against women with disorders of sexual development, and may have shattering consequences for athletes who 'fail' a test." (Simpson et al. 2000: 1568)

In 1990 the International Amateur Athletic Foundation (IAAF) sponsored a workshop that resulted in a proposal for dealing with the testing problems. They concluded that the problem of men competing as women was not a serious issue and that health examinations of both male and female athletes should protect athletes. Any deception would be apparent in these tests, but they would primarily ensure the physical health of these athletes for competition. The IAAF finally voted to eliminate sex testing. (Vines 1992: 39–42) In June 1999, the International Olympic Committee voted to discontinue testing. By the Olympics of the twenty-first century, these tests lost favor.

As these examples show, the misuse of biology, based on a cultural insistence on the inviolability of a preconceived dichotomy, can be profoundly disruptive to social policy and individual lives. This does not mean that the genetic differences between the sexes are insignificant. On the contrary, they are basic to the development of primary and secondary sexual characteristics. The whole basis of the sex and gender categories is established on this foundation. Active research continues to be aimed at establishing the breadth of differences coded in the genes. The next decades will be important in understanding these codes. At this point, however, the lessons of sex and genetics are confusing and debatable. What is known, however, is that the categories will have to go far beyond the XX, XY lesson taught in school.

---

[1] A survey of seven international games in the 1970s and 1980s found that 1 in 504 tested female athletes were defined as ineligible for competition. (Ljungqvist and Simpson 1992: 851.)

Challenges by Intersexed Individuals   While the nature of chromosomal variation was largely invisible until recent advances in Western science, another biological variation has been readily apparent throughout human history. Some people in all parts of the world are born with ambiguous sexual organs. In other words, some babies are born with both male and female reproductive organs or unusual sex organs and thus are not clearly male or female. These people have been called hermaphrodites in the past, and many now refer to themselves as intersexed.[2] The title to a recent article, echoing a phrase originally tied to homosexuality, refers to intersexuality as "the sex that dare not speak its name," reflecting both popular ignorance about these sexual variations and also a repulsion to the condition by those in the United States who do know about it. (Nussbaum 1999: 42) While practices such as homosexuality and cross-dressing, which have formerly been strictly tabooed, have at least become part of the dialogue of American popular culture, intersexuality is still most frequently seen as a secret disorder that should be corrected.

In a now famous classic in the journal *The Sciences*, geneticist Anne Fausto-Sterling defined five sexes. The first sex would be those born with fully female genitalia who develop at puberty into physically unambiguous women. The second are those born with male genitalia and develop at puberty into physically unambiguous men. These first two, then, are the culturally expected configurations. The third sex, however, falls directly between the first two. This third sex, the classically defined hermaphrodite, has both a testis and an ovary. While the adult physical characteristics vary, it is not unusual for these people to have both penises and breasts after puberty. The other two categories, which Fausto-Sterling refers to as pseudohermaphrodites, include "merms" and "ferms." Merms are XY individuals with testes and female characteristics as well, while ferms are XX individuals with ovaries and male characteristics as well. In fact, these categories are artificial because the reality appears to be more complex. Fausto-Sterling agrees: "Indeed, I would argue further that sex is a vast, infinitely malleable continuum that defies the constraints of even five categories." (1993: 21)

Reactions to the Challenge   *Surgery*   While this continuum of sex characteristics has existed throughout the ages, in recent years sex differences became issues for public policy disputes in the developed world. The primary debate centers on the medical treatment of the intermediate individuals. Medical policy called for the correction of the ambiguity as soon after birth as possible. Until very recently, general theory studiously followed the teachings of pioneer John Money and his colleagues, who held that, prior to 18 months of age, a child's gender identity was highly muta-

---

[2]The number of intersexed individuals is estimated at 0.1 percent of the population in an editorial in the *Journal of the American Medical Association* by Jean D. Wilson. ("Sex Testing in International Athletics," *JAMA*, Feb. 12, 1992, vol. 267, no. 6, p. 853.)

ble. While this is currently being strongly challenged in the medical and psychological communities (as discussed later in the case of David Reimer), the idea is still widely asserted.[3] According to this theoretical approach, a sex—with its assumed associated gender—should be selected for a child as soon as possible after birth, and the parents should rear the child unambiguously as a member of the chosen category. Surgery to remove improper sex organs with followup hormone therapy has become the norm. In other words, the child's sexual makeup is "corrected" to one of the two "normal" configurations. The primary rational for this surgery is a real concern about the quality of the lives of intersexed individuals in American society. Parents fear their children's rejection by peers as children and adolescents and as lovers and spouses as adults. Often the parents of the children with ambiguous genitals were not consulted about the nature of the surgery in fear that they, themselves, would reject their own offspring.

Acceptance Recently, individuals who underwent these procedures as infants have challenged their appropriateness. One group of intersexuals founded the Intersex Society of North America with its own advocacy and educational goals. Their general stand is that surgery that is not medically necessary should not be done until such persons are mature enough to make their own choices. At that time the decision to be conventionally male or female, or remain as they are, would be an informed one that they could live comfortably with for the rest of their lives. They also advocate complete disclosure to parents and open communication and support with the intersex child.

Physicians have also joined the discussion. Many agree with the need for parental input and support, but the argument over the need for early surgery is still debated. A 1999 issue of *Physician's Weekly* featured an anonymous "point-counterpoint debate" between two pediatric endocrinologists over the question, Should cosmetic surgery be performed on the genitals of children born with ambiguous genitals? The negative side cited negative outcomes for previous surgeries, trauma of surgery, and the problems of identifying the true sex of the patient. The positive side cited an experience of satisfied patients and rejected the idea of this as cosmetic surgery while asserting the importance of corrective surgery. Clearly a healthy debate has begun.

Other Realities Intersexuality is a human variation not limited to Euro-American society. The recognition and classification of intersexed individuals occur throughout the world during the present and the past. For example, some Navajo, who are a Native American people of the Southwest, trace the "not woman–not man" gendered category *nádleeh* to

---

[3]See the *Merck Manual of Medical Information,* 1997 Home Edition, New York: Pocket Books, pp. 455, 1350.

an origin with intersexed individuals, as seen later in this chapter. The third gender category of India, the Hijra, which is also discussed later, is seen as more purely defined by intersexed individuals. Surely the most well-known intersexed cultural category in Western scholarship is that of the ancient Greeks, the original concept of hermaphrodite.

The word *hermaphrodite* comes from Hermaphroditos, who was, according to Ovid, the mythic offspring of the Greek war god, Hermes, and goddess of love, Aphrodite, who became a half-male and half-female god. One explanation of this god was that the hypermasculinity of the father and the hyperfemininity of the mother allowed for neither to take priority in their child. Another version of the origin of Hermaphroditos recounts that the prayers of a nymph, Salmacis, for the eternal bonding of herself and her lover led to this unity of male and female. In any case, the image of the god in the classical statues of ancient Greece showed a young and beautiful youth with male genitals and full female breasts. According to classicist Aileen Ajootian, as a minor deity in Greek culture Hermaphroditos was revered for powers over fertility and health and was "not a monstrous aberration, but a higher, more powerful form, male and female combining to create a third, transcendent gender." (1997: 228)

Transsexuals

Transsexuals differ from intersexed individuals in an essential way. While intersexuals are born with ambiguous sexual organs, transsexuals are born with sexual organs that they consider essentially mistaken. They accept the idea of the male–female dichotomy but believe themselves to be misassigned. In other words, transsexuals are born as physically unambiguous males or females, but they believe, or know, that they really belong to the other category. Psychiatrists call this "gender identity disorder" and report that in European countries with reliable data 1 in 30,000 adult males and 1 in 100,000 adult females seek sex-change surgery. In these cases, transsexuals resort to surgical reconstruction to change their physiology to one that is more appropriate to their personal identity. Modern Western medical techniques allow the removal of "incorrect sexual organs" and the construction of sexual organs that approximate those of the desired sex. Additional hormonal treatments further transform the physical appearance of the individual. While surgical techniques cannot now transform a person born with exclusively male sex organs into a woman who will give birth to a child nor a person born with female organs into the sire of a child, it can dramatically transform the lives of those who are profoundly motivated to undergo change.

While people around the world may believe that they were born in the wrong sex, and though it would be difficult to prove or disprove the frequency of this condition, there are very few societies in which such people can safely change their physical realities. In other words, the surgery that American and European citizens can use is not available in most parts of the world. Legal, moral, economic, and technological issues restrict these surgeries, even in many industrialized nations. Transsexuality, despite its importance to the individuals affected, has not emerged as an international issue. In America and Europe, however, this condition has received considerable publicity.

The American public first became aware of the possibility of sex change operations in 1950 when the news of the surgery of Christine Jorgensen[4] in Denmark brought headlines across the country. Given the massive publicity she received, her life became an open book, and her future prospects were severely limited. She chose to appear in entertainment venues, but even there her show was often banned as immoral. Despite the discrimination she faced, she supported her decision to "correct" her sex to match her gender until her death in 1989.

Since Jorgensen wrote her autobiography, several memoirs of other transsexuals have appeared in the public eye. Individuals who were born and reared as boys, but who believed that their true genders were female, have written most of these. Often published soon after their surgery, these books tell stories of loneliness, depression, and a sense of alienation that defined the early lives of these people. In a world more accepting than that Jorgensen had to face, these transsexuals portray their surgeries as new beginnings. Each is now free to live her life in an authentic fashion.

A classic autobiography of this genre is *Conundrum* by Jan Morris (1974). Morris, a British writer, asserted that the realization that she was born into the wrong body, that of a boy, was "the earliest memory of my life." (p. 3) In a life that consisted of international adventure, military service, and a long-term, and happy, marriage that included the "fathering" of five children, the certainty of her gender misidentification colored all that happened to her. In the mid-1960s, when her family was growing and stable, she began with female hormone treatments. In 1972 she underwent sex transformation surgery. As part of her understanding family, her wife knew Morris's gender identification throughout the marriage, and a sense that a wrong had been corrected led to contentment at the conclusion of the book. Morris's autobiography is strongly echoed in more recent memoirs of individuals such as Deirdre McCloskey (1999), who lived unhappily as a boy, had male professional and military experiences, had positive love relations with women, and ultimately used hormones and surgeries to become a contented woman.

The lesson that these life histories support is that sex and gender are quite different and that the irregular combination of these in an individual is tragic and must be corrected. They do not support a flexible conceptualization of gender, at least for all individuals, because they suggest that gender is an innate property more powerful than biology. As such they may give strength to the intersex demand that the irreversible sex change

---

[4] I use the names and pronouns for transsexuals here based on their ultimate preferred gender. Christine Jorgensen data is drawn from Califia 1997: 15–29.

wait for a mature decision by the individual rather than being done soon after birth as Money and others counseled.

A recent memoir is sure to add additional fuel to this fire. One of the cases that has been used by Money to support the concept of the flexibility of gender identification in early childhood has become contentious. Journalist John Colapinto (2000) has written the story of David Reimer. Reimer was born one of a pair of identical male twins. David was taken to the hospital at eight months to undergo a circumcision to correct an obstruction. During the surgery, something went tragically wrong and his penis was destroyed. His frantic parents sought out numerous doctors until they came to John Money, who advised them that David could be an abnormal and unhappy man or become a happy woman. Given little other hope, the family followed Money's regime and also allowed him to study both twins over several years. While Money reported that the twins grew into normal and well-adjusted male and female siblings, David's story is very different.

Reimer's story now tells of a childhood of desperation. He rejected his identity as a girl and lived as an outcast who was ridiculed by other children. He rejected dresses and dolls and even urinated standing up. At 12, after years of Money's training, he reluctantly started female hormone therapy but refused any suggestion of female reconstruction surgery. His reaction to his maturing female body increased his depression and emotional turmoil. His parents, who were emotionally fragile from the years of guilt and despair, feared for his life. After consultation with his doctors, Reimer was told at age 14 of his sexual history. This knowledge explained the nature of his confusion, and he decided to live as a boy. Over the following years, he began male hormone therapy, had mastectomies, and finally male reconstruction surgery. Although these did not go smoothly, he eventually was able to live a more satisfactory male life, with a wife and stepchildren.

Gender and sex are complex concepts. Modern medicine and surgical technology have allowed people to make choices that were previously unavailable. Early in this new age, it is obvious that there is a lot to learn before clear conclusions can be drawn about how flexible gender identification is and how biology and culture intersect.

Sexual Orientation

Sexual orientation offers yet another challenge to the dual nature of sex and gender variation. Sexual orientation here refers to focus in sexual desire. How do people select their mates? Most people live heterosexual lives, meaning that they primarily channel their sexual desires toward people of the opposite sex. Men date women and women choose men as dates and spouses. The heterosexual core is the basis of the typical nuclear family that forms the ideological core of American society. A minority of people in society, however, focus their sexual interest also—or exclusively—on those of the same sex. Women date women and men date men.

Permanent relationships and families are established, although civil marriages are not now legally recognized in the United States.

Reactions: Nature or Nurture?   In the past, textbooks would state that sexual orientation was a personal preference and not a biological issue. Some would cite the psychological textbook definitions that some sexual preferences were psychological disorders. At that time, in our recent past, the book could assert that people categorized as homosexuals, gays, lesbians, bisexuals, or similar labels, were choosing, perhaps because of an inappropriate rearing, to place their sexual desires on individuals of their same sex. *The Diagnostic and Statistical Manual of Mental Disorders* no longer defines forms of homosexuality as disorders, and scientific research has suggested biological anchors for sexual preferences. (1994: 493–538) Today, a scientific understanding of the basis of sex preferences can best be seen as a work in progress.

The recent argument over the essence of homosexuality can be seen as a classic clash between those who support *nature* (or biology) as ultimate cause and those who support *nurture* (or culture and upbringing). In fact, however, moral and political issues in American society further complicate this argument. Any nature–nurture argument is inherently naïve because no factor is exclusively one or the other. Even the most deeply physical factor is situated in an environment. For example, the shape of the human hand, which is clearly genetically designed, can be altered because of drugs taken by the mother during pregnancy. Alternatively, all human actions, no matter how they are defined by culture, occur only through the biological form of the individual performing those actions. An individual kneeling to pray is exercising a religious act, which was taught, but the ability to kneel is biological. This means that nature–nurture arguments, even without the sociopolitical underpinnings, are difficult to win. Serious supporters of biological causes for homosexuality have to consider the social setting, and supporters of nurture as a cause for homosexuality have to consider biology. The fact that many vocal supporters of both sides refuse to consider the other raises yet additional issues.

Historically in American society, homosexuality has widely been seen as immoral. Religious teachers have preached against it, and laws have outlawed homosexual behavior. While in recent decades many of these laws have been dropped and many religious leaders have become more sympathetic, homosexual (gay or lesbian) relationships are still not afforded the same benefits or respect as heterosexual relationships. Some leaders of prominent religions remain convinced that the Bible forbids such behavior and, consequently, cannot condone it. The question of nature or nurture as defined plays an interesting role in this cultural environment. If homosexuality and heterosexuality are biologically determined, then there are both religious and legal ramifications.

If, on the other hand, homosexuality is a matter of birth, rather than choice, then the individual cannot be held responsible for his or her orientation. It is not a weakness of character, so the argument goes, because they are who they were born to be. In a religious context, this might be interpreted to suggest that this represents divine intent for these individuals. They could not change who they were by counseling or self-control because their orientation was preordained. From a legal perspective, a biological variation often carries more weight than a personal variation. Laws that protect discrimination against categories of people based on sex, skin color, or physical disability might well apply to sexual orientation if it were biological. Of course, culturally defined categories such as religion are also protected in many laws, but the biological distinctions often provide politically more convincing arguments.

If homosexuality were a matter of choice, then the individual can be seen as choosing a lifestyle that has social consequences. Others who believe this behavior to be immoral can reasonably attempt to change it. Encouraging people to seek corrective counseling or creating negative consequences for those who continue to behave badly can be construed as moral behavior that is for the benefit of gays and lesbians. They should be shown the errors of their choices and be helped to correct them. Legally, a similar thought process can prevail. If, for example, a military general were to believe that homosexual behavior was disruptive to military order, that officer could argue that if a person chooses to be homosexual, that person was choosing not to join the military. That person was being deprived of a military career not because of who he or she was but because of how the person chose to act.

At this point in time, in the current context of American society, a biological basis for sexual orientation appears to convey more protection for gays and lesbians than would a social environment basis. In reality, of course, the truth of this scientific argument cannot be answered in either biological or social terms. Understanding the biological and social underpinnings of sexual orientation in humans will tell us more about being human.

Reactions: Gay or Straight?   Another question often asked is whether homosexuality is universal and, if it is, whether it is universally disadvantaged in society. As might be expected, there is no easy answer. Undoubtedly there are individuals in all societies who have sexual desires for their own sex and many who have sexual relations with both males and females. Surely close emotional or physical partnerships, sexual and asexual, between same-sex individuals exist in widely different societies. It is even clear that in nonhuman primates, same-sex sexual activity occurs regularly. All this speaks to a normality of homosexual relationships. What is not clear is whether all these feelings and activities should be categorized as the same thing or whether different societies should view them in the same way.

Theorists in queer theory (those who study issues of sexual preference) (Turner 2000; Rousseau 2000) have had a lively debate over these questions. Some argue that the definition of gays, lesbians, and straights that has evolved in contemporary society is a cultural artifact of that society and is not applicable to other times or cultures. Certainly group identity and action by gays and lesbians today does not have a long history. Intimate relationships between women and casual sexual relationships between men are common in all eras of European and Euro-American history without labeling any of the participants as gay or lesbian. Likewise, in many societies same-sex relationships are expected in some circumstances, while other circumstances demand opposite-sex relationships. The elite men of ancient Greece, for example, were expected to have wives and children but also to find lovers among young men.

The case of the Sambia described next demonstrates another variation of expectations. The sexual expectations of men among the Sambia are radically different from the expectations of men, both gay and straight, in contemporary America. This case, and others like it, demonstrates that not only is same-sex sexuality found beyond the limits of modern industrial society, but it is found in distinctively different forms. Defining homosexuality in Western terms can hide the variety that actually exists.

The Sambia of New Guinea: A Case Study The Sambia are a people of the New Guinea Highlands and have been studied since 1974 by anthropologist Gilbert Herdt. Among the Sambia, men's lives were centered on the village men's house, where they lived until they married and then continued to visit regularly thereafter. Becoming a man was a ritual process that took many years. Boys progressed through five stages of initiation, beginning when they were just under 10 and ending when they had their first child when they were in their 20s. In Sambia, though, boys became men by being separated from women, cleansed, and then filled with semen by men. Boys were thought to have no internal semen of their own, and they had to be inseminated before they could fulfill their roles as warriors, husbands, and fathers. Young initiates formed a novice–mentor relationship with an older male by whom they were inseminated through oral sex. After a third ceremony took place around their 15th year, these boys adopted the role of semen donor–mentor for a younger initiate. When they fathered their first child, they were expected to end these relationships and focus on their wives and children.

This male–male sexual relationship was highly ritualized and hierarchically structured. It was also temporally limited. It did not create classes of men with differing sexual lifestyles. Instead, all men were expected to have been through the same variety of sexual experiences during their lives. As Herdt summarized: "All males have sexual relations first with boys and later with women as a matter of their socially sanctioned life style." (1997: 85)

BEYOND MALE AND FEMALE

It should be clear by now that sex in humans is a complex reality that challenges any concept of duality. It should be no surprise, then, that gender, the cultural side, is even more broadly variable. Thus far, we have reviewed concepts of gender difference in a variety of ways and in a wide diversity of societies. Before we leave this chapter, however, it seems worthwhile to examine one unusual form of gender diversity that is not part of the American worldview: the formation of a third (or more) gender category.

All societies define at least two categories of people: men and women. These categories are perceived to be situated in biology and appearance. Men sire children and become fathers, while women bear children and become mothers. Others who are childless are generally categorized according to the gender they most resemble and within which they were reared. Along these lines, each culture creates a series of behaviors to which women and men are expected to adhere. How they dress, move, speak, and relate to one another are all culturally determined. This seems obvious because it fits our cultural expectations. What is less obvious to people reared in cultures with just such two categories is that other cultures may calculate more than two genders. In some cultures, there are categories of people who are not men nor women but some other named status.

The expectations for behavior and style for this group are similarly mandated by the society. A member of category X is seen as different than men or women, just like men are seen to differ from women. Two cases, one from India and the other from Native North America, may help clarify this idea.

The Hijras of India

India is the second largest state in the world in terms of population. Traditionally one of the world's strictest status systems, the caste system, maintained a male-dominated society with definite roles for men and women based on caste position, age, and education. The predominant religion of India, Hinduism, ideologically supported the system with promises of better lives in the future for those who followed the rules for their positions as faithfully as possible. The second religion of India, Islam, did not provide support for the caste system but provided a moral teaching that did not contradict the status and gender teachings of India. This strict system might seem a strange place to find a third gender, but, in fact, the teachings of Hinduism, caste, and Indian Islam supported such a category. Anthropologist Serena Nanda (1999) has extensively studied the Hijras, who number about 50,000 and are members of the third gender category in India.

Today Hijras are, at the core, a religious community. The religious base for the Hijras is apparent. They are servants for the mother goddess Behuchara Mata. Mata is a goddess of fertility, and the Hijras are called to

Four Hijras: neither men nor women.

dance at weddings and the births of sons to ensure the continued fertility of the family. While their blessings are necessary, the Hijras also provoke fear because they also can bring curses.

Those born intersexed are seen as natural Hijras. This is their destiny, and they are expected to fit into the cultural norms just as baby boys and girls are. Most Hijras, however, are not born as intersexed and have to become Hijra. These are typically young men who discover that they do not fit the masculine role. Families frequently reject them, and many find themselves searching for their identities and a home. Some find Hijra communities and see in them a place for themselves, while others identify as Hijra from the start and seek out such communities. In either case, when they first reach the Hijra communities, they have just begun their journeys to become Hijras.

The first step for becoming a Hijra is to find a mentor, or a guru, who will take a student, or *chela,* on as a "daughter," pay her fees, and teach her the role. Chelas are indebted to their guru and are expected to give a large portion of their earnings to her and their house. In return she can expect the support of that community. Hijras take on the dress of Indian women and can live and work with their sisters, other chelas of the same guru, and aunts, sisters, and grandmothers of the gurus in the community. They are not women, however. Their dress and appearance is far more flamboyant and sexual than women are allowed. Further, in their Hijra house, men do not control them.

To fulfill her religious duties, a Hijra must be impotent. Those born with typical sexual organs must undergo sex-change surgery. They must physically become neither male nor female in a reproductive sense. A Hijra practitioner, or midwife, will operate on the Hijra, removing all external male genitalia. These surgeries, which have now been outlawed, occur in nonmedical areas and are extremely dangerous. The operation is viewed as a rebirth. When the novice heals, she emerges as a true Hijra.

The Hijra world allows its members to become parts of families with sisters and gurus. They have a religious position in their society and an occupation. Further, their gendered reality is recognized as a category. Hijras demonstrate the legitimacy of their roles, using both the Hindu religious mandate and the history of esteemed eunuchs in the history of Indian Islam courts during the period of Moghul rule.

On the other hand, the role of Hijra is not highly esteemed by the wider population. They are often treated with "a combination of mockery and fear." (Nanda 1999: 9) Other Indians fear them for their abilities to curse people but need them to ensure fertility. While Hijras are paid for their ritual services, most cannot live on these monies. Some Hijras marry men and are supported by them. Some beg in the streets. Many become prostitutes on the city streets, where many men prefer them to female prostitutes. This runs far from the ideal of the Hijra role, but it is the economic reality of many Hijras just as it is for other unfortunate men and women in the poverty of India.

The lives of Hijras are not easy. They have no power or authority other than that given by their religious role. Many are poor, and the category is widely feared and despised. This third gender provides a place for people who could not be happy or successful as typical men or women because they do not fit these roles. Most Hijras who are not born intersexed, reject their male role and physiology but do not become women. The Hijra in many ways resembles the woman's role more than the man's role. Hijras dress in women's clothes, use female words for themselves, and they can marry men. Some can adopt sons and become mother-in-laws and grandmothers. They are not women, however. They are Hijras.

Two-Spirit People

Over the years much has been written about alternate gender people in Native American cultures. Images of individuals in a category sometimes called *berdache* are common in introductory anthropology textbooks. A picture of a pan-Indian figure who is not man–not woman has become part of the folklore of anthropology and gay studies. In recent years, this category, and certainly the term, has come under debate. The term *berdache* has been rejected by some as linguistically and historically derogatory, although others, including Will Roscoe (1998), deny a negative connotation. No consensus term has replaced berdache, and many still find that term insulting. The term *two-spirit* is now widely used, although individual indigenous terms are preferable.

Reviews of the category are far more complex. Recent books, *Two-Spirit People,* edited by Sue-Ellen Jacobs, Wesley Thomas, and Sabine Lang (1997), and *Changing Ones,* by Will Roscoe (1998), summarize the debates and agreements that came from a series of meetings between Native Americans and anthropologists on this question. Issues of gender, sex, and sexuality intertwine in these discussions. Likewise, the relationship of past categories to contemporary lives is central to the debates.

Rather than a broad view, we examine a specific cultural example. The native peoples of North America are often viewed as a unified category, American Indians, but the reality is that Native Americans live in diverse cultures with different beliefs and customs. The same is certainly true of gender ideologies. Although Roscoe asserts, "Alternative gender roles were among the most widely shared features of North American Societies," the cultural specifics of each nation were very different. (Roscoe 1998: 7) The Nádleeh[5] of the Navajo provide a long-researched, but still debated, case.

Nádleeh

The Navajo are today the largest Native American nation in the United States. Their large reservation lies at the Four Corners region of the Southwest, mostly in Arizona and New Mexico. After Spanish contact, sheep herding became the central economic and symbolic activity. Socially, the Navajo are matrilineal and, often still, uxorilocal, meaning that kinship is traced from mother to child and that adult women and their husbands and children live in their mothers' households. The Navajo are a deeply religious people, and their location within a territory bordered by four mountains sets a spiritual as well as geographical locale. Today other economic activities challenge the centrality of herding, and many Navajo live off-reservation.

Most recent researchers are very aware of the rapidity of change in Navajo culture and are uneasy about making blanket statements about the nádleehí role. Most typically, there is discussion of the Nádleehí role in the past and a contrast with the present usage. Following this lead, we start with the picture of the traditional Nádleehí role that has emerged.

A nádleehí was a person who filled a gender role that differed from most men or women. Anthropologist W. W. Hill wrote a classic article describing this role in 1935. In this, he pictured Nádleeh as a category for intersexed individuals who performed sacred rituals and generally led lifestyles common with women. Some who were not born intersexed "pretend to be

---

[5]There are a variety of spellings used in the literature. I use *nádleeh* to indicate the category, nádleehí to indicate a person, and nádleehé to indicate people, following the use of Jacobs, Thomas, and Lang. (1997: 15).

nadle" [nádleeh]. (Hill 1935: 273) In either case, a nádleehí performed typical women's roles such as weaving or washing clothes, typical men's roles such as collecting wood, and role-specific duties such as conflict resolution between men and women. While many scholars and interested Navajo have questioned the specific details of Hill's description, few disagree that the nádleehí was an important member of traditional Navajo society.

Will Roscoe recounted the life of Hastíín Klah, who he refers to as "the most famous nádleehí in Navajo history." (1998: 40) As a friend of traders, anthropologists, and wealthy art collectors, his achievements were well recorded by contemporary scholars. Recognized as a nádleehí when quite young, he was encouraged by his family to pursue his religious and artistic talents. He became an important religious figure who mastered a large number of individual ceremonies. He also became a famous weaver who created a pattern based on sacred sand paintings that has become a standard of Navajo weavings. During his life he traveled throughout the United States from Maine to California and demonstrated weaving at the World Columbian Exposition in Chicago. His skills in weaving, religion, and intercultural communication brought him fame. Many he met in the outside world did not know that he was a nádleehí or even what a nádleehí was. Among the Navajo, he was following a known path for those of his gender. As a mature adult he became a strong advocate for the protection of traditional Navajo culture in the face of rapid acculturation. He became the cofounder of the Wheelwright Museum of the American Indian in Santa Fe, New Mexico, where some of his weavings are displayed. He is remembered as an extraordinary person who fulfilled his role as nádleehí.

Contemporary debates center not on the lives of the nádleehí themselves but on the nature and validity of defining a variety of people into this one category. Anthropologist Wesley Thomas (1997), who is Navajo, argued that there are five, or possibly six, gender roles: woman (the primary gender), man, masculine–female, feminine–male, and nádleeh/hermaphrodite genders. An addition of a female-bodied nádleeh is suggested for future research. For traditional Navajos, the three categories of woman, man, and nádleeh/hermaphrodite prevailed, while in transitional to assimilated Navajos a four-category system prevails with woman, man, masculine–female, and feminine–male. (Thomas 1997: 164–65) Thomas suggests that contemporary medicine has erased the likelihood of nonsurgically altered intersexed people today. (1997: 160) In any case, he argued that the categories are unique and reflected in the view of more traditional Navajos on the issues of homosexuality and heterosexuality. Among these Navajos, sexual relations outside of one's gender category were heterosexual regardless of the physical traits of the individuals. In other words, a sexual relationship between a man and a feminine–male was not homosexual, while such a relationship between two men would be homosexual. As Thomas writes, "People of the same sex and gender are not supposed to have sex with one another according to Navajo tradition. . . . Gender classification, identity, and roles as prescribed by Navajo culture supersede sexual identification in these relationships." (1997: 167)

Anthropologist Carolyn Epple saw the same types of people and behaviors, but she disagreed with the rigidity of the categories and challenged all of them—including man and woman. Epple saw a Navajo world where the philosophy of change[6] and malleability holds forth. All things in this universe are cyclical and interconnected. She quoted one of her informants as, "All males and females are themselves both male and female." (1998: 277) In other words, she concluded that rather than three or more genders, a more appropriate definition would find one reality that has a continuum of possible legitimate variations that changes with situation and time. Rather than showing alternate genders, she believed, the case of nádleeh shows the invalidity of gender categories themselves.

The gender roles of the Navajo clearly differed from those of the colonial European nations that met them. Whether the variations can be best conceptualized as categories or as processes is an interesting theoretical debate, but for our purposes either argument comes to the same conclusion. The idea that there are two immutable genders does not fit Navajo reality.

SUMMARY

This chapter challenged the major assumptions by Western culture that there are only two sexes and only two genders and that those individuals who do not fit perfectly into these boxes are aberrant. Such assumptions should now seem hopelessly simplistic. Many readers will leave this chapter and book feeling that in some ways they know less than they did when they began, and that was intended! The first step in lifelong learning is discarding preexisting barriers to discovery. These misunderstandings not only cloud our understanding of abstract issues, but they can disturb people's lives. The reality of sex and gender in humans is complex and diverse.

Biologically, people can have genetic patterns other than XX or XY and live healthy lives. Socially, these people have been suspected of criminality and barred from athletic competition. Biologically, people can be born with ambiguous genitals and live healthy lives. Socially, they face surgery as infants or cruel treatment if left intact. Perhaps biologically, people develop erotic feelings for people physically like themselves. Socially, these people have been vilified, imprisoned, and worse.

Other cultures have chosen other ways of dealing with these realities, if they deal with them at all. Issues of genetic makeup and

[6]Carrie H. Horse believes that academic scholarship into this religious philosophy and aspects of nádleeh is spiritually inappropriate. (1997: 226)

sophisticated surgical alterations are based in those cultures that have the technology and will to consider them. Matters as seemingly individualistic to us as homoerotic relationships can be integral parts of the life cycle of average people, as among the Sambia. Intersexed people can be identified as that and live their lives in culturally relevant positions.

Human biological realities always exist in cultural context. Likewise, human culture is constricted by the realities of biology. The cases of the Hijras and the Nádleeh demonstrate this. Both categories exist in their respective cultures as types of people who differ from men and women there. People in these categories live lives that differ from those of men and women. These are clearly gender distinctions that go beyond a simple two-category system. In each case, however, biological issues including intersexuality, transsexualism, and sex preference are important considerations.

Sex and gender have been separated in this book. Issues of sex have been isolated for specific study. At this point, it is important to recognize the artificiality of separating these issues. As the cases clearly show, they are highly interrelated in fact. Perhaps as Epple suggested for the study of the Navajo, it may be more valuable to discard these categories completely and see reality in degree rather than kind. Instead of thinking of five sexes or three genders, it may be most useful to see a continuum between male and female and between man and woman that can be culturally expressed in many ways. Societies, however, do not organize people in a continuum. They create categories and mandate sex and gender roles within their own cultural ideologies. Issues of sex and gender will continue to confound people around the world. A way to deal with such confusion is to be aware of the complexity of the issues.

Readings

Ajootian, Aileen. "The Only Happy Couple: Hermaphrodites and Gender." In *Naked Truths: Women, Sexuality, and Gender in Classical Art and Archaeology*, eds. Ann Olga Koloski-Ostrow and Claire L. Lyons. London: Routledge, 1997, pp. 220–42.

Barchas, Patricia R. "Physiological Sociology: Interface of Sociological and Biological Processes." *Annual Review of Sociology* 2 (1976), pp. 299–333.

Califia, Pat. *Sex Changes: The Politics of Transgenderism*. San Francisco: Cleis Press, 1997.

Colapinto, John. *As Nature Made Him: The Boy Who Was Raised as a Girl*. New York: Harper-Collins, 2000.

Diagnostic and Statistical Manual of Mental Disorders, 4th ed. Washington, DC: American Psychiatric Association, 1994.

Epple, Carolyn. "Coming to Terms with Navajo *Nádleehí: A Critique of 'Berdache,' 'Gay,' 'Alternate Gender,' and 'Two-Spirit.'" American Ethnologist* 25, no. 2 (1998), pp. 267–90.

———. "A Navajo Worldview and Nádleehí: Implications for Western Categories." In *Two-Spirit People: Native American Gender Identity, Sexuality, and Spirituality*, eds. Sue-Ellen Jacobs, Wesley Thomas, and Sabine Lang. Urbana, IL: University of Illinois Press, 1997, pp. 174–91.

Fausto-Sterling, Anne. "The Five Sexes: Why Male and Female Are Not Enough." *The Sciences* 33 (March/April 1993), pp. 20–25.

Herdt, Gilbert. *Same Sex, Different Cultures.* Boulder, CO: Westview Press, 1997.

Hill, W. W. "The Status of the Hermaphrodite and Transvestite in Navajo Culture." *American Anthropologist* 37 (1935), pp. 273–79.

Hornblower, Simon, and Antony Spawforth, eds. *The Oxford Classical Dictionary*, 3rd ed. Oxford: Oxford University Press, 1996.

Horse, Carrie H. "Navajo Warrior Women: An Ancient Tradition in a Modern World." In *Two-Spirit People: Native American Gender Identity, Sexuality, and Spirituality*, eds. Sue-Ellen Jacobs, Wesley Thomas, and Sabine Lang. Urbana, IL: University of Illinois Press, 1997, pp. 223–27.

Jacobs, P. A.; M. Brunton; M. M. Melville; R. P. Brittain; and W. F. McClemont. "Aggressive Behavior, Mental Subnormality, and the XYY Male." *Nature* 208 (1965), pp. 1351–52.

Jacobs, Sue-Ellen; Wesley Thomas; and Sabine Lang, eds. *Two-Spirit People: Native American Gender Identity, Sexuality, and Spirituality.* Urbana, IL: University of Illinois Press, 1997.

Lewins, Frank. *Transsexualism in Society: A Sociology of Male-to-Female Transsexuals.* South Melbourne: Macmillan Education Australia Pty. Ltd., 1995.

Ljungqvist, Arne, and Joe Leigh Simpson. "Medical Examination for Health of All Athletes Replacing the Need for Gender Verification in International Sports." *Journal of the American Medical Association* 267, no. 6 (1992), pp. 850–52.

McCloskey, Deirdre. *Crossing: A Memoir.* Chicago: The University of Chicago Press, 1999.

"Medical Examination Has Proved Her Gender as Female." *Sports Illustrated for Women*, 1999.

Merck Manual of Medical Information, 1997 Home Edition. New York: Pocket Books.

Money, John. *Love and Love Sickness: The Science of Sex, Gender Difference, and Pair-Bonding.* Baltimore: Johns Hopkins University Press, 1980.

Morris, Jan. *Conundrum.* New York: Harcourt Brace Jovanovich, Inc., 1974.

Nanda, Serena. *Neither Man nor Woman: The Hijras of India*, 2nd ed. Belmont, CA: Wadsworth Publishing Company, 1999.

Nussbaum, Emily. "The Sex That Dare Not Speak Its Name." *Lingua Franca* 9, no. 4 (May/June 1999), pp. 42–45.

Physician's Weekly, no. 31 (August 18, 1999). XVI.

Roscoe, Will. *Changing Ones: Third and Fourth Genders in Native North America.* New York: St. Martin's Griffin, 1998.

Rousseau, G. S. "Foucault and the Fortunes of Queer Theory." *The European Legacy* 5 (2000), pp. 401–13.

Simpson, Joe Leigh, et al. "Gender Verification in the Olympics." *Journal of the American Medical Association* 284, no. 12 (2000), pp. 1568–69.

Thomas, Wesley. "Navajo Cultural Constructions of Gender and Sexuality." In *Two-Spirit People: Native American Gender Identity, Sexuality, and Spirituality*, eds. Sue-Ellen Jacobs, Wesley Thomas, and Sabine Lang. Urbana, IL: University of Illinois Press, 1997, pp. 156–73.

Turner, William B. *A Geneology of Queer Theory.* Philadelphia: Temple University Press, 2000.

Vines, Gail. "Last Olympics for the Sex Test?" *New Scientist* 135, no. 1828 (July 4, 1992), pp. 39–42.

Wilson, Jean D. "Sex Testing in International Athletics." *Journal of the American Medical Association* 267, no. 6 (1992), p. 853.

Photo Credits

Index